How
Animals
Live

edited by

Peter
Hutchinson

*a series
of volumes
describing
the behaviour
and ecology
of the animal
kingdom*

VOLUME 3

Peter Whitehead

ELSEVIER  PHAIDON

Credits
to Photographers

Elsevier-Phaidon
An imprint of Phaidon Press Ltd.
Published in the United States by E.P. Dutton & Co. Inc.,
201, Park Avenue South, New York, N.Y. 10003

First published 1975
Reprinted 1977
Planned and produced by
Elsevier International Projects Ltd, Oxford
© 1975 Elsevier Publishing Projects SA, Lausanne.

ISBN 0 7290 0025 7

Filmset by Keyspools Limited, Golborne, Lancashire
Printed and bound by Brepols - Turnhout - Belgium

Contents

Introducing the Fishes

Since Neolithic times, wherever the supply was plentiful and fairly easily procured, men have caught and eaten fishes. The actual catching, however, even with a sophisticated rod, line, reel and hook, is not always a simple matter. The hunter's tools, the spear or bow and arrow, so effective against medium-sized mammals on land, proved to be a poor expedient in water. But they demanded patience, which encouraged observation and so brought to fishing some knowledge of the ways fishes live. Gradually, by close attention to such things as fish behaviour, migrations, spawning runs and food preferences, coupled with a remarkable ingenuity in the handling of various fibres, woods, barks, leaves and bones – gradually methods were devised that were more in keeping with a liquid medium and its inhabitants.

Thus, the technical means – the various hooks, traps, wiers, barriers, scoops and poisons – still in use by primitive fishermen are not merely examples of native inventiveness. They are the end result of a long development in which technology and biological knowledge went hand in hand, a kind of dialogue in which each triggered off speculation, experiment and advance in the other. The industrialized nations have brought an even more complex technology to fishing practice, but this would have achieved little without equal advances in fish biology.

As a source of food, fishes are still important, since the world is still a hungry world. For this reason ichthyology, or the broad study of fishes, is by no means an end in itself, whatever esoteric backwaters it may lap. Moreover, the equation TECHNOLOGY + BIOLOGY = SUCCESS has now proved so successful that it often negates itself in over-fishing, while man's other activities offer an increasing threat by pollution of rivers, lakes and seas. One solution is a much deeper knowledge of fish biology.

It is commonly thought that most of the important aspects of the lives of fishes are either known by now or are being actively investigated. The sad truth is that for only a mere handful of fishes do we have exact enough details of breeding and feeding habits to frame rational fishery policies. This applies especially to the tropical fishes, which greatly outnumber in species those of temperate waters. It must be remembered also that, although the majority of fishes are of no direct commercial importance, they still play a vital role in the habitats in which the commercial fishes live. Therefore, the

Fish caught from coastal waters have for many years been an important source of human food. As stocks are depleted, trawlers are forced to fish in increasingly deep waters and new species are being considered as potential food.

Pollution – an increasing threat to fish stocks. On this occasion, dead fishes are being removed from the lower reaches of the Rhine during 1969.

lives of even the most insignificant of fishes may well be of economic importance.

There are, however, certain difficulties in studying fishes. They live in a liquid medium and observation must always be from air into water, usually through a sheet of glass. With even the meanest of land animals, on the other hand, we feel a kind of *rapport*, as if the very act of breathing, albeit by trachea or book-lungs, were a common bond. In fact, it is remarkable how much we have learned of fishes from moribund specimens on the river bank, the ship's deck or back in the laboratory. Henry Thoreau once remarked that some circumstantial evidence is very convincing, as when you find a trout in the milk. Much of our knowledge of fishes is indeed circumstantial, although the arrival of the aqualung and the underwater laboratory have at last made prolonged observations possible. Modern gadgetry has helped in other ways. Fish movements can be followed by sonar or, if the fishes are suitably equipped, by radiotelemetry; their num-

bers can be counted through a fish pass by photo-electric cell; their daily activities can be filmed automatically down to considerable depths; their sounds can be recorded on tape or analysed by transducers; and much of their physiology can be explored with a precision impossible only a few years ago.

Against this must be set the second main difficulty in studying the ways of fishes – their sheer numbers. They represent the largest group of vertebrates, having twice as many species as birds, over three times as many as reptiles plus amphibians, and no less than seven times as many as mammals. Thus a check-list of the mammals of the northern hemisphere is a quite practical undertaking, as is also one for the birds of Europe or North America, whereas a check-list of the fishes of the Eastern North Atlantic and Mediterranean – with its rather restricted fauna when compared with some tropical seas – was only achieved, with considerable difficulty, in 1973. Twenty years earlier Albert Herre

8

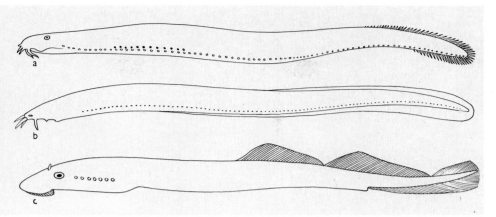

Three types of jawless fishes (Agnatha). (a) The slime hag *Bdellostoma* (b) the hagfish *Myxine* (c) the Sea lamprey *Petromyzon*.

produced a check-list of the fishes of the Philippines, a vastly richer area. Valuable as this work was, there is hardly a fish family included that has not required amendment through subsequent studies.

This profusion of species points to an important aspect of fishes: they are clearly a most successful group. Success in a biological or evolutionary sense can be reckoned in various ways – by persistence, by diversity, by enterprise, or by sheer numbers.

Fishes have certainly shown a remarkable persistence, having colonized the waters of the world since Ordovician times, over four hundred million years ago. Far from being squeezed out by new levels of vertebrate organization, as represented by the amphibians, reptiles, birds and mammals, fishes

A series of sharks, showing range in form: (1) mako *Isurus oxyrinchus* up to 10 ft (3 m) long, North Atlantic and Mediterranean, (2) Smooth hound *Mustelus mustelus*, 3 ft (1 m) long, northwest Europe and Mediterranean, (3) Spurdog *Squalus acanthias* 3 ft (1 m) long, North Atlantic and Mediterranean, (4) Blue shark *Prionace glauca* up to 26 ft (8 m) long, all tropical and subtropical seas, (5) Spotted dogfish *Scyliorhinus caniculus*, up to 2 ft 6 in (0.76 m) long, northwest Europe and Mediterranean, (6) Basking shark *Cetorhinus maximus*, up to 43 ft (13 m) long, North Atlantic and Mediterranean, (7) Hammerhead shark *Sphyrna zygaena*, up to 13 ft (4 m) long, subtropical and tropical Atlantic and Mediterranean.

A stingray, showing the way the large pectoral 'wings' are undulated in swimming.

have remained the dominant group, presumably because they had by adaptation arrived at the best formula for underwater life; their successors were not rivals but went on to found new dynasties on land and in the air.

During their long evolutionary history, fishes have not stood still but have given rise to a vast diversity of forms, not merely to survive physical changes, but to compete successfully with new kinds of animals around them, including other fishes. This diversity is reflected in the number of species existing today. Estimates in the past have often been mere guesses, ranging from 15,000 to 40,000, but recent work suggests a round figure of about 20,000 species, of which about 8,000 or 40 per cent live in freshwaters.

The third mark of success has been the ability of fishes to colonize an extraordinary range of habitats. They are found in both fresh and salt water, sometimes passing freely between the two with an ease still not properly understood. They are found clinging desperately to rocks in the wildest of Indian mountain streams, flitting nimbly amongst coral branches in tropical seas, or hidden in the depths of the oceans some 22,890 ft (7,000 m) or more below the surface; they can live in caverns underground, in highly alkaline lakes, in hot springs or in icy polar seas. In fact, where fishes are absent, it is usually because no ingress exists.

Finally, fishes can be judged successful on account of their sheer numbers. The Peruvian anchovy fishermen, for example, landed some 13 million

Male chimaera *Chimaera monstrosa*, front view and side view, and (top right) upper part of head enlarged showing clasper and lateral line canals.

African lungfish *Protopterus'*, showing the long filamentous pectoral and pelvic fins.

tons in 1964 and the fishery can probably sustain a yield of 7·5 million tons a year without depletion of stocks. This is exceptional, but an average figure of about 10×10^9 (one million million) individuals per species for marine fishes, and perhaps 10×10^6 for freshwater species is a fair estimate. These figures in no way compare with those for insects, but they show that the diversity of fishes is, in most cases, well supported by adequate breeding populations.

So far, the word 'fish' has been used rather loosely, as it is in common speech. In fact, in many European languages it is applied to a variety of animals, usually aquatic but not always (eg silverfish, an insect). Such usuage has a long history. The early naturalists, from Aristotle onwards, were well aware of the differences between fishes and such mammals as whales and dolphins, but the term fish was a convenient one because it described a way of life. It could also serve a rather useful purpose in the Middle Ages when meat was forbidden on Fridays and in Lent. Thus the Goose barnacle *Lepas* was held to be the young stage of the Barnacle goose,

Bichir *Polypterus ornatipinnis* of the Congo Basin, up to 15 in (37 cm) long, characteristically supports itself on its fanlike pectoral fins when resting.

11

whose Arctic nesting sites were then unknown. In this way the goose became a 'fish' and was freely eaten (with a sly wink, for the monks knew quite well what a bird looked like) until the practice was expressly banned by Pope Innocent IV.

A more correct term for fishes would be 'fish-like vertebrates', for there are in fact four major groups or classes of such animals. These differ from each other in so many fundamental ways that it is as misleading to lump them together as it would be to put all the amphibians, reptiles, birds and mammals in one class. Fish-like vertebrates is a clumsy phrase, however, and the word fish will be used here to denote cold-blooded aquatic vertebrates that breathe by means of gills and that have a vertical tail fin. Such a definition excludes whales, dolphins and other warm-blooded mammals that breathe with lungs and have a horizontal tail. The definition is in part contradicted by the lungfishes, some catfishes and others (which can use atmospheric oxygen, in some cases by lungs); by certain tunas and isurid sharks (whose body temperature can rise above that of the surrounding water); by the Ocean sunfish (tail absent in adults) and the

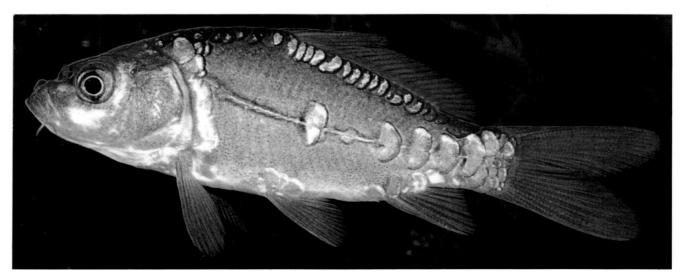

The common Carp of Europe, *Cyprinus carpio*, a typical representative of the order Cypriniformes.

Grenadiers (filamentous tail); and so on. Nevertheless, there are very few fishes that are not instantly recognisable as such, and the presence of gills and absence of limbs distinguishes them from the adults of higher vertebrates.

The four classes of fishes are the Agnatha, the Placodermi, the Chondrichthyes and the Osteichthyes. Of these, the AGNATHA or Jawless fishes are the most primitive, having a skeleton of cartilage and lacking true teeth and jaws. They are represented nowadays by the lampreys (31 species) and the hagfishes (15 species). The PLACODERMI or Placoderms are an entirely fossil group, of which the best known are the arthrodires and the antiarchs; teeth and jaws were present and the skeleton was of bone. The CHONDRICHTHYES or Cartilaginous fishes are represented by the sharks (about 220 species), the skates and rays (about 300 species) and the chimaeras (about 20 species); teeth and jaws are present but the skeleton is entirely of cartilage. Finally, the OSTEICHTHYES or Bony fishes are the dominant class today. One group of these bony fishes, the Sarcopterygii, is now represented only by the coelacanth *Latimeria* and

the seven species of lungfishes. A second group, the Acanthodii, is known only from fossils. The third and most important group of Bony fishes, the Actinopterygii or Ray-finned fishes, contains the bulk of modern fishes (the Teleosts), together with the more primitive Chondrosteans (bichirs, reedfish, sturgeons and paddlefishes – 36 species) and the Holosteans (bowfin and garpikes – 8 species). It is clear, therefore, that it is with members of this third group, the Actinopterygii, that we shall mostly be concerned, and in particular with the Teleosts since all but about six hundred of the species living today are Teleosts.

A general classification of fishes is shown on p 17. A more detailed classification is given on p 154. It shows that the four classes of fish can be subdivided into nearly a hundred orders (each order comprising one or more families, the family embracing one or more genera, and the genus including one or more species). Such a system is necessary if some twenty thousand species of fishes are to be studied and their evolutionary relationships mapped out, but for our purposes it is enough to comment on three large teleost orders (accounting for

The Arapaima, *Arapaima gigas*, of the Amazon basin is one of the largest of all freshwater fishes, reaching a reported length of 15 ft (4·3 m).

over half the total number of fishes) and to list eight other common ones.

The order Cypriniformes contains the Characins (piranhas, tetras, etc of the aquarist) of Africa and Central and South America; the Carps (carps, loaches, suckers, etc) of Europe, Asia, Africa and North America; and the Electric eels of South America. The order Siluriformes or Catfishes is worldwide, chiefly in freshwaters but with some marine species also. The Characins and Catfishes dominate the freshwaters of South America, as do the Carps and Catfishes those of Africa, Asia and North America. Together, these two orders account for about four-fifths of all freshwater fishes. Their success may stem from a number of adaptations, of which one is the possession of a chain of bones (the Weberian apparatus) connecting the swimbladder to the ear, thus enhancing the power of hearing.

In marine shore and continental shelf habitats it is the eight thousand or so species of the order Perciformes or Perch-like fishes that predominate. They have specialized in so many directions that it is difficult to characterize the group, but their mastery of buoyancy and specializations in jaws

Cardinal tetra, *Cheirodon axel-rodi*, one of the many species of characin popular with aquarists.

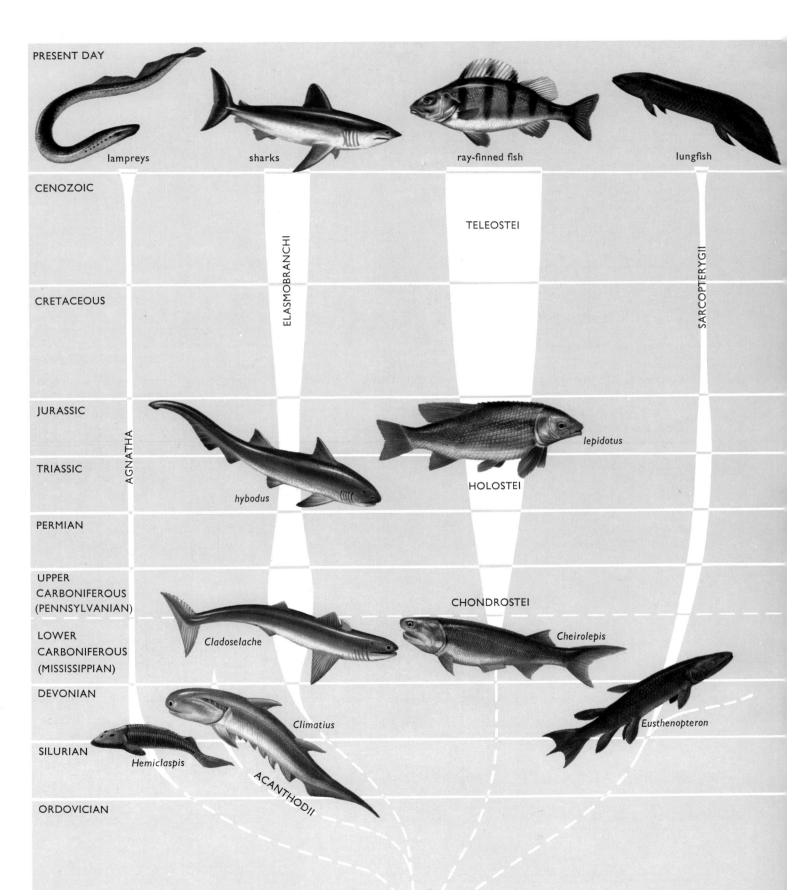

PRESENT DAY

lampreys   sharks   ray-finned fish   lungfish

CENOZOIC

TELEOSTEI

ELASMOBRANCHI

SARCOPTERYGII

CRETACEOUS

JURASSIC

lepidotus

AGNATHA

TRIASSIC

HOLOSTEI

hybodus

PERMIAN

UPPER
CARBONIFEROUS
(PENNSYLVANIAN)

CHONDROSTEI

LOWER
CARBONIFEROUS
(MISSISSIPPIAN)

Cladoselache   *Cheirolepis*

DEVONIAN

Eusthenopteron

Climatius

SILURIAN

Hemiclaspis

ACANTHODII

ORDOVICIAN

Pumpkinseed bluegill, *Lepomis gibbosus*, a representative of the large order of perciform or perch-like fishes.

and fins have certainly contributed to their success.

Of the remaining orders of teleost fishes, the principal ones are the Anguilliformes (Eels), the Clupeiformes (Herrings, Anchovies), the Salmoniformes (Salmons, Trouts, Chars), the Gadiformes (Cods), the Atheriniformes (Flying fishes, Gars, Toothcarps, Guppies), the Pleuronectiformes (Flatfishes) and the Tetraodontiformes (Pufferfishes, Triggerfishes, Boxfishes).

Because of their economic importance, fishes have been studied since earliest times, at first by fishermen but later by naturalists and in the modern era by specialists who may concentrate on just one small aspect of ichthyology. In the last ten years the number of scientific papers published on fishes has almost doubled. We may think ourselves fairly well equipped with theory, technique and active workers, and certainly there is no lack of problems to investigate, often of a very basic nature. In a world of rapidly growing population, there has never been a better reason for studying the way fishes live.

Rainbow trout *Salmo gairdneri*, a popular sport fish from western North America but now introduced into streams in many parts of the world. A distinctive feature of trouts and salmons is the small adipose fin on the back just before the tail.

Classification of Fishes

CLASS			EXAMPLES
AGNATHA Jawless fishes	Cephalaspidomorphi Cephalaspids	Osteostraci*	*Hemicyclaspis,*
		Anaspida*	*Cephalaspis, Jamoytius Birkenia, Pterygolepis*
		Petromyzonida	*Mayomyzon* and modern Lampreys
		Myxinoidea	Hagfishes
	Pteraspidomorphi Pteraspids	Heterostraci*	*Pteraspis, Doryaspis, Poraspis*
PLACODERMI* Placoderms		Thelodonti*	*Thelodus, Lanarkia,* Arthrodires, *Coccosteus* and Antiarchs such as *Bothriolepis*
CHONDRICHTHYES Cartilaginous fishes		Elasmorbranchii	Sharks and Rays
		Bradyodonti	Chimaeras and Rabbitfishes
OSTEICHTHYES Bony fishes	Acanthodii*		*Acanthodes, Climatius,*
	Sarcopterygii		Coelacanths, Lungfishes
	Actinopterygii Ray-finned fishes	Chondrostei	Birchirs, Reedfish, Sturgeons, Paddlefishes
		Holostei	Bowfin, Garpikes
		Teleostei	Teleosts (most modern fishes)

*Entirely fossil groups

Life Under Water

Compared with life in air, conditions under water would seem to offer severe restraints and it is tempting to regard aquatic life as a series of struggles to overcome adverse, even abnormal, conditions. This is true, but only to the extent that air-breathing animals must also struggle to survive. In fact, the relatively greater success of fishes when compared with land vertebrates shows that they have apparently found little difficulty to evolve suitable means to cope with life in water. As we would see it, however, there would appear to be several rather formidable problems.

In the first place, there is the very great density of water, nearly eight hundred times the density of air, and this clearly offers considerable restraint to movement unless the body is specially adapted. Density also involves the effects of pressure, a factor of little importance on land but one which poses for fishes difficulties of buoyancy if they are to live in more than just the surface layers. The question of oxygen supply is even more imposing because of the much smaller amount held in water than in air. Again, land animals, and especially predators, expect to have clear vision for a hundred metres or more, whereas rather few oceans or lakes, let alone rivers, offer conditions even half as clear as this and with increasing depth the light rapidly dwindles to nothing. A further problem concerns the maintenance of the correct balance of internal

salts when the surrounding medium is either more or less salty. Evaporation troubles only a few fishes, but marine fishes have to contend with a tendency to lose water, while freshwater fishes have the reverse difficulty. To all these problems, fishes have found ingenious and often surprising answers.

Breathing Under Water. Oxygen plays an essential role in the production of energy. Most, although not all, energy-producing reactions in living creatures are the result of oxidation of carbohydrates (fats, sugars, starch), the free energy liberated from the breaking of chemical bonds thus being available for maintenance and growth processes. Water, however, contains 30 to 40 times less oxygen than air, even when the water is fully saturated. As a result, considerable ingenuity has been required by fishes in order to ensure an adequate supply of oxygen. Basically, this has involved methods of forcing water to flow over fine blood capillaries where oxygen can be rapidly absorbed by the haemoglobin or respiratory pigment of the blood. At the same time, the waste product carbon dioxide is released into the water. The process is essentially the same as that found in other vertebrates but its efficiency is improved in three important ways, by increase in the surface area, by using the 'counter-current' principle, and by ensuring a constant flow of water.

Typically, bony fishes have four gills. These are

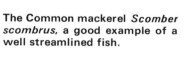
The Common mackerel *Scomber scombrus*, a good example of a well streamlined fish.

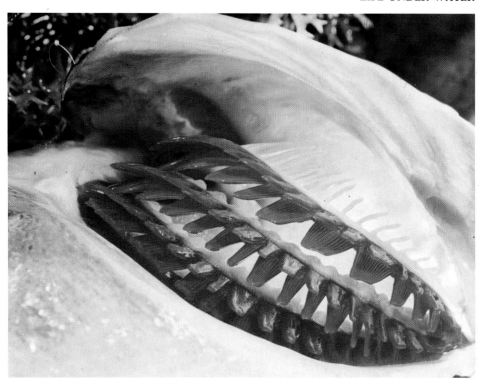

The gills of the bass *Morone labrax.* The gill filaments are borne on bony arches and are protected by the operculum or gill cover (seen at the top of the picture).

bony rods or gill bars placed one behind the other to form a series of arcs or Vs, along the hind edge of which are attached the gill filaments, forming a double series on each gill bar. In most cases water enters the mouth and passes through the gill bars (and thus over the gill filaments) before leaving through a slit behind the gill cover. Although the gill filaments are richly supplied with fine blood vessels, this is not enough for the efficient absorption of oxygen. To increase absorption, the gill filaments are made up of large numbers of tiny, leaf-like lamellae. In this way, the surface area of the gill is increased many thousand times. The importance of such an increase is shown by comparing the extent of the gill surface in fishes of different habits. It has been calculated, for example, that active swimmers such as mackerel or herring may have over 1·55 sq in (1,000 sq mm) of gill surface for every 0·35 oz (1 gm) of body weight – an enormous area considering the comparatively small size of the gills themselves. Puffer fishes or Sea robins, on the other hand, may have only a third or a fifth of this area relative to their weight, and this is clearly related to their more sedentary habits.

A second modification that increases the efficiency of the gills concerns the direction of the flow of blood in the gill lamellae. This is in the opposite direction to the flow of water across the gills. The use of a counter-current principle has the important

result that, at whatever point the blood and water are in contact, the water will have a higher oxygen content than the blood. Thus, blood depleted of oxygen on first entering the lamellae will first meet water from which the oxygen has already been extracted, while blood fully charged with oxygen and leaving the lamellae will be in contact with water entering the system and thus also rich in oxygen. In this way, there will be no danger of oxygen diffusing out of the blood. Considering the rather short distance that water travels over the gills, as well as the speed with which it is moved, the use of a counter-current might seem to be a rather minor modification. In fact, it has been possible experimentally to reverse the flow of blood through the vessels of the gills, with the surprising result that the amount of oxygen actually extracted from the water was only one fifth of that normally absorbed when a counter-current was in operation. The efficiency of the gills can be judged from the fact that fishes are able to absorb up to 80% of the oxygen passing over the gills, whereas we ourselves manage to absorb only about 25% of that inhaled by the lungs.

The third method of increasing the efficiency of the gills is the provision of a constant flow of water. In effect, the cavity of the mouth and the cavity in which the gills lie, work in concert to form a double-chambered pump. Water is sucked in through the mouth, which is then closed, the mouth cavity is

19

compressed and water forced into the gill cavity and out to the exterior through the opening behind the gills. A flap of skin on the upper jaw acts as a valve to prevent the escape of water when the mouth cavity is compressed, while the gill cover or operculum prevents an inflow of water from the rear of the system. Although the appearance is of two separate pumps, the chambers work slightly out of phase with each other and the result is a continuous flow of water through the system. In many bottom-living

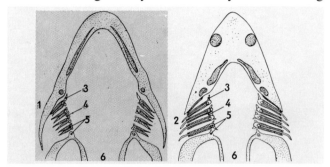

Dissection of head of salmon *Salmo salar* (left) and Spotted dogfish (right), seen from below: 1. operculum, 2. gill slits, 3. gillraker, 4. gill filament, 5. gill bars, 6. pharynx.

fishes, such as the flatfishes, the sucking action of the gill chamber is more important than the squeezing action of the mouth cavity. Presumably this ensures a long steady flow across the gills and a minimum period of disturbance of mud or sand around the fish.

This highly efficient method of breathing has been evolved from a much simpler one, now only found in the jawless fishes. Here, each gill is a small pouch lined with blood capillaries. In the lampreys there are seven pairs of pouches opening to the exterior, while hagfishes have between five and 14 pouches on each side, again opening individually to the exterior except in *Myxine* in which there is a single exterior opening. By muscular action, the pouches

are squeezed empty, refilling with water drawn in when the muscles relax and the pouches expand again. In sharks and rays the gills are more nearly like those of higher fishes but each arch is separated from its neighbour by a partition or septum and each gill opens to the exterior by its own gill slit. Normally there are five gills and gill slits on each side (four in bony fishes) but in one genus, *Heptranchias*, there are seven, and in three genera, *Chlamydoselache, Hexanchus* and *Pliotrema*, there are six. The skeleton supporting the gills in sharks and rays is of course cartilaginous, as are the jaws and other elements in the head, and some of the springiness of the cartilage enters into the pumping action over the gills. Since elastic systems begin fast and then slow down, the flow of water is probably not as smooth as in bony fishes.

The majority of fishes draw water in through the mouth. In the hagfishes, however, a single nostril is used which connects by a passage to the front end of the gut. The only other fishes that have nostrils opening internally are the chimaeras and the lungfishes and in these cases the nostrils are paired. In rays and in some sharks another inlet is used, the spiracle, which is the remnant of the front gillslit of primitive fishes but is lost in the chimaeras and most bony fishes. The spiracle lies behind the eye and thus in the flat-bodied rays it is on top of the head, where it can draw in clean water; were bottom-living rays to take in water with the mouth, sand and mud would inevitably clog the gills.

Breathing frequency is closely linked to both the habitat of the fish and its immediate activities. Some kind of balance must be reached since the faster the breathing the more oxygen can be passed over the gills but the more energy is required to do so. When resting, the rate tends to be slower and in sedentary fishes the gill chamber as well as the gill

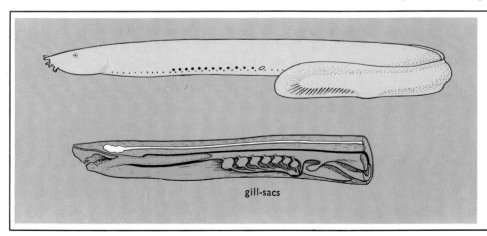

The hagfish *Myxine glutinosa* showing (above) the general form and (below) the way in which the gill pouches are linked to a common external opening.

gill-sacs

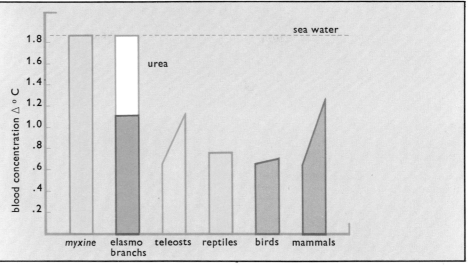

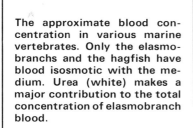

The approximate blood concentration in various marine vertebrates. Only the elasmobranchs and the hagfish have blood isosmotic with the medium. Urea (white) makes a major contribution to the total concentration of elasmobranch blood.

filaments are often relatively large. In certain fast-swimming fishes the pumping action is dispensed with altogether, except when resting, and water is allowed to flow freely into the mouth and over the gills. This occurs, for example, in tunas, in many sharks and in the mackerel which, it is said, will die if prevented from swimming.

The rather small quantity of dissolved oxygen in water has already been mentioned. In fact, a proportion of one part oxygen to 100 parts of water is found in relatively few habitats and the concentration in large areas of the oceans lying below the oxygen rich upper layers may be as low as one part per 4,000. The ability of fishes, under these or even more severe conditions, to extract sufficient oxygen for their daily needs testifies to the remarkable efficiency of their gill system. In shallow waters and especially in swamps, fishes can remedy the situation by gulping at the surface or even by making direct use of the oxygen in the air.

Salt Balance. The next major problem for fishes concerns the regulation of the salt concentration in their body fluids since this has important consequences on their ability to flourish in fresh or salt waters or in both. In essence, the problem is fairly simple. All organic cells have their own internal liquid environment containing various salts and surrounded by a thin membrane. If the membrane is more permeable to water than to salt molecules, then water will pass freely in or out by osmosis, that is to say, by diffusion from the weaker to the stronger solution. Biological membranes are extremely complex and in fact regulate the concentration of sodium, potassium, chlorine and other elements on either side of the membrane, but in principle a multicellular animal such as a fish can be

seen in terms of its water balance. Fluid is contained both within the cells and as a medium that bathes the cells, and is circulated in the blood and lymphatic systems. The skin of the fish is the outer membrane and the key to the process lies in the difference between the concentration of salts within the fish and that outside. This will determine whether the fish will tend to gain or to lose water and from this one can explore the means whereby fishes manage to keep a constant internal environment.

Salt concentration in the body fluids of fishes varies but in general it is lower than that of sea water but higher than that of freshwater. The result is that marine fishes, with blood and other liquids weaker than sea water, suffer from a constant tendency to lose water and must, therefore, drink copiously (10–40% of their body weight daily). In doing so, however, they take in extra salts and these must be excreted. In freshwater fishes, on the other hand, the reverse occurs; the outside medium is weaker in salts and water which they tend to absorb, must be excreted.

The largest and thus most vulnerable surface for diffusion is the skin and in most fishes it is fairly thick and impermeable. The principal sites for the regulation of salt and water are the gills and the kidneys, although the membranes of the mouth and the pharynx are also involved, as is the gut. In marine fishes, sodium, potassium and chlorine, which have been taken in by drinking, are absorbed by the gut and are excreted by the gills, while calcium, magnesium and sulphur are eliminated in the faeces. Freshwater fishes use the gills to absorb salts. The kidneys function as the main regulators of the salt balance. They contain a fine network of tubules

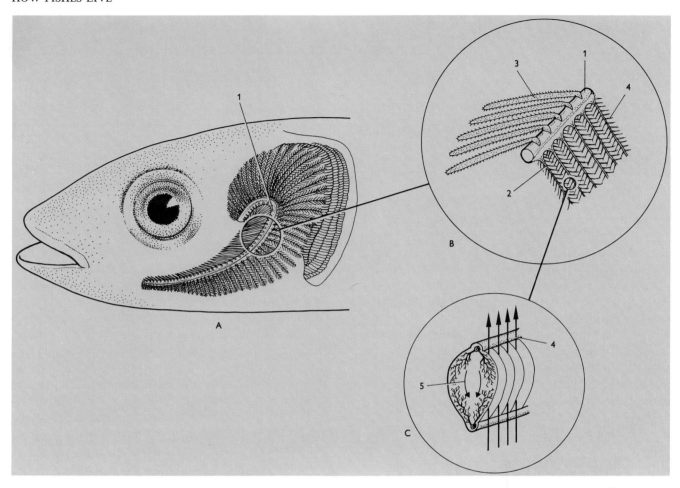

The head and gills of a Flying fish. In (A) the first gill arch (1) is shown in its position beneath the operculum. A close-up (B) shows that the gill arch (1) supports on its hind edge the gill filaments (2) and on its front edge the gill rakers (3). The gill filaments support gill lamellae (4) which are enlarged in (C). Water passes between the lamellae in the opposite direction to the flow of blood through the lamellae (5). In this way the maximum amount of oxygen is extracted from the water.

that connect with the ureter, a tube that leads to the outside. In most fishes each tubule originates in a glomerulus, a small capsule supplied by blood capillaries and acting as a delicate filter. Depending on the needs of the fish, salts can be filtered out and retained or excreted, the organic waste products can be removed from the blood, and water can be retained or rejected.

In hagfishes, which are exclusively marine, the salt concentration in the blood is about the same as that in sea water, largely as a result of high concentrations of sodium and chlorine. Perhaps unexpectedly, the other group of living jawless fishes, the lampreys, which are marine, freshwater and anadromous, have a salt concentration which is one quarter or less that of sea water and they thus face the problems of regulation outlined above for bony fishes. The cartilaginous fishes (sharks, rays and chimaeras) have solved the problem in a most

curious way. Most are marine species and the blood has high concentrations of the two principal elements in sea water, sodium and chlorine. However, this is not enough to bring them into equilibrium with sea water and the balance is made up by an even greater amount of the waste product which most fishes excrete, urea. The result is that they tend neither to absorb nor to lose water. About 50 species of sharks and rays are able to pass into fresh or almost fresh water, where a high salt and urea concentration would be an embarrassment, and these species have between a quarter and a half as much urea in the blood as truly marine species, apparently being able to regulate this during their passage into river mouths. Stingrays wholly restricted to freshwaters probably do not retain urea in the blood.

Urea is found in the blood of some hagfishes, but not in the very high concentrations that occur in the cartilaginous fishes. The coelacanth, however, uses the same system, with urea predominating over sodium and chlorine. In lungfishes, too, urea is allowed to accumulate but only under the very special conditions of aestivation when the fishes survive periods of drought encased in a mud cocoon. In the remaining bony fishes, urea is either absent from the blood or is present in quantities that can have little effect on the water and salt balance.

For the majority of fishes the regulation of salt and water, although a continuous chore, does not demand any unusual strains. These so called stenohaline fishes are confined by their habits and by their physiology to a fairly narrow range of salinities. A few more adventurous ones (euryhaline species) are able to adapt to variations around them. The most striking of these are the anadromous fishes such as salmons, that feed in the sea but breed in rivers, and the catadromous eels that do the reverse. A number of species, such as those that live in estuaries, make the adjustment more frequently. On the whole, the change from salt to freshwater seems to be easier than the reverse process. At least more fishes are capable of making the change in this way. But the adjustment in either direction is a highly complex affair, not yet fully understood, though it is apparently controlled by the endocrine glands. Direct transfer from salt to freshwater usually results in death, but many euryhaline fishes will accommodate if given time. Salts are gained or lost at a certain stage in the process, mainly at the gills, but after a time the concentration of body salts becomes stable. In a species of intertidal blenny, for example, the concentration of sodium and chlorine in the body fluids was found not to alter in dilutions of sea water down to 30%, although at greater dilutions there was a drop. A marine fish must, however, excrete large quantities of dilute urine if it is not to become waterlogged in freshwater, while a freshwater fish must get rid of the excess salts, at the same time taking in water to make up for that lost.

The Rôle of the Swimbladder. The problems of oxygen supply and the regulation of the salt/water balance are certainly major preoccupations for aquatic animals and they have had far-reaching effects on the habits, distribution and abundance of fishes. Yet another preoccupation concerns the sheer density of water and the pressures that it creates. Land animals live at a pressure of 1 atmosphere, that is to say about 14 lbs per sq in (1 kilogram per sq cm). Except when ascending mountains, pressure variations are minute and even at heights it is the shortage of oxygen that causes the real discomfort. In water, however, there is an increase in hydrostatic pressure of 1 atmosphere for every 10·9 yd (10 m) descended, so that at the depths of the oceans an animal is subjected to such enormous pressures as 600 to 1,100 atmospheres. These high pressures have some effect on solutions,

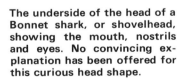

The underside of the head of a Bonnet shark, or shovelhead, showing the mouth, nostrils and eyes. No convincing explanation has been offered for this curious head shape.

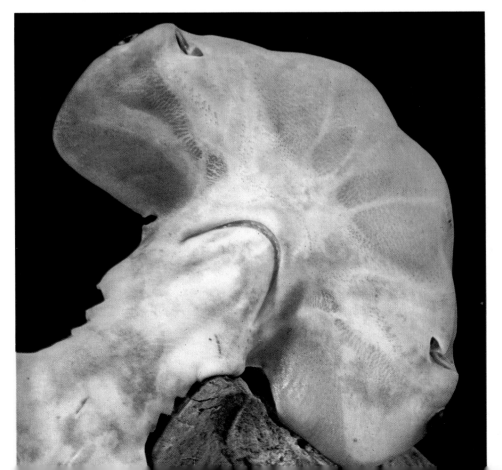

The Lesser spotted dogfish. Dogfish, like all sharks, retain urea in their blood to prevent loss of salts from their bodies into the surrounding water. Most other animals would die if similar concentrations of urea were allowed to build up.

chiefly on viscosity and the solubility of gases, and it has been noted that some crustaceans will actually become more active at pressures of 100 atmospheres; normally, however, these high pressures are detrimental to shallow water forms. For most fishes pressures of only 1 to 10 atmospheres are experienced. These have no effect on the volume of the fish. Problems arise where the fish has a gas-filled swimbladder, since gases are compressible.

Although certain primitive fishes have a lung instead of a swimbladder, the latter is present in most bony fishes and is used as a hydrostatic organ. It is on this bubble of gas that water pressure has its effect. A simple calculation shows that, as a result of the differences in density between air, water and the tissues of a fish, some 5–7% of the volume of a fish must be occupied by air, or gases of some sort, if the animal is to float in perfect equilibrium with its surroundings. The slight range in volume of the swimbladder takes into account the different densities of salt and fresh water since a fish, like a swimmer, experiences greater buoyancy in the slightly denser sea water. This equilibrium or neutral buoyancy works well at the surface, but at a depth of 10 metres the pressure has increased by 1 atmosphere, resulting in a squeezing of the swimbladder, a decrease in its volume, and thus a tendency for the fish to sink. The remedy is, of course, to inflate the swimbladder during descent and to deflate it when rising to the surface again. In this way the swimbladder can be kept at the same pressure as the water outside and its volume will thus remain the same. The ways in which fishes regulate the gases in their swimbladders are often highly ingenious. One can imagine the problems posed in very deep water.

Typically, the swimbladder in bony fishes is a rather carrot-shaped sac, derived during development from an outgrowth above the anterior part of the gut and lying in the upper part of the main body cavity. In many of the more primitive orders of fishes, such as the eels, herrings, salmons and the ostariophysins (carps and catfishes), the connection between the swimbladder and the foregut is retained for life; this condition is most frequently the case in freshwater fishes. In the majority of fishes, however, and especially in the more advanced forms such as the percomorphs, cods and triggerfishes, this pneumatic duct becomes closed during development, a condition more frequently found in marine fishes.

In those fishes with a pneumatic duct it is a fairly simple matter to adjust the volume of the swimbladder merely by 'burping' air when rising to the surface or swallowing air when descending. Seen in this light, it is tempting to think that this must be the origin of lungs, but in fact the reverse seems to have taken place, the hydrostatic swimbladder having evolved from a lung. This method of emptying and recharging the swimbladder can be inconvenient since it forces a fish to rise to the surface where there is often a risk of predators, especially birds. In some species, therefore, a special gas gland has evolved, together with a capillary system, so that the swimbladder can be recharged from gas already dissolved in the blood. This is found in goldfish, carp, pike and eels, the period required to refill an empty swimbladder varying from 12–24 hours in freshwater eels, or 5–7 days in goldfish.

Fishes with a closed pneumatic duct are able as larvae to gulp air and fill the swimbladder initially, but thereafter must rely on a gas gland and other structures for all adjustments. Removal of gases from the swimbladder can be achieved in two ways. In some fishes, such as sticklebacks, gurnards and a number of percomorphs, the hind part of the swim-bladder is separated off by a diaphragm which, by muscular contraction, can be drawn forwards to expand this hind part at the expense of the forward part, thus exposing fine capillaries capable of ab-sorbing gases. In other percomorph fishes, as well as in triggerfishes and many cod-like fishes, there is a special capillary area, known as the oval, for the absorption of gases. Circular and radial muscles serve to dilate or contract the area of the oval and so control the amount of gas lost. Inflating the swimbladder is more difficult since the pressure of gases in the blood is rather low (about one fifth of an atmosphere in the case of oxygen), whereas the pressure in the swimbladder may be as much as 100 or even 200 atmospheres. How can the gases be forced in?

The solution to the problem is essentially that used for the exchange of gases in the gills, that is to say the use of the counter-current principle. The gas secreting cells of the gas gland are supplied with blood through a special capillary system, the rete mirabile, consisting of very fine arterial and venous capillaries lying parallel to each other in a bundle. Thus, gases can be readily exchanged from blood flowing out of the gas gland to that flowing in. In effect, gases under high pressure in the swimbladder

diffuse into the venous capillaries, but in being transported away the gases diffuse back into the arterial capillaries (in which the gas pressure is much less). In this way, the counter-current system not only prevents loss of gases but manages to add those contained in the venous capillaries to that already in the arterial capillaries, with the result that very slowly the pressure of gas in the gas gland becomes greater than that in the swimbladder and gas will actually diffuse in. As might be expected, the length of the capillaries of the rete bear a fairly close relationship to the depth at which the fishes live, the longest so far recorded being in certain deep-sea fishes such as rat-tails and brotulids which are found at depths of over 6,500 ft (2,000 m).

The presence or absence of a swimbladder will be dealt with later when considering its use in swim-ming and its role in the production and reception of sound, but it can be noted that its loss in deep-sea fishes is not a consequence of pressure. Certainly, the swimbladder has been lost in bathypelagic fishes, species that live in depths of 3,300–9,800 ft (1,000–3,000 m) but in the benthopelagic fishes found between 9,800–23,000 ft (3,000–7,000 m) the swimbladder reappears again. The probable reason for this is discussed in the chapter on deep-sea fishes. Getting into Deep Water (see p 110).

The various types of organs, some internal, others external, that assist the buoyancy of fishes and cuttlefishes.

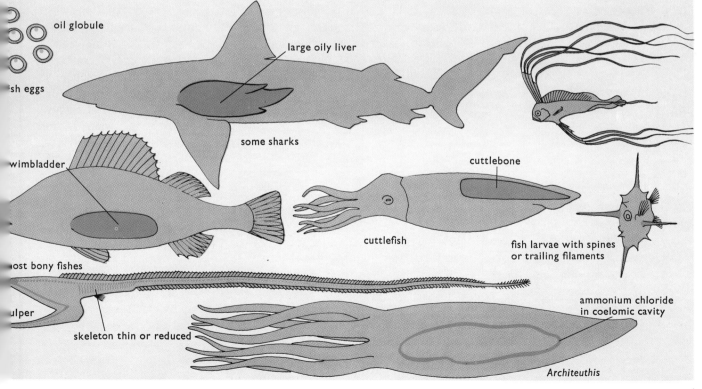

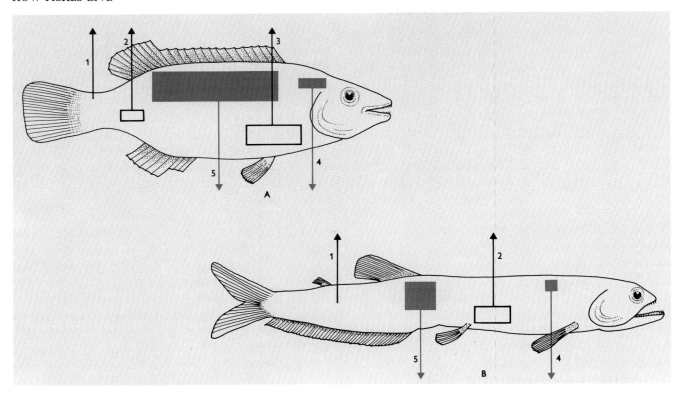

Most fish are able to float at any required depth. In fish with swimbladders (A), components that float are the body fluids (1), fat (2) and gas in the swimbladder (3). The tendency to float is counteracted by the weight of, for example, the skeleton (4) and the protein of the body (5). In fish without swimbladders (B), only the body fluids (1) and fats (2) give buoyancy, and these counteract the weight of the skeleton (4) and body proteins (5).

Underwater Vision. In a sense, fishes have side-stepped the problem of vision under water by relying less on vision than on other senses for the exploration of their environment, for finding food, avoiding predators and communicating with each other. Yet fishes have eyes that are very beautifully adapted to the conditions under which they live.

The range of visibility under water varies considerably, depending on the source of the light and the clarity of the water. Even in the clearest water, however, light falling on the surface is selectively absorbed and scattered, the longer wavelengths,

reds and yellows, being more rapidly absorbed than the shorter wavelengths, greens and blues. Thus, objects take on a progressively greener and then bluer tinge as one descends. At about 300 ft (say 100 m) there is insufficient light for plants to survive, which means that fishes feeding directly on plants must either live above this or else migrate upwards to feed, while those that feed on plant-eating animals, and the successive links in the food chain, are similarly restricted. A kind of twilight zone extends down to 3,300 ft (1,000 m) or so, but even in the clearest oceans light is virtually extinguished

Marine and freshwater fishes showing how the water and salt balance is maintained. In marine fishes salt water is drunk (1) while water is lost from the gills (2), and the body (3). Salt and water are lost in the urine (4), and salt is lost from the gills (5) and in the faeces (6). In freshwater fishes water is absorbed by the body (7) and water and salts by the gills (8). Some salts are lost from the gills (9) and in the urine (10).

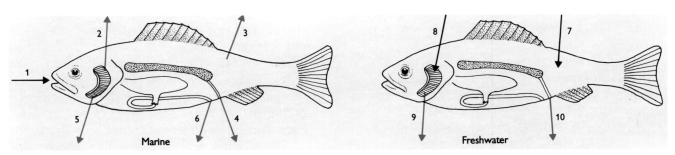

A pike *Esox lucius* in the act of swallowing its prey. In turning its head, the gills, which are normally covered by the operculum, have been exposed.

below this level; it is worth remembering that, by volume, this sunless zone accounts for about three quarters of the oceans. The penetration of light is greatly affected by the turbidity of the water, whether due to silt as in a river or to plant and animal life as in the upper layers of the oceans and lakes.

Hot and Cold Water. A final aspect of underwater life, but not peculiar to it, is the question of temperature. Extremes of heat and cold are nowhere near those experienced on land, the majority of aquatic organisms living between 32° and 95°F (0°–35°C). At one end of the scale, most antarctic fishes live in waters of 32°–28°F (0°––2°C), some species never experiencing temperatures above freezing point. The blackfish *Dallia* and certain Mud minnows *Umbra* are said to be able to survive in solid ice; tests have not confirmed this, but certainly these fishes can withstand very low temperatures. At the other extreme are those fishes that live in hot springs. The small *Tilapia grahami*, a perch-like fish found in the springs that feed Kenya's Lake Magadi, can survive in water of 104°F (40°C) but will die if forced nearer to the source of the spring where higher temperatures are found. However, these tolerances are very rare and the majority of fishes have a rather narrow range of preferred temperature. A classic example of this, although it involves invertebrates as well as fishes, is the catastrophic destruction of marine life off the coasts of Peru brought by the irregular appearance of El Niño, the warm equatorial countercurrent which raises the normal temperature by a mere 13°F (7°C).

Chemical reactions can be greatly speeded by higher temperatures. Biological processes are more complex but as a general rule their rate is approximately doubled for every 18°F (10°C) rise in temperature (van't Hoff's rule or the famous Q_{10} of general physiology). The effect of temperature can

be most easily seen in the time taken for certain fish eggs to develop; trout and salmon eggs can be retarded in this way. Although the direct effect of heat on chemical reactions is overlaid by other factors in the animal as a whole, it is clear that the more frequent spawning of tropical fishes is a reflection of the basic relationship between temperature and chemistry.

Fishes are cold-blooded or poikilothermous vertebrates and are unable to regulate body temperatures against the prevailing temperature of the water around them. As a result, their metabolism tends to become sluggish if the temperature drops and in very many cases their distribution is limited by water temperatures. An even greater limitation is that of breeding grounds, the adults being able to tolerate a greater range of temperature than the eggs or larvae. For example, the swordfish ranges well into temperate seas where the water temperature is as low as 54°F (12°C), but in the breeding season it returns to tropical waters of 77°–82°F (25°–29°C). In the majority of fishes the blood is at approximately the same temperature as the surrounding water, the heat generated by muscular action being rapidly lost. In tunas and bonitos, however, body temperatures may be as much as 18°F (10°C) higher than that of the water around them and since these are extremely fast and powerful fishes the advantages of 'warm' muscles are clear. This also enables them to range into colder seas. Heat is retained in these fishes by the same counter-current principle described earlier for oxygen exchange, although here it is heat that is being recycled by the close apposition of veins and arteries. Two of the most powerful sharks, the porbeagle and the mako, also have body temperatures higher than the surrounding water.

These aspects of underwater conditions – oxygen, salt concentration, pressure, visibility, density and temperature – will be mentioned frequently in succeeding chapters with regard to breeding, feeding and other activities of fishes. It should be borne in mind, however, that none is a separate factor, or rather, that all the structures and physiological systems that cope with the outside environment are intimately connected. Thus, tolerance of high temperatures seems to be connected with an ability to withstand high salt concentrations, while the normal depth range of a fish may be overridden by temperature considerations. Again, structures such as the gills may be involved in a variety of activities, namely the exchange of gases, salts and heat, while the limiting factors in a fish's life may be different at different times or stages in its life span. Like any other organism, a fish represents a complicated self-regulating system in which every facet ultimately has a relationship with all others.

Going Places

It was stressed, when dealing with the problem of pressure, that water is a dense medium, being volume for volume, nearly eight hundred times as heavy as air. While this poses certain difficulties for a static fish, the problems are greatly increased when the fish attempts to move. Somehow it must accelerate a heavy load of water back along its body, but without the advantage a land animal has with its fixed points from which to push. At the same time, however, the land animal has to counter the powerful tug of gravity, a force that for fishes is comparatively slight although not negligible. Locomotion, whether in defiance of gravity or of the viscosity of the medium, demands great ingenuity if the maximum result for the minimum effort is to be achieved. In fishes, swimming has involved questions of streamlining, or organization of muscles, nerves and skeleton, of the role of fins, and of buoyancy.

Streamlining. Typically, fishes tend to have a fusiform, cigar-shaped body. This is not merely an adaptation for speed but is the ideal shape for travelling from one place to another with the least amount of effort. It is noticeable that in fusiform fishes, such as trouts, herrings, salmons and minnows, the head tapers more abruptly than does the tail. This is not wholly essential, for although much must be packed into the head, a projecting snout can on occasions be developed (as in the swordfish). The fact that tapering or pointed snouts are rare suggests that, from a hydrodynamic point of view, they may be unnecessary. Indeed, they could even be a liability. A stick held straight out against a fast current will vibrate; turned a few degrees to the side, its resistance to the water will be felt but it will cease to vibrate; the 'swords' of swordfishes are slightly bent, presumably for this reason.

A fish's body is constantly changing its shape, but experiments on solid models can be revealing. By towing cones through water and measuring their resistance it has been shown that the taper *after* the widest point is more important than that before. Thus a cone drawn through the water backwards causes less drag than one drawn forwards by its point. This seems rather surprising, but the resistance to water pushed aside in front is much less than the drag of eddying water behind. Thus, most fusiform fishes have the widest point of the body not halfway along the body but somewhat in front of this.

A fish, of course, is not some kind of cigar pulled through the water. It is a living, moving body that by its own contortions must propel itself along. For this reason, fishes must depart from hydrodynamic ideals and instead of a truly cylindrical body most have a body that is slightly compressed or oval in cross-section. This is most noticeable towards the tail where the principal propulsive surfaces are to be found. Swimming is achieved by passing a series of waves down the body, the size of the waves (their amplitude) becoming progressively greater. At the same time, the head oscillates slightly from side to side as the fish 'snakes' its way through the water. The undulations of the body produce, in effect, a series of inclined surfaces that travel down the body, pushing outwards and backwards against the water. As a result, water is thrust aside and the fish moves forward. Various ideas have been put forward to suggest exactly how this happens, one being that the undulations of the body produce small whirlpools or vortices, the fish then 'elbowing' its way forward between the alternate vortices as in a roller-peg system. Whatever the exact mechanics may be, however, the wave motion of the body is the characteristic basis for forward movement in most fishes.

Even without watching fishes swim, it is apparent from their shape that some are able to undulate their

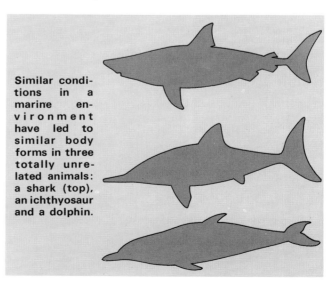

Similar conditions in a marine environment have led to similar body forms in three totally unrelated animals: a shark (top), an ichthyosaur and a dolphin.

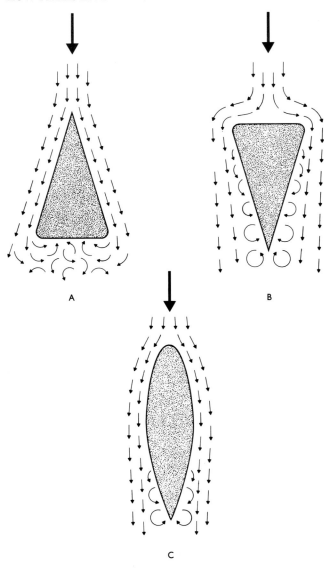

If a cone (A) is suspended in a current of water, eddies causing drag, or resistance, develop at its hind edge. In a similar way, a reversed cone (B) produces eddies along its sides. The streamlined fish can be likened in shape to two cones put end to end (C). This shape causes very few eddies and consequently offers least resistance to the water flowing past it.

bodies much more strongly than others. Taking a trout or a minnow as the norm, the extremes in flexibility and stiffness may be represented, on the one hand, by an eel and, on the other, by a boxfish encased in its armour. The body of an eel can be, and is, thrown into more than one complete wave as it swims along; in the very elongate eels or in a fish such as the oarfish *Regalecus* there may be three, four or five waves passing down the body at any one time. The boxfish is a rather specialized example since the body plays no real part in locomotion, apart from some small movements at the

base of the tail, but a tuna is a good example of a flexible but stiff-bodied fish, the flexure of the body being confined to the last third of the body. Clearly, the manner in which these various types of fishes swim must vary considerably. In the case of eel-like fishes, the sinuous body is usually (but not always) an adaptation for sliding into or through small crevices; in any event, the multiplication of waves down the body, like the multiplication of legs in a centipede, results in slower progress. The stiff-bodied tuna, however, is certainly adapted to swift and powerful swimming, as can be judged not only by its performance but by several other adaptations to be described below. Between these extremes in flexible and stiff bodies there is a great variety of intermediates, but it is important to realize that, although movement from place to place with the minimum effort is desirable, often it may take second place to more pressing problems, such as camouflage or defence.

To produce a series of waves down the length of the body requires some very neat engineering. The vertebral column, evolved from the flexible rod of cartilage or notochord of primitive chordates, is essential to prevent the body from buckling when the muscles on either side contract. The units of the column, the individual vertebrae, are so designed that the column can bend just the required amount and no more. In the freshwater eels there may be over 100 vertebrae, whereas there are about 30 in most perch-like fishes and only 14 in some boxfishes. To the vertebrae are attached muscles whose role is essentially to attempt to shorten the distance between sets of vertebrae, thus producing a curve, first one one side of the body and then on the other. This is achieved through the arrangement of the muscles into segments matching the number of vertebrae, each segment tapering forwards and being overlapped by the one in front. In fast-swimming fishes the segments form complex cones whose outline just below the skin is in the form of a single or double V. This matter of overlapping blocks of muscles is important. It means that by triggering the muscle blocks in sequence, a smooth wave can be sent down the body. Since much depends on using the waves to push water back along the body, exact control of the muscles forming the waves is essential. In many fishes requiring the abrupt co-ordination of muscles for a hasty get-away, there

This picture of a Leopard shark *Triakis semifasciata* shows ▷ clearly how the large pectoral fins act as hydrofoils as the fish swims towards the water's surface.

are two large neurons at the hind end of the brain from which arise a pair of giant axons or nerve fibres that run the length of the spinal cord, sending off side branches at intervals. This is the Mauthnerian system, present in certain bony fishes, and in amphibians with strong tails, but not found in sharks. By short-circuiting the normal system of nerves, the Mauthnerian fibres can send extremely rapid messages for sudden muscle contractions. As might be expected, the system is not found in eels or sluggish bottom fishes. Surprisingly, it is not well developed in tunas, possibly because they already swim extremely fast and do not require sudden spurts.

The main blocks of muscles along the flanks of fishes may make up over half the weight of the fish, hence the importance of fishes as food. If a kipper is peeled of its skin and examined closely, it will be seen that most of the muscle is light coloured but that there is a narrow band of dark purple muscles running down the length of the fish. Similarly, the breast of a chicken is white but the muscles of the legs are largely red-brown. These are two different kinds of muscles serving different purposes. The white muscle functions anaerobically by converting glycogen to lactate and is largely used for spurts of energy. The red muscles, on the other hand, function aerobically, that is to say they obtain their energy by actively oxidizing fats, which is twice as efficient, weight for weight, than by using carbohydrates; the red colour comes from the oxygen transporter, myoglobin. The red muscles are used for sustained cruising. As might be expected, many oceanic fishes, such as mackerel and tunas, have a large proportion of red muscle, whereas bottom-living fishes like the plaice, or lurkers like the pike, have a preponderance of white muscle.

Fins. So far, nothing has been said of the fins of fishes, although these are obviously of great importance in swimming. For propulsion, the caudal or tail fin plays a key role. If the tail is cut off a trout the fish can still swim but the oscillations of the body are greatly speeded up. In this case the tail is serving to damp down the oscillations. It does more than this, however. It provides a flat bearing surface against which a final thrust can be given and it also acts as a rudder. It has been shown that the percentage of total thrust contributed by the tail is 45

The head-on view of the perch, a member of the large group of spiny-finned fishes, shows the paired fins clearly. The pectoral fins lie on either side of the body just behind the head and act as brakes and also aid steering.

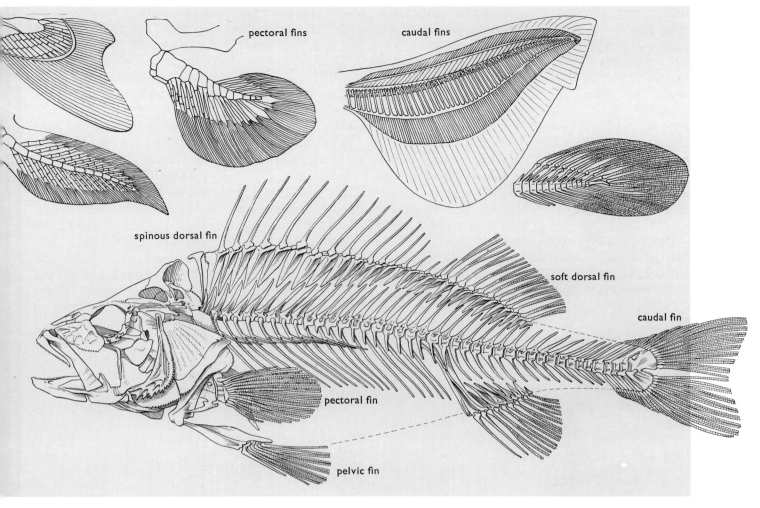

spinous dorsal fin

soft dorsal fin

caudal fin

pectoral fin

pelvic fin

pectoral fins

caudal fins

Pectoral fins (left) of Frilled shark, Australian lungfish and cod, and caudal fins (right) of sturgeon and tenpounder. The skeleton (below) is of a perch, a typical bony fish.

in the bream *Abramis brama*, 65 in the goldfish *Carassius auratus*, 84 in the dace *Leuciscus leuciscus* and no less than 90 in the Yellowfin tuna *Thunnus albacares*. These differences are related both to the manner in which the fishes swim and the actual shape of the tail. In the bream or the goldfish, for example, the body is fairly strongly flexed and the tail is rather broad, whereas in the tuna the body is bent only in the latter part and the tail is lunate and much deeper than broad, a high aspect ratio. In the bream, the goldfish and the dace, the tail is rather soft and at each sweep the upper and lower edges are in advance of the more flexible rays in the centre. This means that even at the finish of one sweep the rays in the middle of the fin are still moving across and exerting a thrust. It also means that the fish can manoeuvre with great delicacy, each ray in the fin being under individual muscular control. In tunas, the fin rays are much more rigid, but these fishes

have far less need to make the complicated turns imposed on those that live in a restricted environment. In most fishes the upper and lower lobes of the tail are symmetrical but in many sharks the upper lobe is much larger and extraordinarily so in the Thresher shark. This produces a lift in the tail region which is counteracted by the use of the pectoral fins as hydroplanes; the tail of the thresher shark does not seem to make hydrodynamic sense but is apparently used to thrash the water in order to concentrate shoals of fishes on which the sharks feed. In certain other fishes, such as the whiptailed loricarid catfishes, the upper lobe of the tail is drawn out to a long filament, while in the tripodfish *Benthosaurus*, it is the lower lobe that is filamentous and provides, with similar filaments from the pelvic fins, a tripod on which the fish can rest on the bottom. Finally, the Ocean sunfish *Mola* gradually loses its tail during development and a number of

33

fishes, grenadiers, Rat-tailed anchovies. African lungfishes, have the tail reduced and tapering to a virtual filament. Clearly, movement is not wholly dependent on a tail, although progress may be slower without it.

The waves that pass down the body of a fish increase in amplitude towards the tail and corresponding with this the amount of turbulence increases also. If the tail is to be efficient, both for propulsion and for steering, then the turbulence must be reduced. One way in which this may be done is the siting of small finlets along the upper and lower profile in the hind part of the body, each finlet helping to modify the flow of water over the body as the tail thrashes from side to side. Another method seems to be the provision of small lateral keels on either side where the tail joins the body, as in the swordfish or the Mackerel sharks.

Vertical fins – the one or more dorsal and anal fins – serve to stabilize the body against rolling, may contribute to the reduction of turbulence, and certainly provide a pivot or bearing surface for making turns. In sharks, these fins are permanently erect, but in bony fishes they can usually be depressed for fast swimming but are erected when the fish makes a turn or is merely swimming back and forth as in an aquarium. In the more primitive of the bony fishes the dorsal fin is short-based and set somewhere near the centre of gravity of the fish – presumably the best position in which it can act as a pivot. In fishes such as the pike that require a sudden thrust of speed, the dorsal and anal fins are set far back on the body. In the more advanced perch-like fishes both dorsal and anal fins are usually rather long-based and the leading rays are spiny; possibly these spiny rays act as 'cut-waters,' but certainly they provide the kind of rigidity required in a highly manoeuverable fish and they must, in addition, serve a purpose in defence. As in the case of body shape, however, it must be remembered that these fins may serve other functions, so that their position and shape may not be entirely determined by hydrodynamic considerations. In the anglerfish, for example, the first spiny ray is modified into a fishing rod, in the live-bearing toothcarps the anterior anal rays form a gonopodium or intromittent organ for transferring sperm to the female, while in some bottom-living fishes the dorsal fin to a greater or lesser extent may aid in camouflage.

The shape and position of the paired fins, the pectoral and pelvic fins, is largely governed by the buoyancy of the fish, which in turn depends on whether a swimbladder is present. In the cartilaginous fishes – the sharks, rays and chimaeras – there is no swimbladder and since the fish is a little heavier than water it will sink unless constantly moving. The skates and rays have come to terms with this and spend most of their time on the

In most fishes the tail is the main propulsive fin (A). Some others (B) use their pectoral fins, the tails only providing extra speed when required. Trigger-fishes (C) swim by undulating their dorsal and anal fins, and pufferfishes (D) by supplementing these motions with movements of the pectoral fins. The sunfish (E) and seahorse (F) do not use their tails and rely solely on other fins for propulsion.

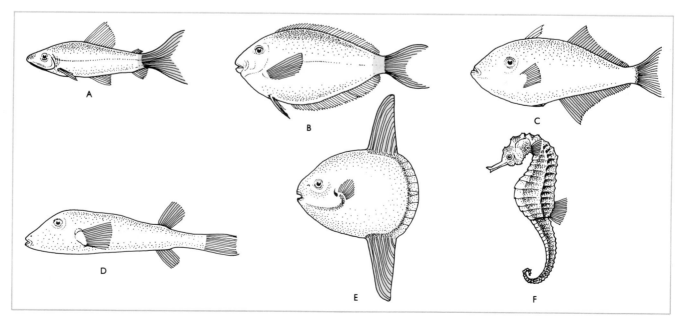

Reminiscent of the magic carpet, the Thornback ray moves gracefully through the water using wave-like movements of its expanded pectoral fins.

bottom. When they do move it is the large wing-like pectoral fins that supply the driving power, the tail acting chiefly as a rudder. Many sharks, on the other hand, must constantly keep on the move. Their pectoral fins are set low on the body and are spread more or less horizontally, thus providing a planing surface that lifts the front of the body against the downward thrust imparted by the tail. Slight adjustments of the pectorals can send the fish up or down, or aid in braking, while the twisting of only one pectoral can help in turning. Some sharks have partially solved the problem of sinking by using the liver as a buoyancy organ. The specific gravity of most fishes (the weight in grammes of one cubic centimetre of body tissue) is about 1·06–1·09, that is to say, more than either freshwater (1·00) or sea water (1·026). Sharks usually have very large and oily livers whose specific gravity is correspondingly low (0·86). Since the liver may comprise 20% of the weight of the shark, one can see how species like the Basking shark or the Whale shark can lie almost motionless at the surface. Yet another buoyancy method has been used by sharks. In a captive Sand shark *Odontaspis taurus* it was found that the fish gulped air at the surface and was then able to hold its position in the water while remaining motionless.

In all fishes that possess pectoral fins (absent for example in some eels) the fins are set just behind the head. In the bony fishes the pectorals are quite mobile and although usually folded into the sides of the body during fast swimming, can be used in a most delicate manner for turns, braking, rising, sinking or back-paddling, when stationary, against the outflow of water from the gill openings.

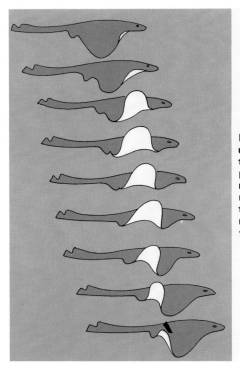

Rays swim by undulation of the wing-like pectoral fins, not by lateral movements of the body as in most other fish.

35

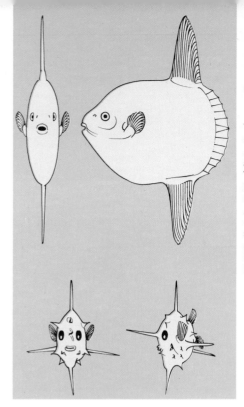

The Ocean sunfish *Mola mola*, head-on and side-view. The juveniles, like those of a related species *Masturus lanceolatus* shown below, are quite unlike the adult in shape.

In sharks and in the more primitive bony fishes the pelvic fins lie somewhere near the midpoint of the body. The early naturalists termed such fins abdominal as opposed to the thoracic pelvic fins of advanced bony fishes, which lie just behind, below or even just in front of the pectoral fin bases. The position of the pelvic fins is very significant because it is correlated with the ability of the fish exactly to control its buoyancy by adding or removing gas from the swimbladder. As explained in the previous chapter, the advanced perch-like fishes are masters of controlled buoyancy, so that the most intricate turns, pitches, yaws or rolls can be performed under the guidance of the fins. The most manoeuverable of these weightless fishes are those that have a rather short and deep body, as opposed to the slender fusiform bodies of trouts, salmons and herrings. In such fishes the pelvic fins have moved forward from the primitive abdominal position to below the pectoral fins and in this position the two pairs can act in concert. Fishes such as perches, butterfly-fishes or sunfishes *Lepomis* can suddenly stop short in their tracks – a thing impossible for a large shark – by spreading the pectoral fins. However, this immediately lifts the front of the body. The low-set pelvic fins act in the opposite way, producing a downward drag. The combination of the two produces a perfect brake. Since the elaboration of the swimbladder into an exactly controlled hydrostatic organ is a major trend in the evolution of fishes, the early naturalists placed great importance on the position of the pelvic fins in their classifications.

36

Swimming. Methods of swimming are varied and much depends on how and where the fish finds its food. Does it migrate to reproduce? Does it flee from predators or prey on other fishes? Does it live an open, active life or does it lurk, hide or bury itself? The speed of predators is largely dependent on the speed of their prey but for fishes, unlike predators on land, the prey is usually considerably smaller than the predator. As a general rule, the larger a fish the faster it can swim (usually $1\frac{1}{2}$ to 2 times as fast as a fish half its length), therefore it is more economical to feed on small animals. The actual speeds of fishes are difficult to record, especially when the fish is too large to be placed in a tank and have its progress measured against a current of known speed. A stickleback of 10 cm may swim at 1–2 mph, a Sea trout at 5–6, a Striped bass *Roccus* at about 12, a dolphinfish *Coryphaena* at about 20, and a tuna at 40. Experiments have shown, however, that top speeds are only briefly sustained, perhaps for 20 seconds or less. The cruising speeds of the fishes mentioned here are very much less, a burst of speed being necessary only for pursuit or escape.

The really fast or powerful fishes are extremely efficient in their use of energy. Comparison between the performance of a 7 ft (say 2 m) Blue shark and a submarine showed that, weight for weight, the shark required six times less driving power. As mentioned earlier, tunas and some large sharks are able, by a heat counter-current system, to retain heat in their muscles, thus increasing the speed of the muscle chemistry. Yet another means of getting the most out of swimming activity is by reducing the drag caused by friction between the body and the water. A study of dolphins (mammals – but the same holds true for swift fishes) showed that they were able to achieve speeds that, theoretically, were impossible if one calculated the motive power available and the resistance caused by friction. The solution to this paradox lay in the behaviour of water in the layer bounding the fish's body. Normally, this layer is turbulent and creates drag, but under special conditions a thin layer of water adheres to the body so that in effect water is moving past water and the friction is much reduced. How a boundary layer is maintained is still not clear. Sharks have bodies roughened by small denticles;

The European seahorse *Hippocampus guttulatus* swimming ▷ in typical upright position. These curious fishes swim by movements of the dorsal and pectoral fins.

Mediterranean seahorse *Hippocampus guttulatus*.

do these serve to 'anchor' a boundary layer? In the tuna-like fishes, on the other hand, the scales are small, often absent, over most of the body. The answer to this problem would be of the greatest interest to ship designers.

Although the motive power for most fishes comes from undulations of the body culminating in lateral sweeps of the tail, the other fins may also be used in propulsion, chiefly by the rather slower-moving fishes. Rowing movements of the pectoral fins are used by some fishes, for example surgeonfishes, and in the pufferfishes the pectorals are used in the manner of propellers. Triggerfishes tend to use undulations of the dorsal and anal fins; the gentle undulation of the dorsal fin in the African bichir gives this fish a majestic, effortless appearance as it

cruises along; in the knifefishes (Gymnotidae) and the Electric eel it is the anal fin that is undulated. A most curious method of swimming is found in the Ocean sunfish *Mola*. In this fish the tail degenerates, the body becomes disc-like, and the muscles formerly serving the tail reinforce those attaching to the high dorsal and anal fins. This huge fish, which may reach a ton in weight, apparently sculls itself along with the two vertical fins but is occasionally reported floating on its side at the surface. In some fishes the armour encasing the body is too stiff for lateral movements and all propulsion must come from the fins. This is clearly the case in the boxfishes. In seahorses movement results from rapid vibrations of the small pectoral and dorsal fins, the two being beautifully coordinated to keep the fish in an upright position. Another group of fishes that swim vertically are the shrimpfishes (Centriscidae), sometimes moving in small shoals or sheltering between the long spines of Sea urchins. Here again, movement is by rapid vibrations of the fins, the body being inflexible. In skates and rays the flattening of the body makes lateral movement impossible, except for the tail. Instead, the pectoral 'wings' are undulated and in the enormous but harmless Manta rays or devilfishes, which may reach 10 ft (3 m) between the pectoral tips, the power is such that the fish can leap clear of the water and return with a resounding splash.

Not all fishes are concerned with speed but those that live in rivers and streams are involved in a constant battle to keep their position, even if they have no ambitions to ascend. Usually such fishes are spawned near the edges of the river, where conditions are quieter, and only venture into the stream when they are larger. In torrential hillstreams, however, such escape is impossible and members of several fish families have evolved methods of keeping their place against the rush of water around them. Examples are found amongst the naked catfishes (for example, *Astroblepus*) of the Andes and the carps, loaches, suckers and catfishes of Africa, India and the Indo-Australian Archipelago; in most cases only a few adventurous members of a family have fought their way into the torrents, but in the Himalayan region an entire family of loaches, the Homolopteridae, have become adapted to this

way of life. In all such fishes the belly is flattened and the back rounded, so that water cannot pass under the fish and lift it up and away. In addition, many have frictional ridges on the ventral side to prevent the fish from slipping backwards and a suction disc formed by folds of skin, by specialized pelvic fins, or by a round suctorial mouth. The paired fins are set low on the body and if not used as a sucker can still aid the fish by preventing water from flowing underneath.

Fishes that ascend rivers to spawn, such as salmon, may require power not merely to battle against a fast current but to negotiate waterfalls. Large salmon can leap a fall of up to 10 ft (3 m), although often the fish enters the fall and swims up the last bit. The ability to leap such heights depends on a very rapid underwater acceleration, a last powerful thrust with the tail, and the sudden emergence into a medium hundreds of times less dense. For the salmon there is good reason to jump, but what can be said of the tarpons, the mako sharks and even the large Basking shark? These can leap over 6 ft (say 2 m) into the air but, like the huge Manta ray, can hardly be troubled by predators. Even quite small Grey mullets are adept at leaping and are difficult to catch with a seine net, so that in this case at least, jumping is probably a means of escaping potential enemies. Some of the blennies leap from one rock pool to another at low tide, showing an extraordinary ability to land exactly in the next pool and not on the dry rock.

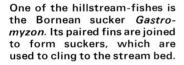

One of the hillstream-fishes is the Bornean sucker *Gastromyzon*. Its paired fins are joined to form suckers, which are used to cling to the stream bed.

Flight. In all these instances, once the fish has left the water, it behaves essentially like an inert missile and there is no attempt to prolong the flight or alter its direction. In the South American hatchetfishes (Gasteropelecidae) the body, as the common name implies, is highly compressed and deep, the chest housing large muscles for the pectoral fins. These small fishes leap from the water and vibrate the pectoral fins rapidly enough to produce a distinct buzzing noise. The flight is only of short duration, but presumably the pectorals help to prolong it. This is perhaps the nearest that fishes have approached to true flight, in the sense of 'wing' flapping to maintain height. The classic flyingfishes are in fact not flyers but gliders. They belong to the group of fishes that includes the sauries (Scombresocidae), the garfishes (Belonidae) and the half-beaks (Hemirhamphidae), all of which leap from the water and skitter along the surface. In doing so, they can to some extent change direction, but the tail remains in the water and provides the motive power. In the flyingfishes, however, the pectoral fins are enormously expanded and in some species the pelvic fins are also enlarged. Rising fast to the surface with the paired fins folded, the fish either leaps straight out or taxis for a moment at the surface by rapid vibrations of the tail. At the same time, the pectorals and pelvics are extended and the fish rises into the air. The flight may last up to half a minute and cover a distance of about 1,300 ft (say 400 m). Like some oceanic birds, flyingfishes probably make use of updraughts of air in the troughs of waves, while in a stiff breeze they can rise 20–30 ft (6–9 m), often landing on the decks of ships. Hunted by dolphinfishes and some of the large tuna-like fishes flight offers them a temporary escape.

The so-called Flying gurnard of the Atlantic and Mediterranean, *Dactylopterus volitans*, is another fish with very large pectoral fins which in this case are also highly coloured. When disturbed it will suddenly spread its fins and the following flash of colour, together with the enormous increase in the apparent size of the fish, is probably enough to deter a potential predator. This species has a rather heavy body, so that the 'wings' may be for defence rather than flight; certainly there is insufficient musculature to flap the pectoral fins. In the freshwater butterflyfish *Pantodon* of Africa, on the other hand, the body is also rather robust when compared with that of a flyingfish, but the pectorals can be flapped and the fish definitely leaves the water for short periods. These, like the hatchetfishes, are often kept by aquarists who are sometimes not aware that the tank should be covered.

While the majority of fishes swim, some bottom-living forms have evolved ways of creeping, crawling and burrowing. The gurnards, for example, have a number of finger-like pectoral rays with which they creep along, while the frogfishes (Antennariidae) and related batfishes (Ogocephalidae) have a muscular base to the pectoral and finger-like 'hands' that are used both for crawling and for clinging to rocks and weeds. The mudskippers (Periophthalmidae) have similar muscular pectoral fins. These fishes both skitter along the surface of the water and also sit on mudbanks, sticks or rocks. The body is supported by the pectoral fins and these are used rather in the manner of crutches when the fish

Freshwater hatchetfishes are capable of short flights, the deep chest housing muscles that vibrate the pectoral fins.

40

African butterflyfish, *Pantodon bucholzi*, can fly for short distances by vibrating its pectoral fins.

moves around. Another fish that crawls on dry land is the celebrated Climbing perch *Anabas testudineus*, reputedly a tree-climber but most likely deposited in trees by fish-eating birds. This fish uses not only the paired fins but also the spiny gill covers as anchors, while the body is flexed from one side to the other. Similarly, certain African catfishes *Clarias* use the pectoral fins to 'elbow' their way forwards over damp ground, whereas the snakeheads (Channidae) use rowing motions of the pectorals. Since progress is slow, such fishes can only survive by means of accessory breathing organs capable of utilizing atmospheric oxygen. Freshwater eels, although lacking such organs, are able as young elvers to wriggle their way up almost vertical surfaces where there is only a mere skin of water, while the adults can work their way through damp grass using the same writhing movements as in swimming. The feat of the elvers is matched by that of certain Andean catfishes *Astroblepus*, mentioned earlier in

Climbing perch, *Anabas testudineus* does not climb but can make quite long journeys overland.

connection with their ability to live in torrential conditions. By the use of a suctorial mouth and a suction pad formed by folds around the pelvic fins, these fishes can climb vertical or even overhanging rocky walls.

Although not necessarily a method of locomotion, burrowing is done by a number of bottom-living fishes. Most eels tend to work their way through small openings in order to find refuge, but the Garden eels spend their time buried in the sand with the front part of the body exposed and swaying, as they search for food. At the first sign of danger they disappear so rapidly back into their burrows that they are extremely difficult to catch. The mud-minnow *Umbra* is a highly efficient burrower, able to make its way rapidly through mud or sand, whereas the flatfishes sometimes actively burrow in search of food, but more often shovel or fan the sand on top of themselves for camouflage.

Many fishes remain in the locality in which they were spawned whereas others travel considerable distances, either regularly to breed (migration) or in the course of their search for food or more amenable conditions. For the most part, reef fishes remain close to their 'home' reef. Tagging experiments on a reef off Florida showed that the fishes were almost invariably recaptured on their home reef, some reappearing in the traps as many as 40 times. This can be contrasted with the wide-ranging oceanic fishes, such as the sailfish, sword-

41

With head raised and pectoral fins spread, the fish 'taxis' over the surface, the lower lobe of the tailfin still in the water.

fish and many of the tunas, or the regular spawning migrations of anadromous fishes like salmon or catadromous fishes like the freshwater eels. The Sockeye salmon of British Columbia, for example, not only ranges far out into the Pacific but migrates inland for over 700 miles, travelling at the rate of 30 miles a day; the Chinook salmon has been recorded over 1,000 miles up British Columbian rivers, having presumably travelled considerable distances in the ocean before reaching the river mouth.

From what has been said, it is clear that fishes are truly masters of their medium, although it has taken several hundred million years to achieve this. The ancestors of modern fishes, just as the sharks of today, were faced with two problems, gravity and viscosity. Once the first was solved and weightlessness achieved through the development of an efficient swimbladder, then the way was open for all kinds of experiments in manoeuverability. The result was the modification of fin and body shapes or the release of these for purposes other than swimming. It is not surprising, therefore, that the greatest diversity is found in the most advanced fishes, the spiny-rayed perch-like fishes that comprise nearly half the present day total of known species.

Feeding

The success of fishes, in terms of their diversity and numbers, is to a large extent a measure of their success in finding adequate food, sometimes in the most unlikely situations. Within any given environment there are obviously a limited number of organisms on which fishes can feed, including other fishes. The evolution of each new species of animal, however, both creates new feeding problems while providing yet another potential source of food for those already present. Thus one can see that the web of food relationships grows more complex as the diversity of organisms increases. At the same time, the complexity of food relationships makes the experiment of tapping new food resources worthwhile, leading as it does to the evolution of new forms and thus a further addition to the food web. The results of this 'explosion' in complexity can be seen in some of the African lakes, where 100 or more rather closely related species, descended from only a few original colonizers, have developed a most extraordinary range of feeding habits, from filter-feeding to fish eating, not to mention such bizarre specialists as fish scale eaters and eye-biters.

As much as any other aspect of fishes, feeding demonstrates very clearly the strong correlation between structure, function and habits (morphology, physiology and ethology). Each member of this triad is intimately bound to the other two, not only by the day to day running of the system but in an historical sense by their mutual development from an earlier system.

The Mouth. As far as structure is concerned, this is clearly the most important element. In the most primitive fishes, no true jaws were present, a condition still seen in the lampreys and hagfishes. In both of these modern representatives of the jawless fishes (Agnatha) the mouth is a rather funnel-shaped aperture. In lampreys it is in the form of a disc bearing rows of horny teeth and leading down to a pair of scraping toothplates and further teeth on a muscular tongue. With the sucker-like disc the lamprey attaches itself to its prey (usually another fish) and rasps at the flesh. Hagfishes lack the disc with its circles of horny teeth, but have a well-developed rasping tongue with which they bore into the flesh of dead or dying fishes, often disappearing right inside the carcass.

The suctorial and rasping mouth is no doubt efficient, but it offers very little scope for modification into any other sort of mouth. Such mouths reappear among the bony fishes, for example, the catfishes that browse on algal-covered stones, but here they represent merely one of innumerable possibilities opened up by the evolution of jaws. With the development of cartilaginous or bony struts around the mouth came the ability to seize, to bite, to nibble and to chew, in a word, to perform the many complex jaw movements employed by fishes in feeding. This led to the evolution of predators armed with strong teeth and like any new instrument of war, gave a sharp impetus to the evolution of better methods of defence and escape.

The River lamprey *Lampetra fluviatilis*, one of the few remaining species of jawless fishes (Agnatha).

In sharks, rays and chimaeras the jaws, like other parts of the skeleton, are entirely of cartilage, but there is no question of their inferiority to bone in respect of strength; the almost effortless ability of the Great white shark to shear through a man's arm or a leg is well documented. In chimaeras, rays and the majority of sharks the mouth is on the underside of the head and overshot by the snout. The position of the mouth, as in all fishes, gives an indication of the normal feeding posture; skates and rays scavenge along the bottom, while sharks must approach their prey from above. The Whale shark, the largest of all fish-like vertebrates and reaching a length of 50 ft (15 m) or more, is an exception and has a terminal mouth adapted to feeding on plankton.

The jaws of bony fishes, although superficially similar to those of the cartilaginous fishes, have a different evolutionary history, as will be outlined later. In essence, however, they function in the same manner, the bottom jaw being snapped upwards against the top jaw for biting, although many other kinds of movement are also possible. The lower jaw acts as a pair of single rigid elements, but the upper jaw comprises two pairs of bones, the premaxillae in front and the maxillae behind. The evolution of the mouth in bony fishes has been largely a matter of excluding the maxillae from the gape of the mouth and developing them into levers for opening the mouth even wider. At the same time the premaxillae have been loosened and by a system of levers, ball-joints, ligaments and muscles have been made protrusible. The protrusile mouth is a most important development. It becomes well-developed in a number of families, reaching an extreme in the John Dory *Zeus faber* and in the leiognathids or slip-mouths, in which a fish of 2·5 in (6 cm) can shoot its mouth outwards and downwards a centimetre or more. One advantage of mouth protrusion is that the fish can feed off a slope without having to stand on its head, in which position it could be vulnerable to attack. Thus surgeonfishes, which have non-protrusile jaws and which feed at all kinds of angles, also have sharp defensive spines at the base of the tail. More important, perhaps, is the fact that when the jaws are protruded, the mouth cavity is enlarged, with the result that water is sucked in. In this way the fish can both pluck its food from the bottom and suck it in. The efficacy of this method of feeding is shown by the very frequent occurrence of protrusile jaws amongst bony fishes.

Once the mouth had become supported by bones, it became possible to angle the jaws in the direction in which food was expected. In most fishes the mouth is terminal, but in fishes that take their food from the surface, such as the toothcarps, the jaws point upwards, while in bottom feeders the jaws are on the underside of the snout, so that the fish can swim horizontally in search of its prey. A further development was the extension of the snout to form a tube, with the jaws at the end of it, as in the elephant snoutfishes of Africa or certain of the butterflyfishes (Chaetodontidae) of coral reefs. In both cases the long snout is used to probe into crevices and, in the case of the African fishes, into mud. The flutemouths offer another example of this type of tubular snout and it is seen yet again in seahorses, the prey being sucked into the mouth in pipette-like fashion.

Although a few fishes, such as the dreaded pirhanas of South American rivers, bite off pieces from prey larger than themselves, in most cases the prey is relatively small and can be taken into the mouth or swallowed whole. The mouth is therefore of moderate proportions, that is to say, its height and width when open do not exceed the fish's girth. In certain deep-sea fishes, for whom an encounter with a potential meal is rather less frequent than in the heavily populated upper waters, the jaws (and of course the stomach) are adapted to swallowing and accommodating fishes that are in fact larger than the predator itself. The classic example is *Chauliodus sloanei*, in which the anterior vertebrae are modified to enable the head to be thrown upwards when seizing its prey. This greatly enlarges the gape of the mouth. At the same time as the lower jaw is depressed, the heart and gills are drawn away from the area to prevent them being damaged by the struggling prey. As a result, these fishes are able to swallow others of their own size, or even larger. A slight tilting of the head generally occurs in bony

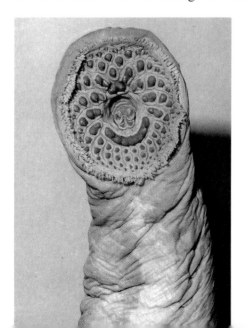

The suctorial mouth of the Sea lamprey.

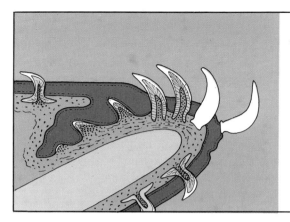

◁ Section through a shark's jaw showing stages in the development of a tooth to the point where it is about to be shed and replaced by one behind.

John dory *Zeus faber* ▷ seizes small fishes with a sudden protrusion of its telescopic jaws.

fishes when the mouth is opened for feeding, but in the coelacanth and its fossil relatives there is a most curious intracranial joint which allows the front part of the skull to bend upwards automatically when the mouth is opened; this widens the gape of the jaws while enlarging the mouth cavity, both of which are of value in swallowing large prey.

The Teeth. Having developed bones to support the edges of the mouth, the next logical step was to arm the bones with teeth. In most sharks, which are essentially carnivorous or scavenging fishes, the teeth are triangular or awl-shaped and lie in a single series around the perimeter of the jaws. Behind the outer teeth are further series of replacement teeth. Rather few observations have been made on the frequency with which teeth are lost and replaced, but in the Lemon shark *Negaprion* individual teeth seem to last for about 10 days. In the Nurse shark *Ginglymostoma*, two or three series of teeth may be in use at any one time and a development from this is to combine many rows of teeth into a kind of flat pavement for grinding or crushing food (shellfish, crustaceans and so on). Pavement teeth are rather rare in sharks, but are found in the Smooth hounds *Mustelus* and the Comb-toothed sharks *Hexanchus*. All skates and rays have a pavement of teeth. The Port Jackson sharks are most unusual in having flat crushing teeth at the back of the jaw and sharp biting teeth in front. In the chimaeras the teeth are in the form of three flat plates, usually armed with points, and presumably the fishes can both seize and crush their prey. In the Great white shark, a species that reaches 21 ft (6·4 m) in length, the triangular teeth may be 2 in (5 cm) in length. Terrifying as this monster is, it is dwarfed by its fossil relative that is known to us only by its 4·6 in (11·7 cm) teeth.

The teeth of sharks and rays are confined to the jaws and are rather stereotyped – pointed, triangular, pavement. In the bony fishes, on the other hand, teeth may be present on many of the bones of the mouth or throat and they show an extraordinary diversity in shape, size and function. Thus teeth may be found on the tongue, on the sides and roof of the mouth, on the bones that make up the basket of struts on which the gills are hung (those at the rear forming the pharyngeal or throat teeth), and in some cases merely as isolated tooth patches lying in the skin that lines the mouth. The jaw teeth are used principally for seizing, cutting, nibbling, wounding, crushing and piercing. The teeth in the mouth cavity crush or break up the prey, compress the mouthful into a manageable lump, prevent its escape or ensure that its progress is towards the throat. The pharyngeal teeth are both for combing, grinding or crushing the food, and for pushing it backwards. The jaw teeth themselves may be long and canine-like, flat and sharp-edged, fused into a beak, round and molar-like, fine and comb-like, massive, delicate or minute. Before describing the way in which these various types of teeth are used, mention should be made of the gillrakers, because of their highly important role in feeding. The gillrakers are typically small spines along the front edge of the gill arches. If the gill arches are seen as a series of four or five hoops in the gill cavity, each overlapping the one behind, then the gill filaments trail from the hind edge and the gillrakers point forwards along the leading edge. In this way the gillrakers turn the gill arches into a kind of basket and where the gillrakers are fine and close-set the whole apparatus operates much like a sieve.

Fishes can be grouped into two main feeding categories – the plant feeders and the animal feeders (remembering that by plants and animals we also mean the often minute floating creatures of the plankton). A third possibility, found in the grey mullets (Mugilidae), is feeding on detritus that settles at the bottom. This takes the form of the

45

Piranhas, South American river fishes, are credited with unusual ferocity. Some, such as the Red piranha, are kept as aquarium fishes, but can cause trouble in mixed company.

remains of animals and plants, and perhaps the bacterial flora which is actively breaking it down. Mullets have a mouth adapted to scraping and sucking food from the bottom. The gillrakers are long, close-set, edged with minute spines and joined at their tips, thus making a sturdy sieve to trap fine particles, as water is forced out through the gill openings. Like a plankton net, the particles are washed backwards and in some way are sufficiently concentrated for the fish to swallow without taking in water as well. The stomach is gizzard-like and serves to break up larger particles before the food is passed to the long intestine. Stomach and intestine seem to contain mostly mud, but evidently these fishes are able to extract nourishment from the organic matter it contains.

Plant-eaters or herbivorous fishes are in the minority, but they constitute an important element in the general web of feeding relationships. They are also of great significance to fisheries because they

Gnathonemus elephas, one of the Elephant snout fishes that truly lives up to its name. Most species have a less pronounced 'trunk'.

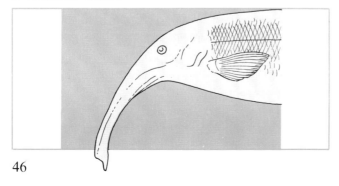

convert plant matter directly into animal protein without the intervention of some intermediate step or steps. Since only about one tenth of the food consumed by an animal actually contributes to an increase in its weight – the rest being expended in maintenance activities – it is obviously an advantage in farming if the steps in the food chain are as few as possible. Thus cows are more productive per hectare than lions; similarly, ponds of Grass carp yield more than those stocked with predatory Black bass.

The Grass carp of China feeds on higher plants, cropping the edges of rivers or feeding on grass cuttings or waste leafage from crops when grown in ponds. So rapid is its growth rate, up to 1 lb (0·45 kg) per month, that it has become a popular pond fish throughout much of southeast Asia and parts of Africa. As with all carps, there are no teeth in the jaws but very strong pharyngeal teeth in the throat, with which the plant matter is macerated. Some of the tilapias of Africa feed on higher plants, as many a novice has discovered after his aquarium has been stripped of expensive waterplants by *Tilapia zillii*. A much greater number of herbivorous fishes make use of small or microscopic plant life. In some species food is gathered by scraping algae off rocks or leaves and in such fishes the jaw teeth are usually small, numerous and comb-like. Among the cichlid fishes of Lake Nyasa are many examples of rock-scrapers and plant-scrapers that leave a neatly mown swathe behind them. Certain of the catfishes and carps practice scraping. These usually have the mouth on the underside of the head, and the upper lip is often modified into a pad or a horny scraper. Collected in bulk like this, the food can be fairly easily passed to the throat and swallowed, but certain fishes feed partly or wholly by filtering minute plants or animals from the water, and the problem arises of how to concentrate the food into a mass large enough to swallow. The actual filtration is often achieved by means of very numerous, fine and barbed gillrakers, as in the mullet. It appears that in such fishes mucus is secreted in the mouth and streams over the gillrakers, entangling the microscopic plants; the stream of water must then force the mucus back towards the throat. In a number of unrelated fishes – the osteoglossid *Heterotis*, certain characins and certain herrings and anchovies – pouches (epibranchial organs) are developed in the throat and these probably concentrate the food into a bolus ready to be swallowed. It is still a puzzle whether unrelated fishes could all hit on the same

Archerfish *Toxotes jaculatus* and, right, showing how an insect is shot down with drops of water.

ingenious answer to the problem, or whether the potential to develop an epibranchial organ is something they have all inherited from a remote common ancestor.

In plant-eating fishes the stomach is sometimes absent or much reduced, although a muscular, gizzard-like stomach may be present where mud or sand particles are taken in, to assist perhaps in grinding the food. The intestine, on the other hand, is usually very long, many times the fish's length, and must necessarily be coiled. Digestion of plant material depends on the physical rupture of the cell walls to release their content. In the case of minute algae this is not possible and a number of cichlid fishes, which have no enzyme capable of dissolving the cellulose walls of green and blue-green algae, pass this potential food through the gut in such an unharmed state that cultures of the algae can be raised from the fishes' faeces. Other cichlid fishes feed mainly on diatoms, which, having a cell wall of silica, are equally minute and even more indigestible. In this case, however, the fishes can make use of such food because the cell wall is already perforated and can allow digestive juices to enter.

In many herbivorous fishes, the peritoneum or lining of the body cavity is black. This is especially noticeable in the carp-like fishes (Cyprinidae), the plant-eaters having a dark peritoneum and the species that feed on animal life having the peritoneum silvery or speckled. A black peritoneum is also found in many deep-sea fishes, but these cannot be herbivores since plant life is restricted to the well-lit upper layers. The explanation seems to be that the dark peritoneum prevents the passage of light. In herbivorous fishes light is thought to be detrimental to the processes of digestion; in the deep-sea fishes, on the other hand, the light is coming from inside, for these fishes feed on luminous organisms and it would be unwise for a fish to advertise its presence by a glowing stomach.

Animal Feeders. Fishes that feed on other animals are in the majority. They show a diversity in feeding habits commensurate with the enormous variety of animals on which they prey. At one end of the scale are those that merely filter out small animals from the myriad floating members of the plankton, while at the other are those whose mouths, jaws and teeth are adapted for making an individual choice of meal. Curiously enough, the filter feeders are not all small fishes. One of the largest of these fishes is the Basking shark, a species that grows to more than 30 ft (9 m) in length. It has very numerous bristle-like gillrakers that become erect when the mouth opens and act like a sieve. When feeding, the fish cruises with its mouth open and it has been calculated that a specimen of about 23 ft (7 m), cruising

The Great barracuda *Sphyraena barracuda*, found on both sides of the Atlantic, has a reputation for ferocity.

47

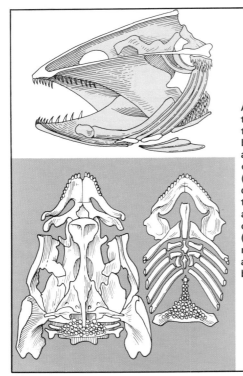

A vertical section through the skull of a bowfin (top), a ventral view of the skull (left), and a dorsal view of the lower jaw and gill arches of a wrasse (right). Pharyngeal teeth are indicated by (P).

at 2 knots, will strain some two million kg of sea-water per hour. After feeding, the stomach will contain a tighly-packed mass of planktonic animals and quantities of mucus, the latter presumably used in collecting the food and later being resorbed. An odd feature of the Basking shark is its loss of gill-rakers in winter and apparent regrowth of them the following spring. It has been suggested that, since winter plankton densities are very low in northern waters, the energy expended in trying to collect food would not be balanced by the energy derived from the food, so that the fishes do better to retire to the bottom, shed their gillrakers and quietly await the bloom of plankton in the spring. This does not explain, however, the loss of gillrakers and presumably cessation of feeding, in the rich waters off central California where Basking sharks are present throughout the year.

The largest of all plankton feeders is the Whale

Bluefish, *Pomatomus saltator*, found in both the Atlantic and Indo-Pacific and well known for its ferocity when feeding.

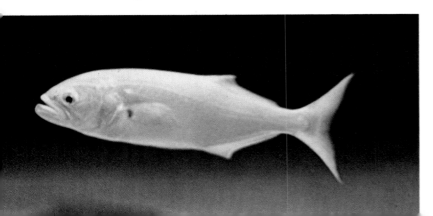

shark. This huge but harmless species feeds in much the same way as the Basking shark but in this case the sieving device is in the form of cartilaginous rods supporting a fine mesh of spongy tissue between the gill arches. Whale sharks, like Basking sharks, spend much time at the surface. They have been seen with their heads at or above the surface, slowly rising and sinking so that water pours into the mouth. On at least one occasion, Blackfin tuna, presumably feeding on the same small fishes as the Whale sharks, have been seen to leap right into the open mouth of the latter. This might also explain the presence of quite large tuna in the stomachs of the rather lethargic Whitetip oceanic shark, a species that has been observed swimming at the surface with its mouth open in areas where tuna shoals were attacking schools of small sardines.

A very large number of fishes, both in freshwaters and in the sea, feed on moderate-sized animals, including other fishes. Some fishes are specialists and take only or mainly one kind of food. The squaretail *Tetragonurus*, for example, seems to live almost entirely on jelly-fishes. Others, like the cod, seem to take whatever is abundant, be it a fish, a crustacean or a mollusc. For this reason studies of stomach contents may not indicate the preferred food so much as the food actually available at that time. Species like the Common carp are even more generalized feeders, and while mainly subsisting on vegetable matter, will also eat small fishes, insects, worms and crustaceans. Jaws and dentition match the food. Pike have a formidable array of teeth, both in the jaws and lining the mouth, those on the roof of the mouth being flexible and allowing the prey only one choice of direction, as frogs, fishes and waterbirds discover. Fishes such as the barracudas and the bluefish have sharp chopping teeth, used as much to maim their prey as to reduce it to manageable proportions. At the other end of the scale are the fine, bristle-like teeth of the butterflyfishes (Chaetodontidae) and some of the African cichlid fishes that are used for delicately plucking small animals from the bottom or from crevices.

Specialist Feeders. Although the permutations in jaws, teeth and habits are almost limitless, there are certain species whose feeding is highly specialized and these have long excited the interest of naturalists. Some species, because of their real or reputed danger to man, have found their way into literature and folklore. Others again, formerly overlooked, have shown remarkable adaptations once their habits have been studied under water.

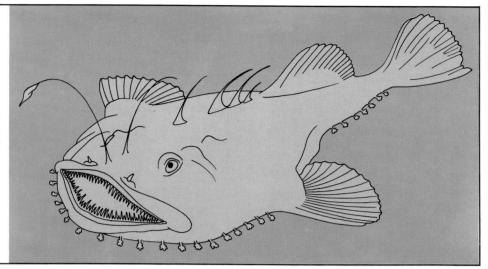

The anglerfish *Lophius pisca-torius*, showing the fishing rod and bait used in catching its prey.

One of the best known specialists is the archerfish *Toxotes jaculatus*, renowned for its ability to shoot droplets of water at insects above the surface. When an insect is spotted, the fish pushes its snout out of the water and squirts a fine jet along a channel formed by the ridged tongue and grooved palate. Since the eyes of the fish are still under the water, the apparent line of sight caused by refraction must be modified to produce the correct trajectory. Archerfishes are able to make this compensation and usually hit with the first shot; if they miss, they will alter their position and try again. However, it appears that the force of the jet cannot be properly controlled and on occasions the insect may be knocked out of reach. Kept in an aquarium, they will often shoot at spots or blemishes on the glass.

The next example might seem rather mundane since its feeding habits are in no way remarkable,

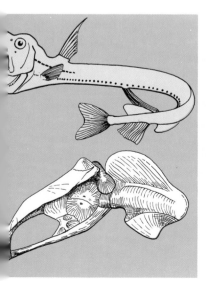

The viperfish *Chaulio-dus sloanei*, a deep-sea species which throws back its head when striking at its prey. A remarkable adaptation to this is the enlargement of the first vertebra (below). This vertebra, several times larger than any of the others, serves to take the strain when the head is thrown back and also acts for attachment of the muscles required for this action.

but it does give an excellent lesson in the importance of finding out just what a particular fish does eat. The fish in question is the gambusia *Gambusia affinis*, often called the guppy or millionsfish in Trinidad and the other Caribbean islands where it occurs. When world-wide attempts were being made to eradicate mosquitoes in countries where malaria and other diseases were rife, the gambusia was held to be the answer because of its partiality to mosquito larvae. Indeed, it did score some notable successes, but what was overlooked at the time was that it also fed on the eggs and fry of other fishes. The result was that it gradually wiped out most or all of the native species of mosquito-eating fishes and took a heavy toll on other species as well. In one experiment a pond with 11 goldfish and 250 guppies remained more or less stable over five years. The guppies were then removed, with the result that the next year the goldfishes had increased to 30 and the following year were nearly double that number. What was even more striking was that after seven years the weight of goldfish in the pond was three times the original weight of goldfish plus guppies. Thus the guppies, unrestrained by the normal checks in their own environment, were able to cut down the stock of a larger and stronger fish.

Rivalling the archerfish in specialization are the anglerfishes, a group that includes deep and shallow-water forms. In all of them the first dorsal finray is modified into a fishing rod or *illicium*. In the Common angler *Lophius piscatorius*, the first ray is well forward on the snout and is thin and flexible, with a small flap of skin at the tip (known as the *esca*, from the Latin for bait). Lying in the sand, the fish dangles the flap of skin in front of its large

49

mouth until small fishes are attracted to it. Suddenly the mouth, with its sharp needle-like teeth, opens wide and the prey is sucked in. Aristotle, over 2,000 years ago, was the first to record this remarkable habit. The ceratioid or deep-sea anglers are even better equipped. A mere flap of skin would be of little use in dark or twilight waters, and so in this case the *esca* or lure is luminescent. In the genus *Linophryne* there is also a tree-like luminescent barbel hanging from the chin. In *Ceratias* and *Lasiognathus* the illicium can be slowly retracted so that the prey is drawn towards the mouth before being seized. The ultimate sophistication is shown by the bottom-living *Galatheathauma*, found at depths of about 13,000 ft (say 4,000 m). In this fish the luminous organ is actually inside the mouth.

Specialization of this kind, in which some other body part is used for feeding, is not common, but there is growing evidence that the swordfish as well as marlins use their 'spear' for transfixing their prey. In two well authenticated cases Black marlin have been found with tunas in the stomach that had clearly been speared before swallowing, while bales or rubber from ships torpedoed during the war were reported to have broken-off marlin spears embedded in them. Certainly, the swordfish is well known for ramming wooden boats and ships, although this would seem to stem more from aggression, or even negligence, than from hunger. In sawfishes and saw sharks the snout is prolonged into a flat blade with teeth down either side. Although this weapon is probably used in the obvious way – to slash at prey – rather few observations have been made.

The diet of carnivorous fishes does not normally include man, not only because man is a comparatively rare visitor, but because few predatory fishes

A species of parrotfish *Scarus*. Note the parrot-like beak with which this fish feeds on corals.

A marine butterflyfish *Pomacanthus arcuatus*, a typical ▷ inhabitant of coral reefs where competition for food is high.

take on opponents larger than themselves. Some exceptions have been mentioned already, of which the South American piranhas are a good example. Travellers' tales speak of men and large animals having the flesh picked off their bones before they could make good their escape and although such stories may be exaggerated, there is no doubt of the ferocity of these fishes. The piranhas are characins (Characinidae) with short, powerful jaws and sharp cutting teeth, the largest species reaching almost 16 in (40 cm). They swim in shoals and, by repute, the smell of blood will bring hundreds in for the kill, the piranhas then falling into a kind of 'feeding frenzy.' A similar kind of frenzy is seen in the bluefish *Pomatomus* of the Atlantic, a species that has been described as an animated chopping machine. These fishes will cut and tear into shoals of fishes only slightly smaller than themselves, leaving a trail of blood and fragments behind. Another rapacious fish, and one that is much feared in certain parts of the world, is the Great barracuda *Sphyraena barracuda*. Reaching over 6 ft (2 m) in length and armed with rows of large shearing teeth, this pike-like fish certainly appears formidable, although skin-divers often say that its reputation is overrated. Nevertheless, more than two dozen attacks on swimmers have been attributed to it in the last century. Skin-divers probably pay more respect to the Moray eels, of which some species grow to at least two metres and perhaps nearly three. These large eels live in crevices or holes in coral reefs and on occasions can be extremely aggressive. It is popularly believed that morays will not release their grip once they have bitten, thus being potentially able to drown the unfortunate skindiver. It is also thought that their bite is poisonous. Neither of these are true, but there is no doubt that the bite is strong and can cause considerable damage. However, attacks are usually the result of provocation, not an attempt to feed.

Morays, barracudas and piranhas have reputations for attacking man, but in popular mythology it is sharks that are considered the real man-eaters. To some extent the myth that tropical waters seethe with hungry sharks only too ready to snap off an arm or leg has been exploded. Numerous films and reports by skindivers show that sharks are frequently timid and can be frightened off by some kind of aggressive behaviour on the part of the swimmer.

Nevertheless, shark fatalities occur every year and in certain areas, such as the eastern shores of Australia, considerable sums are spent on safeguarding bathing beaches by means of barriers, tanglenets, look-outs and so forth. In 1958 a Shark Research Panel was set up in the United States to compile statistics on shark attacks, to promote research on sharks and to study the possibility of shark repellants. The panel documented about 50 shark attacks per year but were able to list only 27 species as culprits out of over 200 known species. The largest and most terrifying of these is the Great white shark. Variously estimated to reach 30–40 ft (say 10–12 m), the largest measured specimen was was only 21 ft (6·4 m) and tooth marks on whale carcasses raise the maximum length only to 26 ft (8 m). Even at this size, however, the fish can very easily dispose of a swimmer, usually by amputation of a limb. More attacks have been accredited to the Great white shark than to any other species; some of these attacks have been on small boats. The Mako sharks *Isurus*, known also as Blue pointers, and the Tiger shark *Galeocerdo* are equally dangerous, as

also are certain species of Hammerhead shark *Sphyrna*. The Blue shark *Prionace* has a perhaps unjustly bad reputation, but some of the Grey sharks *Carcharhinus*, and in particular the White-tip oceanic shark *C. longimanus*, probably deserve more respect. It is in the nature of things that a man-eating shark can only rarely be identified with certainty, so that the Shark Research Panel advised caution even in the case of quite small and apparently harmless species.

Sharks have been said to consume their own weight in food per day, but this, frankly, is nonsense. In captivity, Lemon sharks *Negaprion* of 10 ft (3 m) have consumed and apparently thrived on food weighing only 3·5% of their body weight *per week*, while juveniles took about 10%. Stories of their voracity are, however, well-founded. Hammerhead sharks, for example, seem undeterred by stingrays, whose barbed spines are sometimes found embedded in their jaws or in the skin of the mouth. Some very curious objects have been found in the stomachs of sharks. The stomach of a Grey shark of three metres was found to contain eight legs of

The Five-bearded rockling *Ciliata mustelas*, a relative of the cod, is abundant off the coasts of Europe and uses its barbs, four on the snout and one on the lower jaw, to locate its food.

mutton, half a ham, the hind quarters of a pig, the front half of a dog (with the neck encircled by a rope), 298 lb (135 kg) of horseflesh, a ship's scraper and a piece of sacking. A Tiger shark, caught off Senegal, had swallowed a native drum which had evidently been in the stomach for some time. One of the most curious cases of this kind took place in 1799 when an American privateer was chased by a British man-of-war in the Caribbean. The Yankee captain threw his ship's papers overboard and would have been acquitted at the subsequent trial had not the papers been recovered from the stomach of a recently caught shark; as it was, the captain was convicted solely on the evidence of the 'shark papers,' as they were called. An even more dramatic case was the affair of the 'Shark Arm Murder' in Sydney, in which the tattooed arm of the victim was found in a shark and provided convincing evidence that this was not merely a case of misadventure.

Although sharks can swallow bulky objects, the indigestible things must either remain in the stomach or be rejected by everting the stomach through the mouth. This is because the intestine contains a spiral valve which increases the absorptive surface area. This valve may resemble a spiral staircase, or a series of cones one inside the other, or it may resemble longitudinal coils rolled back on themselves. A spiral valve is a primitive feature and in simpler form is also found in the more archaic bony fishes (lungfishes, bichirs, sturgeons and bowfins). By passing through the spiral, the faeces are given a characteristic shape, so that from fossil faeces (coprolites), the shark can often be identified.

Much has been learned in recent years of the diets of fishes from observations under water and in aquaria. One of the strangest examples concerns certain cichlid fishes of the African lakes whose stomachs were found to contain nothing but fish scales. It seemed incredible that a fish could subsist on such a diet but one species kept in an aquarium would feed on nothing else. Scale-eaters of this very enterprising family of freshwater fishes have now been found in three of the African lakes (Malawi, Victoria and Tanganyika). In one of the species, the diet is augmented by nipping small pieces of fin from other fishes, while two other species mimic the appearance of their prey, presumably so that they can approach without alarming the host. The scales, which may be 1 cm in diameter, are curled and passed down the gut, to be reduced to a structureless pulp.

An important aspect of feeding in fishes is the extent to which it affects the environment. Since

The Fire eel, one of the spiny eels popular with aquarists, burrows in sand during the day and breathes through its elongate snout at the tip of which lie the nostrils. In spite of its protruding snout, the Fire eel feeds successfully with an otherwise unmodified mouth.

one animal may be preyed on by several others, and itself prey on several others, the ramifications of the food chain, better termed a food web, can be extremely complex. Although a kind of balance of forces maintains the general shape of the web, a sudden increase in one species can have profound effects on some apparently distant member of the web. A very direct effect on the environment is brought about by certain coral reef fishes. In many of the islands of the West Indies, a conspicuous band of bare sand about three metres in width separates the reefs from the beds of sea grasses (mainly *Thalassia* and *Cymodocea*). This results from heavy grazing by parrotfishes *Scarus* and *Sparisoma* and surgeonfishes *Acanthurus* that use the reef as shelter. When an artificial reef of concrete blocks is constructed in the middle of such sea grass beds, an exactly similar bare, sandy strip forms after only nine months. Another effect of reef fishes is the production of sediment. This is produced by species which have little difficulty in grinding up the hard parts of crabs, sea urchins, shellfish and even coral. Triggerfishes (Balistidae) and filefishes (Monacanthidae), have small but very powerful jaws and grinding pharyngeal teeth; parrotfishes

A naked catfish *Synodontis flavitaeniatus* with its four whisker-like barbels which serve a sensory function in detecting food.

(Scaridae) have sharp beak-like jaws and similar pharyngeal teeth, while the sparids (Sparidae), often have flat, molar-like teeth in the jaws. In addition, some of the herbivorous surgeonfishes have a gizzard-like stomach and often take in sand or coral fragments to grind up their plant food and make it more digestible. The effect of all these grinding fishes is to produce enormous quantities of bottom sediments. In Bermuda, for example, it is estimated that fishes deposit roughly a ton of calcareous material per hectare every year.

Our knowledge of the feeding habits of fishes is still far from complete. The first step is to make a qualitative assessment of the kinds of food on which a particular fish feeds. Next comes a quantitative analysis, which leads, on the one hand, to an understanding of the web of feeding relationships that surround the fish, and on the other to a calculation of the nutritional value of the food and its correlation with growth. At the highest level, a study of feeding is a study of interrelated energy systems.

Breeding and Development

Among the vertebrates, fishes are unique in their variety of breeding patterns. Normally, the entire process from fertilization to the hatching of the fry takes place externally: the female lays her eggs, the male fertilizes them, and they are then left to develop on their own. For the vast majority of fishes this has evidently proved a perfectly satisfactory arrangement. There are, however, a number of highly interesting variations on the theme. In some fishes the eggs are fertilized within the female, necessitating an act of copulation. These eggs may then be extruded at a later stage, or they may develop and hatch within the mother. In the latter case the young may even be nourished by the mother in a manner approaching that of mammals. A more bizarre variation, however, is the occurrence of hermaphrodite fishes, all individuals of a species having both male and female reproductive organs, of which both are truly functional, either in turns or in a few cases simultaneously. Finally, there are even species in which only a single sex occurs. Thus, in reproduction, as in other spheres, fishes show amazing diversity.

Gonads, Eggs and Sperm. In most fishes the reproductive organs or gonads are paired structures and they lie within the body cavity below the kidneys. The testes of the male, popularly called the soft roe, are usually elongate yellow or cream-coloured tubes that become enlarged and often flattened at maturity. Each testis leads back by a fine tube to the genital pore. By squeezing a fully ripe fish a white stream of spermatozoa, the milt, can be made to exude through the pore and this is what occurs during mating. The ovaries or hard roe are more sac-like and as the eggs ripen they become easily visible. The ovary narrows into an oviduct or tube leading either to its own external opening or to a common opening with the excretory pore; in some fishes, such as the trouts and salmons, the eggs are released into the body cavity and through movements of the fish's body are forced into a funnel-like opening of the oviduct and thus to the outside. As in the male, a ripe female will extrude eggs if squeezed and it is in this way that eggs and milt can be stripped from fishes and fertilized artificially in a fish hatchery. Fertilization usually takes place in the water but this is perhaps not quite so haphazard as might appear since the parents usually perform some kind of mating ritual whereby eggs and sperm are shed at about the same time.

In addition to their obvious function of generating the sex cells or gametes, the testes and ovaries are also important sites for the production of hormones responsible for the secondary sexual charac-

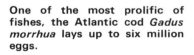

One of the most prolific of fishes, the Atlantic cod *Gadus morrhua* lays up to six million eggs.

ters of fishes. Removal of the gonads may prevent the proper development of breeding colours or inhibit aspects of breeding behaviour, while the injection of hormones from the testis of a male can in some cases cause a female to develop male secondary sexual characters. In most fishes the male is rather smaller, sometimes considerably smaller, than the female, although in the cod and the haddock the reverse is true. One of the most obvious of secondary characters is colour, the male (and in some cases the female also) becoming more highly coloured in the breeding season. In the guppy *Poecilia reticulata*, for example, the female is rather drab while the much smaller male has all kinds of variable spots and patterns of orange, blue, blue-green and white. Fin shape often differs between the sexes, either as a feature of sexual display, as in the elongate dorsal fin in male dragonets *Callionymus* and the 'sword' of male swordtails, or, in the case of an enlarged anal fin, for the purpose of disseminating eggs or sperm. In many of the carp-like fishes (Cyprinidae), the males develop curious tubercles on the snout during the breeding season – the so-called pearl organs – but one of the most remarkable changes is that found in male salmons in which the snout and the lower jaw become elongated and hooked towards each other. In addition to such physical differences between the sexes, there are also highly important differences in their behaviour during breeding. As in other animals, each partner has a specific role to play, the function of these roles being to ensure that as many eggs as possible are fertilized. Some examples of breeding behaviour are given later.

The number of spermatazoa produced and released by the male during breeding is enormous, just as in most other animals. However, the number of eggs produced varies widely and is dependent on several factors, the chief of which are the likelihood of survival and the amount of yolk necessary for the development of the embryo. The ling is usually cited as one of the most prolific species; a fish of about 5 ft (1·5 m), produces as many as 28 million eggs. A cod and a turbot, albeit half that size, are recorded as laying respectively 6 million and 9 million eggs. These are fishes that release buoyant eggs which float up to the surface layers and so there is clearly great wastage, resulting as much from the failure of sperm to encounter an egg as from the toll taken by predators. If a fish population remains at a stable level, then obviously only two eggs need survive to become mature breeding adults; in the case of the ling, for example, some 27,999,998 eggs can be destined to perish each time without the population declining. In other fishes the number of eggs laid by a female may amount only to hundreds or tens of thousands, as in the sole (about 600,000) or the herring (20,000–40,000). Fishes that produce relatively few eggs, numbered in hundreds or even less, usually have some means of protecting their brood.

In some of the cyprinid fishes that spawn in rivers and streams (genera *Barbus*, *Labeo*), the eggs are about 1 mm in diameter but swell up to four times that size on contact with water, with the result that they are more easily caught by currents, swirled away and deposited over a wide area. Among the bony fishes, some of the largest eggs are those produced by the sea catfishes (family Tachysuridae), the eggs being as much as 0·8 in (2 cm) in diameter. These are dwarfed, however, by the 19 eggs of no less than 3·5 in (9 cm) in diameter found in a female coelacanth of about 6 ft (1·82 m) in length. At the other extreme there are gobies that have eggs of only about 0·4 mm in diameter, but this is near the limit in reduction for egg-laying fishes. Thus some

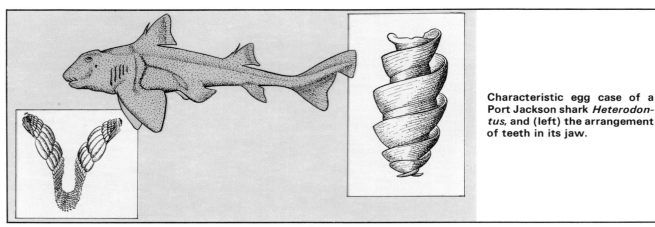

Characteristic egg case of a Port Jackson shark *Heterodontus,* and (left) the arrangement of teeth in its jaw.

The familiar egg cases of the Common skate, *Raja naevus.*

of the dwarf gobies of the Philippines, such as *Mystichthys luzonensis*, or the smallest of all fishes, *Pandaka pygmaea* (adult size 11 mm), must manage by producing fewer eggs (about 20–40 only). In those rays and sharks that do not produce live young, the eggs are large and are enclosed in a horny case, those of rays being the familiar 'mermaid's purses' of the sea shore. The largest on record belonged, as might be expected, to the largest of all fishes, the Whale shark, a species that reaches at least 50 ft (about 15 m). Only one egg case has been found and this measured 12 in (30 cm) in length; the embryo inside was 14 in (36 cm) long and was such a perfect replica of the adult that there could be no doubt about its identity.

Embryos and Larvae. The development of fish embryos usually follows a fairly standard pattern, with the early appearance of a distinct head and series of segments (myotomes) that will eventually form the muscle blocks. Nerves, blood vessels, a heart, eyes and other organs gradually develop and the muscle segments are reinforced by a cartilagin-

ous rod, the notocord, around which the vertebrae will later form. The vertical fins (dorsal, caudal and anal) are represented by a continuous fold of skin and small pectoral fin buds may appear at this stage. At hatching, the larva is a rather helpless creature which can subsist for a time on the remaining yolk until the mouth and gut become fully formed. In some fishes, especially those of tropical waters, the embryonic development is incredibly rapid and may be achieved in a mere 24 hours. The speed of development, however, is closely linked to temperature, a fact that was noted and put to good use in the last century when salmon and trout were being introduced into New Zealand. Packed in moss between layers of ice, the hatching time could be extended to as much as three months, allowing ample time for a long sea voyage.

As it grows and begins to feed, the larva starts to take on the appearance of the adult. The dorsal and anal fins are often set rather far back on the body in the larva, presumably because their role in swimming is to provide thrust; at a certain stage in development the fins move fairly rapidly to a more forward position. In general, the larval form is a series of compromises: it is an adaptation to larval conditions but it must have the potential to assume, in miniature, those features necessary for adult life. In most fishes, the transition to adult form is fairly gradual and is evenly matched by a transition to adult conditions of life, but in a few families of fishes the change is abrupt and can be termed a metamorphosis. In eels, for example, the larva or leptocephalus is a transparent ribbon-like or leaf-like animal which, for its volume, has achieved almost maximum surface area. As a result, minimum effort is required to avoid sinking, enabling the leptocephalus to drift for long periods in ocean currents. The European freshwater eel, spawned in the area of the Sargasso Sea, drifts 3,000 miles and takes two years before it reaches river mouths in Europe. Its metamorphosis, which takes place in autumn, is a remarkable process. The leaf-like body shortens and becomes round in cross-section, the needle-like larval teeth are shed and replaced by short conical teeth, and after a while the body becomes pigmented. Henceforth the young eel will live in freshwaters and in conditions that could hardly be more different from those at sea.

A leptocephalus larva is found not only in eels (about 22 families united in the order Anguilliformes), but also in the so-called Spiny eels (Notacanthiformes) as well as the tenpounders and ladyfish (Elopiformes), suggesting that perhaps the members of these three orders share a common ancestor. Certainly, the larvae are very similar, so that when a giant leptocephalus of 72 in (183 cm)

Stages in the life history of the mackerel *Scomber scombrus*. (A) a fertilized egg containing an embryo; (B) a newly hatched larva with large yolk sac; (C) an advanced larva which has lost its yolk sac; (D) a young fry in which the dorsal fin is starting to develop and (E), the adult mackerel.

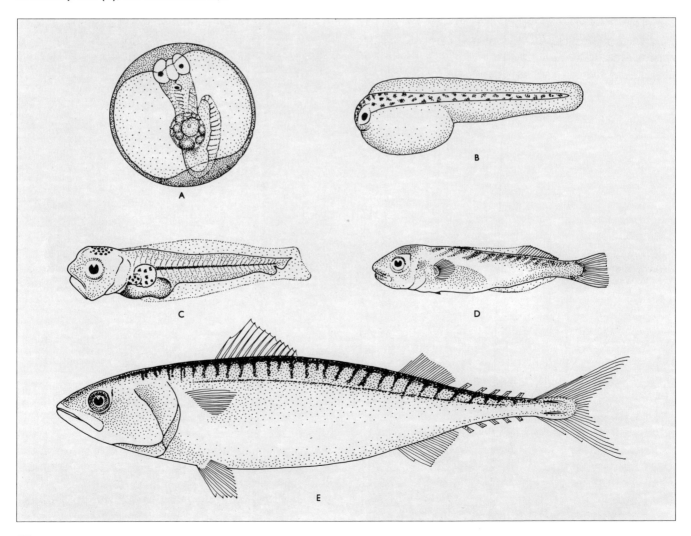

was caught off Cape Town some believed that it must belong to an eel and that, assuming the subsequent ten-fold increase in length normally found in eels, then the adult must be a sea monster of some 60 ft (18 m). It is now thought to be the larva of a Spiny eel (Halosauridae) whose size is not exceptional. Another example in which the larva differs markedly from the adult and also has an extended larval life is found in lampreys. The worm-like ammocoete larva, popularly known as a Pride, has rudimentary eyes and instead of the suctorial mouth of the adult it has a horseshoe-like mouth fringed by a fine net of barbels through which it strains its food. The ammocoetes live buried in tubes in the mud or sand for as much as seven years, after which they undergo a metamorphosis quite as striking as that of the eel leptocephalus; eyes appear, as also the circular suctorial mouth of the adult, while the filter-feeding apparatus becomes associated with the pituitary gland. Sea lampreys then migrate to the sea, where they spend their adult life, but the non-parasitic species become mature almost as soon as they have metamorphosed and thus breed and die without feeding.

Quite as striking as the metamorphosis of eels is that undergone by the larvae of flatfishes (Pleuronectiformes – soles, plaice, flounders). The adults are unique in having both eyes on the same side of the head, the fish being asymmetrical and lying on either its right or its left side. The larvae, however, are perfectly normal and it is only in the course of development that one eye migrates across the head, the jaws and other bones of the head become twisted, and the juvenile fish comes to rest on the bottom, lying on its 'blind' side.

Other larval specializations include the development of long streaming finrays, as for example in the dealfishes; the provision of spines or vanes on the body, as in the sunfishes (family Molidae); adhesive organs on the head for anchoring the larva, as in some species of the cichlid genus *Tilapia*; and external gills, which are found in the bichir and the lungfishes. Ernst Haeckel's dictum that *ontogeny repeats phylogeny*, that is to say, the development of the individual recapitulates its own evolutionary history, must be tempered by the fact that embryos and larvae frequently show adaptations suitable only to this early period of their lives.

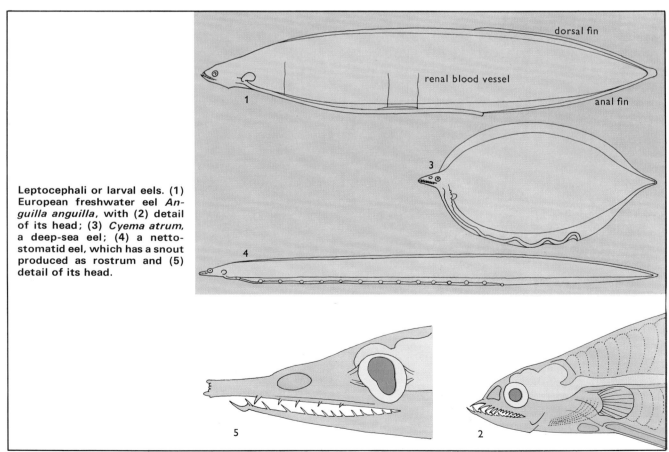

Leptocephali or larval eels. (1) European freshwater eel *Anguilla anguilla*, with (2) detail of its head; (3) *Cyema atrum*, a deep-sea eel; (4) a nettostomatid eel, which has a snout produced as rostrum and (5) detail of its head.

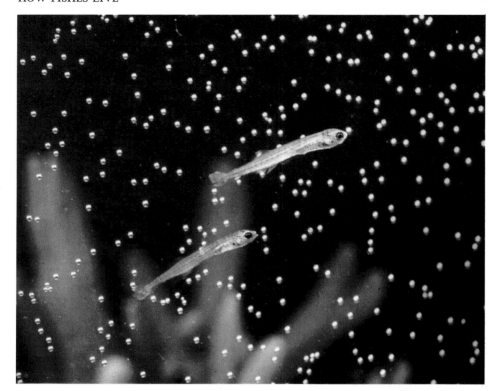

Very young fry of the Thick-lipped grey mullet *Crenimugil labrosus.*

Maturity and Courting. After a longer or shorter period of growth, a fish attains maturity and the gonads ripen for the first time. Unlike mammals, fishes continue to grow after maturity so that a breeding population may contain fishes of widely differing sizes. In some circumstances – usually under adverse conditions – the onset of maturity may be advanced and a dwarf population produced, as for example among certain populations of *Tilapia* confined to crater lakes in Africa; a rather similar phenomenon occurs in an overcrowded goldfish pond. Carried over many generations, and given isolation, this dwarfing may become genetically fixed and thus remain long after the original conditions that produced it have gone.

The ripening or maturation of the gonads is part of an extremely complex series of events that must be synchronized not only with what is happening with other members of the species but with those environmental conditions necessary for successful spawning. Many species breed only once a year and at a particular time, but others, such as the herring, breed at different times of the year (in fact, there is almost no time at which ripe herring cannot be caught in the North Sea). In many cases, and especially in temperate waters, ripening of the gonads seems to be tied to rising water temperatures, although increasing day length can also play a part.

The final trigger that sets off spawning is often difficult to determine, especially in the ocean where conditions are fairly stable. In rivers and lakes the first flush of flood water is usually the signal for fish to move upstream to the spawning grounds. Actual spawning, however, involves a close interplay between the necessary environmental conditions and inherent patterns of behaviour in the fishes. The term 'courting' is appropriate for the first stage.

Courting ensures that male and female are absolutely ready to discharge their sex products at about the same time. Both eggs and sperm are viable for only a limited time and conditions are often such that sperm must be squirted around the eggs fairly quickly before the latter drift or are swept away. A good example is seen in the marine dragonet *Callionymus* in which the highly coloured male swims excitedly around the rather drab female, erecting his fins and showing off his fine colours. If the female accepts, the male lifts her towards the surface by means of his pelvic fins and shortly after they climb vertically with their anal fins brought together to form a gutter into which eggs and sperm are shed. Such individual courting is much more common among freshwater fishes but· the same result is achieved whether the courting is done by pairs or by a number of fishes in a shoal: it is still a pattern of behaviour essential to the success of spawning. Courting can also play an important role in preventing the accidental crossing of two different species. In Africa, for example, certain shallow lakes may contain six or more species of *Tilapia* whose spawning grounds overlap. Although closely related and extremely similar in general appearance, the species are kept separate at breeding time by the rather different breeding colours of the males, reinforced by slightly different patterns of behaviour when a female is encountered. In this kind of situation, the wrong colour or the wrong response will turn courtship into aggression.

Nesting and the Young. Associated with courting are some often highly specialized patterns of behaviour which help to ensure fertilization and the protection of the eggs. These can be grouped under the general term 'nest building.' The female salmon, for example, scoops out a shallow depression in the stream bed into which the eggs are laid and are fertilized. The eggs, which sink and stick to the bottom of the 'redd,' are then loosely covered with fine gravel and are thus both protected and well aerated. In salmon, courting, nest building, egg-laying, and fertilization form a progressive sequence

in which male and female behaviour patterns reciprocate. In this case the sequence ends with the covering of the eggs, but in a number of fishes one or both of the parents then remain with the eggs and protect them from predators. In the African cichlid fish *Tilapia zillii*, for example, the eggs are adhesive and although frequently laid outside the saucer-shaped nest are subsequently guarded and aerated by fanning movements of the pectoral fins. Eggs which fail to develop are taken into the mouth and spat outside the brooding area thus preventing subsequent contamination by bacteria and fungus as the dead eggs decompose. An unusual form of nest is that found in the Labyrinth fishes (Anabantoidei), of which the Siamese fighting-fish is a good example. In this species the males become extremely pugnacious during the breeding season, advertising their right to a particular territory by a brilliant metallic red and blue breeding dress whenever another male approaches, although combats between males in aquaria, which form the basis of wagers in some eastern countries, are perhaps more fierce than in nature. If a female approaches, the colourful display serves to bring her to a state of

This view of a flatfish with its head raised waiting for prey, shows clearly the position of the eyes which come to lie on the same side of the head during development.

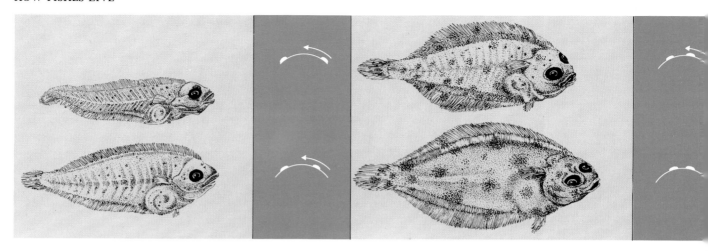

Metamorphosis in a flatfish. The eyes of a young flatfish are at first in the usual place but one of the eyes soon moves to the top of the head and over to the other side.

readiness to lay the eggs. The nest prepared for this is made of bubbles of air blown from sticky mucus by the male. The process of egg-laying is complex because the eggs are heavy but yet must be made to stick to the floating bubble-nest above. This is achieved by the male first turning the female upside down and releasing sperm, then swimming below her and as the eggs are extruded, fertilized and dropped, taking them into his mouth and with a further sticky secretion fixing them into the nest. The male continues to guard the nest and if any of the larvae fail to stick the male replaces them.

Another elaborate nest-builder is the Three-spined stickleback *Gasterosteus aculeatus*. Here again, it is the male that does the construction, gathering small pieces of plants or algae, pressing them together with a sticky secretion and finally tunnelling through the pile to make a passageway in which the female will deposit the eggs. Having fertilized the eggs, the male remains and fans a stream of water through the nest in order to aerate them. He remains guarding them after they have hatched and returns straying larvae to the nest until such time as they are able to fend for themselves.

One of many colourful varieties of the millionsfish, *Poecilia reticulata*, better known as the guppy, bred by aquarists. Compared with the colourful male, the female is rather a drab fish.

A male stickleback with his red breast prepares to greet a female. When she enters his territory, he leads her to spawn in the nest he has built.

The fishes mentioned so far must clearly co-ordinate male and female behaviour patterns if spawning is to be successful, but there is a certain amount of flexibility as far as the environment is concerned. In the grunion *Leuresthes tenuis*, a silverside found along the coast of southern California, breeding behaviour must be very closely correlated with tides since the eggs are buried as far up the beach as possible on one high tide and are released from the sand and hatch on the next high tide. In this way, the eggs are relatively unmolested by predators. Unfortunately, the regularity of the runs and the vulnerability of the adults as they spawn on the wet sand between waves, has led to man becoming one of the chief predators.

While some fishes, such as bullheads, gobies, blennies, lumpsuckers and toadfishes, actively guard their eggs, yet others have evolved ways of attaching the eggs to their bodies. In the pipefishes and sea horses the male has either a special brood pouch on the under side of the body or tail, or at least a soft-lined groove into which the eggs are deposited by the female. In seahorses, which have a proper pouch, the extrusion of the hatched larvae resembles an act of birth and may take some hours to accomplish. Another variant of this kind of care for the young is seen in the discusfishes *Symphysodon* of the Amazon and Rio Negro basins. The eggs are guarded, fanned and mouthed by the parents and when hatched are transferred to various surfaces where they remain attached by a short thread. When the fry become free-swimming, however, they make for their parents' sides and feed there on special mucus secretions for a month or more; the parents are said to be adept at flicking their bodies to transfer the juveniles to the other partner.

Many fishes hide their eggs in one way or another, usually by burying them in sand or gravel as in the grunion and salmons. One of the most ingenious methods of protecting the eggs is that evolved by the bitterling *Rhodeus amarus*, in which the eggs are deposited in the mantle cavity of the freshwater mussel. To achieve this the oviduct of the female bitterling becomes extended into a long tube which serves the purpose of an ovipositor. The stream of water drawn in by the mussel for normal breathing purposes also aerates the bitterling eggs, which later hatch and escape. The mussel, like other bivalves, snaps its two shells together when touched, but the female bitterling has a way of nudging it with its mouth to make it open. The association between the two animals is even closer, however, since the mussel spawns at the same time and its larvae become attached to the bitterling's gills, or elsewhere, to be carried away and to drop off when ready to settle on the bottom.

Species that manipulate the eggs with their mouths have already been mentioned, but so far this has merely involved the transfer of eggs or the removal of dead ones. In a number of fishes, such as the marine Cardinal fishes (Apogonidae), jawfishes (Opisthognathidae) and some catfishes (Ariidae), as well as in the freshwater cichlids, the practice is carried a stage further and the eggs are kept in the mouth and incubated there. This occurs in many of the species of the African cichlid *Tilapia*, where it is associated with nest building. The nest is usually a shallow, saucer-shaped depression excavated by the male who both guards it from other males and displays over it to attract females. Successful courtship leads to the female depositing the eggs in the nest, the male swimming over the eggs to fertilize them, and finally the female sucking the eggs (and sperm) into her mouth where they are kept even after they have hatched and grown into quite active larvae. In order to ensure fertilization, some species of cichlids have evolved ingenious ways of enticing the female to take sperm into her mouth. These are in the form of an egg dummy, being either a highly

Common dragonet, *Callionymus lyra*, spawning. The male is larger and more brightly coloured than the female.

coloured male genital papilla or tassel, or else spots on the male's anal fin that simulate eggs. In gathering up the eggs, the female will snap at the dummy and thus suck in sperm.

A final and very curious example of egg-laying and parental care is that shown by the Splashing tetra *Copeina arnoldi*, a South American characin. A pair of fish move into shallow water where branches overhang and then, leaping clear of the surface, attach themselves belly uppermost on the underside of a leaf. Clinging momentarily, they lay and fertilize some eggs before dropping back into the water and then repeating the process. Once this is done the male remains nearby, splashing the eggs to keep them moist.

Internal Fertilization. In all the fishes mentioned so far, fertilization has taken place after the eggs have left the ovary, but there are quite a number of fishes that practise internal fertilization and retention of the eggs for at least a part of their development. Curiously enough this has not been a general evolutionary beginning or end point but is found in fishes that are quite unrelated, although within families or groups of families a certain trend can be seen. Internal fertilization – the rule in sharks, rays and chimaeras, but also occurring in a number of bony fishes (teleosts) – requires an act of copulation and some organ for injecting the sperm into the female. In sharks, rays and chimaeras the males have modified appendages to the pelvic fins, known as claspers or mixopterygia, and these are thrust either singly or together into the cloaca of the female, the sperm passing down a groove within the two claspers. In some species, such as the Basking shark and certain chimaeras, the sperm are held together in a distinct capsule, a spermatophore, which presumably prevents loss during the transfer to the female. Once fertilized, the eggs are enclosed in an egg capsule or shell but thereafter one of three things may happen.

In the simplest case the egg in its horny capsule is extruded and continues its development in the sea, the embryo being nourished solely from its yolk sac. This is known as *ovipary* and it is typical of dogfishes, Port Jackson sharks, some carpet sharks and the Whale shark. The second possibility is that the egg capsule is thin and temporary, the fish hatching within the mother and continuing its development

but being nourished by its yolk. This is called *ovovivipary* and it is found in a number of sharks such as the sand sharks (Odontaspidae), the thresher sharks (Alopiidae) and all the squaliform sharks. In some cases the yolk may not provide enough nourishment for the developing embryo, but this is solved in the porbeagle *Lamna nasus*, the mako *Isurus oxyrinchus* and the Sand shark *Odontaspis taurus* by allowing the embryo to feed on the yolks of unfertilized eggs around it. The third possibility, and one that has fascinated biologists since the time of Aristotle, is that, as in mammals, the embryo develops a kind of placenta. In the Smooth hound *Mustelus canis*, for example, the yolk sac becomes applied to the wall of the uterus of the mother and as the yolk is used up, a system of blood vessels develops which brings nourishment to the embryo and at the same time removes waste products. Not only does this 'placenta' function in the same way as the placenta of a mammal, but it is connected with the shark embryo by a long tube, the equivalent of the umbilical cord. This type of reproduction, which is termed *vivipary* or 'live-bearing', is found in the Smooth hounds and dogfishes (Triakidae), the Grey

sharks (Carcharinidae), the Blue shark *Prionace* and the hammerheads (Sphyrnidae).

Typical of the live-bearing bony fishes are the toothcarps of the family Poeciliidae, which includes such well-known aquarium fishes as the mollies *Mollienesia*, the guppy *Poecilia reticulatus* and the swordtail *Xiphophorus helleri*. In these fishes the male has a long copulatory organ, known as a gonopodium, formed by modification of the third, fourth and fifth rays of the anal fin. By means of the gonopodium, sperm is transferred to the female in a gelatinous mass and the eggs are fertilized within the ovary. In most species birth takes place after about a month and then the next brood is fertilized, but in certain highly specialized toothcarps there may be as many as eight successive broods developing simultaneously in the ovaries of one female, a phenomenon known as superfoetation. This is the case in *Heterandria formosa*, but here the brood has been reduced to only a single individual produced every three to eight days during the breeding season. Coupled with this has been a trend towards reduction in yolk to the point that the mature egg of *Heterandria* consists almost entirely of a single oil

◁ Male Siamese fighting fish show off their fins, so important in the display behaviour that preceeds courtship.

Territorral disputes in cichlid ▷ fishes sometimes develop into a show of strength, an aggressor seizing its rival by the mouth.

The Kissing gourami, *Helostoma temmincki*. This apparent sign of affection is in fact a ritual in asserting territorial rights and mate selection.

◁ A clingfish, the Cornish sucker *Lepadogaster lepadogaster*, clings to a rock whist guarding its eggs. In one South African clingfish fertilization takes place inside the female's body, although eggs are afterwards laid.

globule and measures only 0·2 mm in diameter.

With reduction in the amount of yolk available, the embryo must be nourished in other ways. Bony fishes have not developed the complex 'umbilical cord' of the viviparous sharks, but in some cases small outgrowths from the yolk sac or the lining surrounding the heart serve to absorb nutrient secretions from the mother. However, the period of gestation during which the eggs are retained and develop inside the female varies considerably between species or families of species and it is also difficult to draw the line between those fishes that are ovoviviparous and those that might be considered truly viviparous. It would seem that, in comparison with sharks, the bony fishes are still, as it were, experimenting with the method.

Yet another remarkable experiment made by fishes is sex reversal, the fish either starting as a male and later developing into a fully functional female (protandrous, or 'early male'), or more commonly *vice versa* (protogynous, or 'early female'). Sex reversal is found in the Serranidae – groupers, jewfishes, sea perches – and two common examples are the Scribbled perch *Serranus scriba* and the Comber *S. cabrilla* of the Mediterranean and Eastern Atlantic. Where male and female colour patterns differ strongly, as in the parrotfishes (Scaridae), the fish usually makes a colour change. On occasions it may not, so that where the juveniles also have their own colour pattern, and where this is sometimes retained by mature males, the problem of identifying the breeding elements in a population can become extremely complex. Even more baffling are the few fishes that function as hermaphrodites. Instances of herring, mackerel or hake having both male and female reproductive organs are not unknown, but in certain species testes and ovaries are present in all adults and are active simultaneously. One well known case is the Sea perch *Serranus subligarius*, found commonly off the coasts of Florida. Each adult can act as either male or female or as both sexes at the same time. During spawning the fish acting the part of the male has broad, dark vertical bands on the body while the female is unbanded. In

The Common discusfish *Symphysodon discus* transfers the ▷ newly hatched larvae to a convenient surface, where they remain attached by a short thread.

Male and female bitterling, a species renowned for the way that it uses the freshwater mussel as a repository for its eggs.

an aquarium two unbanded fishes will display until one is cornered, when it will then take on the banded male colouration, court the unbanded 'female' and fertilize the eggs. Thereafter the sex roles may be reversed once, or even several times.

Hermaphrodites are found, not only among the Sea perches, but also in members of the Sparidae (Sea breams). The most extraordinary case, however, is that of the small toothcarp *Rivulus marmoratus* from Florida and some of the Caribbean islands. This species shows the ultimate in herma-

phroditic breeding. Like *Serranus subligarius*, it has testes and ovaries that develop at the same time, although a few individuals may start and remain as males while others become males after first acting as hermaphrodites. What makes this toothcarp unique, however, is that it is able to fertilize itself and apparently does so in nature. The proof of this can be found by grafting experiments, for there is no rejection of transplanted tissue such as normally occurs between individuals even as similar in hereditary material as brothers or sisters. In other

Siamese fighting fish *Betta splendens* at bubble nest, shown at the top of the picture.

One of the best known live-bearing fishes, the Variegated platy *Xiphoporus variatus*.

words, the offspring are genetically identical to each other and to their single parent.

As shown already, the toothcarps have tried various reproductive methods, ranging from normal egg-laying to complete viviparity and from a normal complement of males and females to self-fertilizing hermaphroditism. This is not the limit of their experiments, however, for there are even species in which only a single sex occurs. In the so-called Amazon molly *Mollienesia formosa*, found in coastal and inland waters of north-eastern Mexico and Texas, only females occur. These are able to breed by using the males of two related species, *Mollienesia sphenops* in one part of their range and *M. latipinna* in another part. Experiments have shown that only females are produced and, of even greater interest, that although sperm from the other species is necessary to induce development of the embryos it does not contribute to inheritance. This is the nearest approach made by fishes to parthenogenesis, such as is found in aphids, in which the male gametes play no part at all. Two or three other species of toothcarp *Poeciliopsis* produce all-female broods, but in this case there are also females that can produce both sexes.

Reproduction is the most fundamental activity in all living matter. It not only perpetuates the species: it produces (except in unisexual organisms) a degree of variation in the offspring which is the basis for evolutionary change. For this reason, many aspects of the way that fishes live are, in essence, ways of ensuring successful breeding.

A male swordtail and young females. This male started life as a female and, after giving birth to several broods, underwent a change of sex and became a fully functional male. The sword is used in sexual displays.

Defence and Self-preservation

If feeding is a constant theme in the lives of fishes, then defence is the other side of the coin, since all fishes are at least potential food for other animals around them. None is immune from attack, at some stage in its life, so that the more fishes have diversified in order to play new roles in the environment, the more new risks they have opened up for themselves. When the flatfishes forsook a free-swimming life and took to a more sedentary existence on the bottom, they immediately became vulnerable to all those predators that crawl or skim over the sea floor. Camouflage became more effective than direct flight, while the sharp spines of the anterior part of the dorsal fin, still found in primitive members such as *Psettodes*, became the flexible finrays of the more specialized forms. Thus, the means of defence must keep abreast of other modifications if new ways of life are to succeed. Some adaptations are obvious, such as the development of barbed spines that can be erected in case of danger, but others are much more

subtle and depend on quite small facets of behaviour whose value can only be determined by careful observation.

Size and Shape. One solution to the problem of defence is to be larger than any potential enemies. The Whale shark, for example, reaches at least 50 ft (15 m) in length and it is doubtful that at this size it has any serious rivals, although Killer whales could perhaps be considered as a possible threat. At any rate, these huge beasts have a surprising disregard for what is going on around them. On several occasions Whale sharks basking at the surface have been so unaware of approaching shipping that they have been rammed, apparently before knowing anything was upon them. Basking sharks and the Ocean sunfish *Mola* are other large fishes that laze at the surface. It is significant that none of these has large teeth or spines, their bulk being the main guarantee of safety.

The majority of fishes grow to about 4–12 in

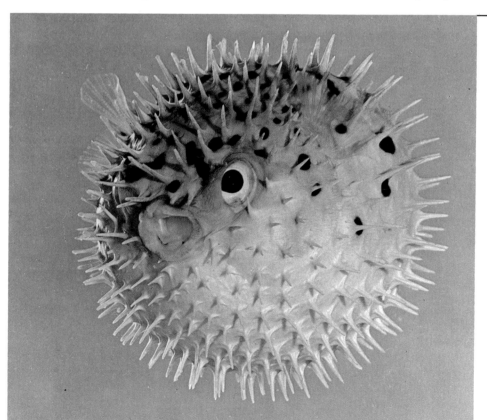

The Globefish *Diodon hystrix*, with body inflated and spines erect, becomes an impossible mouthful for many predators.

Surgeonfishes – this one is *Zebrasoma veliferum* – are so named for the sharp knife-like spine at the base of the tailfin, which can be erected for defence.

(10–30 cm), so that even those that achieve 6 ft (say 2 m) in length are relative giants and their size alone must be a factor in their defence against all but a few species. Size is not, however, attained overnight and one must presume that fishes that are large have adopted other and successful methods of self-preservation in the interim. Two groups of fishes that overcome this problem are the pufferfishes and globefishes (families Tetraodontidae and Diodontidae), which can inflate themselves with air or water and thus double or treble their bulk. What appears at first to be a tasty mouthful suddenly becomes as awkward to nibble as an apple in a tub of water; the presence of short and erectile spines makes many of these species even more unappetizing.

In many of the primitive fishes – for example, the placoderms – the head and front part of the body was encased in a stout armour of bony plates, thus leaving the tail free for swimming movements. Later fishes reduced this armour in the interests of mobility, but the bony box around the braincase and the bony plates covering the delicate gills are still retained. The majority of modern fishes have scales on the body but these are usually thin and flexible and thus offer only moderate protec-

tion. Scales, however, have proved extremely adaptable, providing spines for the puffers and globefishes and an armour of bony plates for fishes of many different families. Packed close together and thickened, the scales can provide a tough outer covering to the fish, reaching an extreme in the boxfishes (Ostraciodontidae), in which the body is quite rigid and may be further protected by spines projecting forwards and backwards, as in the cowfish *Lactophrys*. The pipefishes and seahorses (Syngnathidae) are protected by hard rings on the body, while the shrimpfishes (Centriscidae) have a bony cuirass that is compressed along the belly to form a knife-edge.

Weapons. In most fishes at least the first or outer ray of each fin is slightly stiffened if not actually spiny. This is presumably necessary to strengthen the fin against vibration or crumpling during swimming, but it also opened the way for the development of spines as a means of defence. A typical example is the Three-spined stickleback *Gasterosteus aculeatus*, which has three quite large spines along the back, as well as a spine in the anal and pelvic fins. Experiments have shown that if a stickleback is seized by a pike or perch it will lock its spines erect and remain quite motionless. The predator will

Upsidedown - catfish *Synodontis nigriventris* of Africa, lacks the silver belly usual in fishes that swim the right way up.

then reject it and after a few such experiences will take care to avoid sticklebacks as food. If a pike is starved, however, and presented only with sticklebacks, it will learn to rotate them in its mouth until the head is pointing down the throat and the spines are less effective. An interesting comparison can be made with the Ten-spined stickleback *Pygosteus pungitius*, which has 10 much smaller spines and is far easier to swallow than its relative. The Three-spined stickleback is much the bolder of the two species, selecting more open nesting sites and having more conspicuous breeding colours. Relatively few comparative experiments have been carried out but they are essential if the value of defensive mechanisms is to be assessed and understood in terms of an animal's total biology.

The perch-like fishes may have 10 or more spines in the dorsal fin, but these must be considered only partly defensive since they are also important in supporting the fin membrane when the fin is used during turns or other manoeuvres. The dorsal spines, however, are frequently modified for almost exclusive use in defence. The dorsal spine is long, barbed and capable of being locked into an erect position in many of the catfishes and can only be depressed if carefully lifted forwards and upwards before being eased back. Catfishes have similar spines in the pectoral fins, so that when these too are erected the front of the fish forms a spiny triangle of

perhaps twice the normal girth of the fish, and the would-be predator has much the same problem as with the pufferfishes. The triggerfishes (Balistidae) have a short but similar dorsal spine which is locked into position by the base of the succeeding spine; only by lowering the second spine will the first become unlocked. Spines in the pelvic and anal fins are less elaborate but can also cause damage when the fish is struggling to escape.

Spines are not confined to the fins but can develop on almost any part of the body. In many of the perch-like fishes the bones covering the gill chamber – chiefly the operculum or gill cover itself, but also the pre-operculum and the bones below the eyes – have serrated edges. The defensive value of this is arguable, but in some fishes the serrations are developed into definite spines and when such fishes, for example the soldierfishes (Holocentridae), are handled the gill covers are spread outwards to great effect. A curious bony projection – a horn more than a spine – is developed on the forehead in adults of the so-called unicornfishes *Naso*. Beginning as a mere bump, it may become longer than the snout in some species and presumably it plays some role in defence or aggression. The unicornfishes belong to the family Acanthuridae, or surgeonfishes, whose members have a sharp spine on either side of the caudal peduncle (base of the caudal fin). Normally the spines lie flat against the body but they can be erected and can lacerate the fingers if the fish is handled carelessly.

Weapons for attack and weapons for defence are sometimes difficult to separate and often they sèrve the same ends. In general, attack is associated with two rather different activities, feeding and breeding. The first is directed at another species, or a quite different animal, and has the object of killing and swallowing. Thus the weapons of attack are usually centred round the mouth and in most cases occur simply in the form of teeth. Exceptions may be the 'sword' of swordfishes and marlins, which aquarium observations suggest may actually be used to spear fishes – as distinct from the probably accidental spearing of wooden ships for which these fishes are famous – and the toothed snout or 'saw' of saw-fishes, which may be used to slash at prey. Aggression in breeding involves disputes over territory or over a mate and in the second case at least, if not frequently in the first, it is directed at members of the same species. In this event, the weapons are the same for each contestant and the confrontation is highly ritualized, the loser rarely being killed but merely being 'persuaded' to yield. In these battles the mouth forms an obvious weapon – for biting, fin nipping, wrestling – but fins and spines may also come into play.

Camouflage. The most universal of all methods of defence in fishes is concealment by means of colour, and the most frequently used system is that of countershading. Since lighting is always from above, thereby casting shadows on the undersides of objects, fishes have evolved the reverse pattern, the back being dark and the belly lighter. This helps to eliminate the shadow under the fish but equally important perhaps, it makes the fish blend with the darkness of the water when seen from above and with the lightness of the surface when seen from below. A striking confirmation of the importance of this method of camouflage is shown by the Upside-down catfish *Synodontis batensoda* of the Nile which habitually swims upside-down and has the normal colour pattern reversed. Many open-water sea fishes have silvery flanks. Seen from below, and at various angles, the silver reflects the light at the surface and the flanks take on the same hue as the water above, rendering the fish almost invisible. In some of the herring-like fishes of tropical waters, the belly is sharply keeled to form a knife-edge and this serves to eliminate all but a hairline of shadow along the belly of the fish. It has been suggested that fishes with light-organs along the belly may in some cases gain a measure of concealment by appearing light when viewed from below.

Herrings *Clupea harengus* showing typical pattern of countershading, the back being dark and lower flanks and belly light.

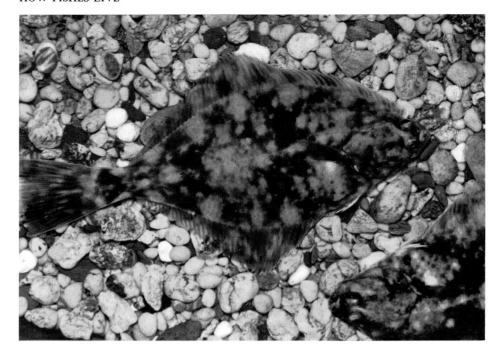

Flounders *Platichthys flesus,* on pebbles. Their colours change to blend with the sea-bed.

Countershading is essentially the result of trying to match the background whether the fish is viewed from above or below. In fishes of open seas, for example, the back is rather green-blue while in fishes of freshwaters the back is usually more green-brown. In fishes that spend their time in midwater the elimination of shadow that results from this colour pattern is obviously important, but fishes that lie mostly on the bottom have developed even more sophisticated ways of blending into the background. Some of the best examples are found among the flatfishes, which are capable of assuming approximately the colour of the bottom and may be able to vary the spots on the back to match the sand,

gravel, pebbles or stones on which they lie; in the laboratory, specimens of the flounder *Paralichthys* have been placed on variously dotted or chequered surfaces and have made quite creditable attempts to assume the same pattern.

This kind of blending camouflage is best developed in those fishes that live on the bottom, or at any rate lie fairly still against their background. The Sargassum fish *Histrio histrio*, which spends its life among the drifting fronds of the Sargassum weed, is mottled in browns and yellows and speckled with small white spots so that its presence among the weed is extremely hard to detect even by an observer who has been told that there is a specimen present.

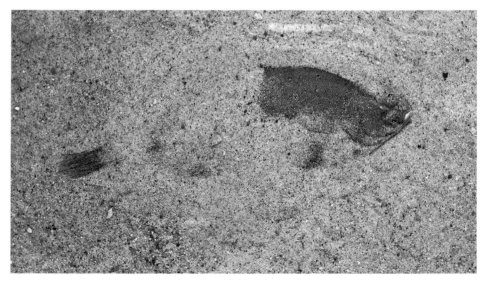

Dab *Limanda limanda* half-hidden under sand it has flipped over itself with its fins.

Other experts in this type of protective concealment are the bottom-living scorpionfishes (Scorpaenidae) and anglerfishes (Lophiidae and Antennariidae). The venomous and much-dreaded stonefish so closely resembles a weed-covered piece of coral that it is not until one has inspected it closely and seen its two rather beady eyes that the rest of the fish becomes visible. Yet another method of camouflage is simply to dispense with colour and to have a transparent body, as in the glassfish *Chanda ranga* of India, Burma and Thailand. Although the eyes, gillcovers and elements of the skeleton are still visible, the fish is extremely difficult to see.

Fishes may also be more or less visible but not noticeable. Thus the vertical bars on the flanks and fins of angelfishes *Pterophyllum* tend to match the appearance of the shadowy stems of water plants among which these fishes live. The eye of the predator is probably carried up and down beyond the outline of the fish by the insistent effect of the vertical bars. This is also an example of disruptive colouration in which stripes or other patterns run counter to the profile of the fish and thus disguise its shape. This same principle seems to be used by many of those highly coloured fishes of coral reefs. Quite commonly the eye is concealed by a black vertical or horizontal bar and in some species there is a false eye or ocellus on the hind part of the body, presumably to deceive a predator. It must be remembered, however, that colour also serves other functions and that the total colour pattern may comprise elements for advertising the possession of a particular territory or for attracting a mate, as well as for camouflage.

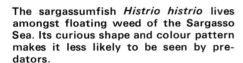

The sargassumfish *Histrio histrio* lives amongst floating weed of the Sargasso Sea. Its curious shape and colour pattern makes it less likely to be seen by predators.

In rather few fishes is there an attempt to mimic a definite object; more often the fish merely blends into the background. A bizarre example is the Sea dragon *Phycodurus eques* of Australian seas, a seahorse whose colours and little leaf-like appendages give it an almost exact resemblance to a piece of floating seaweed. Juvenile batfishes *Platax* of the Indo-Pacific appear to mimic floating Red mangrove leaves, not only in their colouring and shape but in their habit of drifting motionless when chased

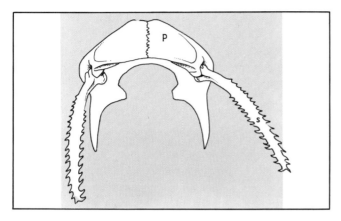

The pectoral girdle (P) and the pectoral spines (S) in a catfish to show the way the spines can be erected (right side of picture) and then locked in that position.

by a predator. An even more realistic leaf mimic is the leaf-fish *Monocirrhus polyacanthus* of the Amazon in which the resemblance to a dead leaf is heightened by a small stalk-like barbel on the chin. In fishes that mimic, unlike those that attempt concealment, the fish remains perfectly visible but is misidentified.

Misidentification involves two different things. The animal may be mistaken for something of no particular interest, such as a piece of seaweed to a carnivorous predator, or it may be mistaken for an object to be avoided. The spreading of the large and colourful pectoral fins by the so-called Flying gurnard *Dactylopterus* may suddenly suggest to a predator that instead of a normal-looking fish he is confronted by an animal large enough to fight back. Similarly, the black spots on the gill covers in some fishes may, when the gill covers are spread outwards and the fish seen head-on, suggest to a predator the eyes of a very much larger fish and one best left alone.

Fairly close resemblances between two different species are not uncommon and in the past these have been cited as cases of mimicry. The mimic, however, must be shown to live habitually with the species mimicked and to gain from the association, otherwise it is much more likely that the two species have arrived at the same colour and general shape quite independently and presumably under the same environmental pressures. One of the best known cases of true mimicry is the Common sole *Solea vulgaris*. It has black markings on the upper-side pectoral fin and when danger threatens the fin is lifted. Since the young soles live in sandy bays inhabited by the venomous weeverfishes *Trachinus*, whose black dorsal fins advertise their threat to predators, one must conclude that the soles gain a measure of protection from their deception. An even more striking case of mimicry concerns the Snake eel *Myrichthys colubrinus* and a Sea snake *Platurus colubrinus*. In their shape and banded colouration, the two are almost identical in appearance. The bright colours advertise the poisonous bite of the snake, so that the eel is presumably also left alone by predators.

A few fishes are also suspected of mimicking noxious invertebrates. One of these is the batfish *Platax pinnatus* of the Indo-Pacific, in which the juveniles with their deep bodies and broad dorsal and anal fins are edged with a bright orange band. A 16 mm juvenile has been observed lying on its side and undulating its fins in a way that made it strongly resemble a turbellarian worm. Since these worms exude excretions that are unpleasant to predators, it would seem that the young batfishes gain protection also. The juveniles of certain species of sweetlips *Plectorhynchus* are also conspicuously coloured and they swim head-down and with exaggerated and unfish-like movements that suggest a soft-bodied invertebrate.

Another type of mimic is the small blenny *Aspidontus taeniatus*, which bears a strong resemblance to the wrasse *Labroides dimidiatus*. Not only is the normal adult colour of the wrasse mimicked, but so too is the rather more brilliant blue of the juveniles and, even more extraordinary, the colour variants of the wrasse are also mimicked. These take the form of either a dark stripe at the base of the pectoral fin or a dull orange-red area in the middle of the body. The wrasse is a cleaner fish that removed parasites from larger fishes without being attacked and the mimic thus enjoys the same immunity. Cleaner fishes, like the venomous Sea snake, far from trying to hide, actually advertise their presence by bright colours, the one because of its usefulness, the other because of its danger to predators.

Poisons and Venoms. From earliest times men have been aware that certain fishes are poisonous to eat. Until fairly recently, this has mainly been blamed on poor preservation, although it has for some time been generally recognized that at least in Moray eels and pufferfishes there is a special toxin present. It is now known that quite a large number of fishes harbour poisonous substances either in their flesh or in a particular organ such as the liver, the intestine or the gonads. Such poisons have mainly been assessed according to their effects on human beings, or else with cats, rats or mice as test animals. There are numerous accounts in early Chinese and Japanese literature of the dangers of eating certain pufferfishes, while Pierre Martyr included a description of fish poisoning in his early 16th century account of the West Indies.

For such poisonous properties to be useful in the fish's defence, however, it is essential that the danger be understood by potential predators, otherwise the fish will continue to be eaten at the same rate by predators as its non-poisonous fellows. One of the principal means of advertising the unpleasant consequences of being eaten is by colour, for a fish that stands out from its background must clearly have good reason to be conspicuous. Certainly, some of the eels and pufferfishes advertise themselves by striking colour patterns, but this warning might equally apply to the bite of the eels and the difficulty of attempting to swallow the puffer. Moreover, many fishes are poisonous to man that either resemble non-poisonous relatives or appear to have no special means of advertising their noxious qualities. Much more work is needed before the link between toxicity and defence can be properly established.

The main groups containing toxic fishes are the pufferfishes (Tetraodontidae), the Moray eels (Muraenidae), the mackerel and tuna-like fishes (Scombridae) and the herring-like fishes (Clupeidae).

Pufferfish poisoning appears to be the most violent and serious. About half an hour after eating a poisonous puffer the lips, tongue, finger tips and toes become numb and the patient suffers from headache, vomiting, dizziness and gradually increasing paralysis, finally passing into a coma and sometimes dying within 24 hours. The effects of the other types of poisoning are no less distressing, although the percentage of fatalities is lower (about 10% in cases of eel poisoning). Curiously enough, the flesh of pufferfishes (sold as *fugu*) is considered a delicacy in Japan, where specially trained chefs prepare it in a way that is said to render the flesh harmless, even though many who eat it still die. The poison of the tuna-like fishes is not an inherent property of the flesh as such but appears to be generated by bacteria once the fish is dead and if there has been some delay in either cooking or preserving it.

At one time many cases of fish poisoning were blamed on spoilage and bacterial action because this seemed to explain yet another category of fish poisoning in which fishes normally regarded as perfectly safe to eat suddenly caused severe illness and often death. This form of poisoning had distinctive symptoms (severe diarrhoea, joint and muscular pains, itching, confusion between sensations of heat and cold) and was known as *ciguatera*, a name derived from the Spanish for the marine snail *Livona pica*, which could on occasions cause the same symptoms. Sometimes a whole area of reef would have to abandoned by the fishermen because previously edible fishes were now poisonous, but the reef would later recover and be fished again. It is now believed that *ciguatera* poisoning results from the fishes eating a toxic blue-green alga. The most poisonous fishes are the large fish-eating barra-

The Sea dragon *Phycodraco eques* is the most bizarre of all the seahorses and bears a striking resemblance to the classical Chinese dragon.

By being transparent, the glassfish *Chanda ranga* achieves near invisibility.

The lionfishes, members of the genus *Pterois*, advertise their venomous nature by striking colour patterns. Pectoral as well as dorsal spines can inject poison. ▷

cudas, Horse mackerels and groupers that feed on the browsing reef species. Presumably in these cases the poison is not eliminated and, like DDT, becomes more and more concentrated as it is passed upwards through the food chain.

Obviously, the earlier a predator can be discouraged the better. Defensive spines, as for example those of the Three-spined stickleback, are not totally effective since a number of individuals are probably maimed before being rejected. Poisonous spines provide a better protection and have been developed in over 50 species belonging to several groups of fishes. Some of the best known are the stingrays (Dasyatidae) and Eagle rays (Myliobatidae), which have a serrated spine, sometimes two or even three, pointing backwards on the base of the tail. A pair of grooves on the underside of the spine contain venom-producing tissue which can cause

very severe pain and even death. In chimaeras and in the Spiny dogfish *Squalus acanthias* and the Port Jackson sharks *Heterodontus*, the dorsal spines carry venom-producing tissue and these too can cause a painful wound. Four groups of bony fishes are particularly noted for their venomous members. In many of the catfishes the sharp and often serrated dorsal and pectoral spines can inject a poison whose effects vary from an unpleasant sting to an almost unbearable pain that may last many hours. The venom of the weeverfishes *Trachinus*, is even more virulent, producing effects both on the blood and the nervous system. In this case the poison glands are associated with the spines of the first dorsal fin and also with a spine on the gill cover. As already noted, the fishes lie partly buried in the sand and the black dorsal fin probably acts as a warning to predators. The toadfishes have a similar set of spines

A Glass catfish *Kryptopterus bicirrhus*, sometimes known as the Ghost fish, hovers among plants and is almost invisible due to the transparency of its body tissues.

The Spotted triggerfish *Balistoides conspicillum*, of the Indo-Pacific, is one of a number of species responsible occasionally for ciguatera poisoning.

in the dorsal fin and on the gill cover but in this case the spines are hollow and thus resemble the fangs of a snake. The fourth major group containing venomous species is the Scorpaeniformes or scorpionfishes, of which two genera deserve special mention. The zebrafishes (otherwise known as turkeyfishes, lionfishes or firefishes, genus *Pterois*) are among the most colourful of all venomous fishes and presumably rely on this as a warning to potential predators. The venom apparatus comprises no less than 13 dorsal spines, three anal spines and two pelvic spines, each armed with a groove containing poisonous tissue and so potent is the poison that even long preserved specimens should be handled with great care. Undoubtedly the most dangerous of all venomous fishes, however, are the stonefishes (Synancejidae) and especially members of the genus

Synanceja of tropical seas. As in the zebrafishes, all the fin spines can inject poison, but the stonefishes are far more dangerous. In the first place, they are remarkably well camouflaged and can be easily trodden on even by those on the look out. Secondly, the venom is extremely powerful and can lead to death due to heart failure. As in the case of fishes with poisonous flesh, much more work is required on the effects of fish venom on their natural predators.

Electricity in Defence. Fishes are the only vertebrates capable of producing electricity and although the electrical discharge generally serves other purposes (capture of prey, communication, location of objects), it seems reasonable to suppose that it can in some cases be used for defence. Electric organs are described more fully later, but mention can be made

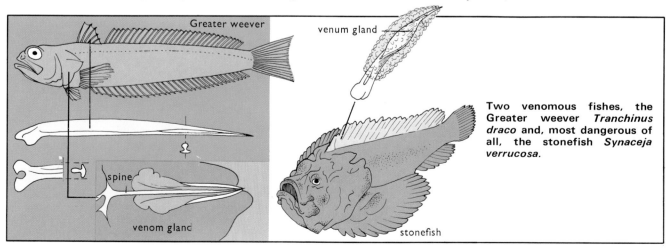

Two venomous fishes, the Greater weever *Tranchinus draco* and, most dangerous of all, the stonefish *Synaceja verrucosa*.

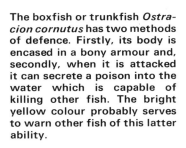

The boxfish or trunkfish *Ostracion cornutus* has two methods of defence. Firstly, its body is encased in a bony armour and, secondly, when it is attacked it can secrete a poison into the water which is capable of killing other fish. The bright yellow colour probably serves to warn other fish of this latter ability.

of the Electric rays *Torpedo*, the Electric eel *Electrophorus* and the Electric catfish *Malapterurus,* since all of these have large electric organs capable of stunning other fishes and thus presumably of deterring predators.

Behaviour. On the face of it, many fishes appear to be rather ill-equipped for the struggle against predators, yet they have evolved methods of self-preservation quite as effective as those of their armoured, spined, venomous, poisonous or electrical relatives. Such methods often rely as much on behaviour as on available equipment. Swift fishes, such as the tunas, can be out-paced by rather few of their enemies, while many normally slow-moving fishes can show a surprising turn of speed when pursued. Other species can suddenly leap out of the water, as do the freshwater hatchetfishes *Argyropelecus* of South America or the sauries and Grey mullets of the seas. The glide of the flyingfishes probably provides at least temporary bafflement to its enemies. Fishes such as eels, by their slipperiness and contortions of the body, may well free themselves from predators, although they are better adapted to hiding in crevices.

Hiding is one of the best means of defence provided that the surroundings offer suitable holes. Ideal conditions are found on coral reefs and numerous species take advantage of the cracks, openings, cavities and passages. In general, reef fishes show distinct day and night patterns of activity and as daylight fades the night feeders emerge from their hiding places while those active

in the daytime take their places. In the Caribbean the cardinalfishes *Apogon binotatus* and *A. townsendi* hide in crevices and holes but at a little after six o'clock in the evening they emerge for their nightly foraging, returning by six o'clock in the morning. Damselfishes, such as *Chromis cyaneus* and *Pomacentrus partitus*, on the other hand, feed during the daytime and seek shelter at night. Other fishes, and in particular some of the gobies, rarely stray far from their crevice, even during the day. From hiding in the interstices of coral it is only a short step to taking refuge inside another animal; such fishes are called inquilines or 'lodgers.' The Tusked goby *Risor ruber* and the Yellowline goby *Gobiosoma horsti* of the Caribbean live inside sponges and perhaps rarely make excursions outside.

One of the most unusual means of defence – if indeed it is one – is found in some of the parrotfishes (Scaridae). At night certain species secrete a mucous envelope around themselves, producing quantities of mucus from special glands near the gill cover. Such fishes browse over the reef during the day but at night remain immobile in their mucous cocoons until the morning changeover at dawn. It is thought that the cocoon prevents predators such as Moray eels from detecting the parrotfish by smell. The production of so much mucus, presumably every night, would seem to be a considerable waste of protein but evidently its value in protection outweighs this. Another fish that produces a coating of mucus is the clingfish *Lepadichthys lineatus* of the

Red Sea. Its skin is a continuous layer of giant mucus-producing cells which, within seconds, can envelope the fish in a thick slimy layer. These fishes live on or among the arms of shallow-water sea lilies (crinoids), feeding on the host and on its copepod parasites. The mucus may well serve to protect the fish against the rough surface of the crinoid.

The methods of defence so far described have been individual ones, but in fishes as in other animals, excepting man, the act of self-preservation is merely an instinctive expression of the much greater need to preserve the species. Thus individual efforts are sometimes combined into collective efforts. One example of this is the 'fright reaction' shown by some members of the carp-like and related fishes (Cypriniformes). Special cells in the skin of fishes such as minnows *Phoxinus*, will release a chemical into the water when the fish is attacked or damaged and on smelling this the remaining fishes will flee. The sight or smell of a pike does not prompt an instinctive urge in the minnows to flee from danger, but once they have learnt to associate the pike smell with fright reaction the bid to escape becomes automatic. Another collective method of defence is shoaling. Although this would seem to offer ideal conditions for a predator, it is more likely that the sight of thousands of exactly similar bodies makes it difficult for a predator to choose which to attack. In addition, some shoaling fishes, such as the herring-like *Jenkinsia* of the Caribbean, form themselves into tightly packed masses and in this state resemble a single large individual. Another case of collective mimicry has been reported in the catfish *Plotosus lineatus*; a swarm of dark juveniles was seen in a tidepool in East Africa arranged in a symmetrical mass with heads pointed outwards, the whole giving the impression of a large black sea anemone.

As in all other aspects of the way that fishes live, defence and self-preservation must be regarded as something of a compromise. The fish cannot be entirely organized for defence since it must also succeed in feeding, breeding and coping with the exigencies of the aquatic environment. In fact, survival of the species depends on many facets of structure, function and habit, of which some play a major role in defence but many combine several roles in the total organization of the animal. Fin spines, for example, are probably necessary both for defence and for support of the fin, while eye spots on the hind part of the body may not only confuse a predator but also serve as display signals in courtship. In trying to decide on the function of a particular structure it is important to bear in mind the total biology of the animal.

The Senses

Like any other animals, fishes have a constant need to assess the environment and to make suitable adjustments in their behaviour and the functioning of their bodies. If conditions are not satisfactory, then the fish must either compensate or move elsewhere. Similarly, the search for food, shelter or a mate requires constant monitoring of information. Among the factors to be measured are temperature, light, colour, dissolved gases, pressure or depth, chemical composition of the water, intensity of water currents, odours, sounds, vibrations, electrical activity in other fishes, and all those aspects of the environment that can be investigated by touch. This does not exhaust the list, but it gives an idea of the impressive amount of data required by a fish in order to carry out its daily activities. Obviously, some kinds of information are more important to a particular fish than others. In sharks, for example, it has been claimed that, were a thimbleful of blood to be diluted in the entire water-body of Lake Constance, their sense of smell is so acute that they would be able to detect it. This may be an exaggeration, but it is certainly true to say that for sharks, smell is very much more important than sight in searching for prey.

Fishes gather information either through special-ized sense organs, such as the nostrils or the eyes, or by fairly widely dispersed nerve endings in the skin. Sensory organs serve to concentrate information and thus enable the fish to respond directionally. For the same reason, much of the information is gathered in the head region. The data is brought by sensory nerves to various parts of the brain for assessment and then the necessary messages are sent to appropriate parts of the body. Some regions of the brain deal with specific types of information (olfactory lobes for smell, optic lobes for vision) but other parts have the important task of coordinating different sets of data and building up the great complexity of memory and learned behaviour. In general, the brains of sharks and rays show less variation and elaboration than those of the bony fishes and this reflects the difference in their adaptability and diversity of habits. The success of the bony fishes can be correlated with the evolution of a much more complex brain. However, the size of the brain may be misleading. In a large shark it may weigh only two or three thousandths of the total body weight; in a pike it may weigh about one thousandth; and in an elephant snoutfish *Mormyrus*, it may weigh about one fiftieth. The *Mormyrus* is not thereby the more intelligent, for a large part of its

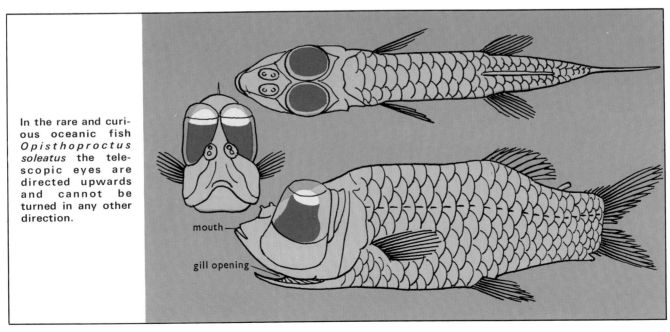

In the rare and curious oceanic fish *Opisthoproctus soleatus* the telescopic eyes are directed upwards and cannot be turned in any other direction.

mouth

gill opening

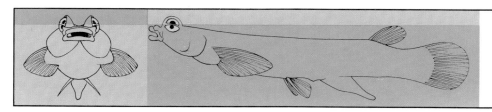

The Four-eyed fish *Anableps tetrophthalmus* showing the double structure of the eyes, the upper half being adapted for vision in air and the lower half for vision in water.

brain is made up of the cerebellum, which in this case seems to be associated with electrical sensing. Similarly, the relative size of a shrew's brain is about twice that in an elephant, but its organization is less complex.

Investigation of the senses in fishes is by no means easy. A certain amount can be learnt from the structure of a sense organ but this must be backed up by experiments in aquaria and observations in the field. In this respect, modern advances in electronic and other research methods have sometimes made it possible to challenge previously held theories on the function or range of a sensory system.

Sight. For man, possibly the most highly prized sense is vision. Human eyes are large, well protected in a bony socket and situated so as to give maximum binocular sight. In fishes, vision may be of equal importance for some activities but it often provides a rather restricted amount of information and must be supplemented by other senses. Turbidity and, in deeper water, the absorption of light in the upper layers, prevent many fishes from enjoying the accurate vision of a land animal. Nevertheless, the use of colour patterns for concealment, for courtship or for asserting territorial rights shows that

vision generally plays an important role in a fish's life. In some cases the differences in colouration that apparently prevent cross-breeding between related species are quite small and evidently depend on careful observation. Again, courtship displays may comprise rather slight nuances of behaviour that must be correctly interpreted. By placing fishes in aquaria or by using mirrors, other senses can be eliminated and the effects of signalling postures, colour patterns and the approach of potential enemies assessed.

Most fishes have well-developed eyes which are basically much like the eyes of other vertebrates, that is to say, there is a transparent protective covering, the cornea; an opaque iris, which regulates the amount of light entering the eye; a lens; and a retina of light-sensitive cells lining the back of the eye. The cornea has the same refractive index as water and light rays pass through without being refracted. The lens differs from our own in being spherical and protruding somewhat out of the iris, with the result that light can enter the eye from extremely wide angles. This, together with the usual placing of the eyes on the side of the head, enables the fish to see backwards almost down the length of the body and at the same time forwards and across

(A) Lateral line in three Bony fishes with section across lateral line of the greenling. (B) Neuromasts in the lateral line system register the movement of water or mucus by the degree to which the gelatinous cupola is deflected, thus stimulating the nerves at its base.

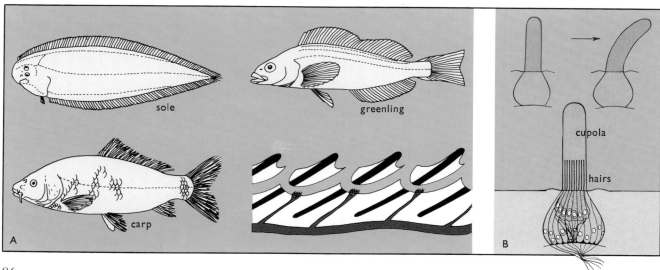

the snout so that there is a small area of binocular vision straight ahead. In man and other mammals, as well as in birds and most reptiles, an image is focussed on the retina by altering the curvature of the lens. In fishes, and also in amphibians and snakes, this cannot be done; to focus, these animals must move the whole lens either backwards or forwards. In bony fishes and in lampreys the lens is moved backwards to accommodate for seeing at a distance, while in sharks (and in amphibians and snakes) the lens must be moved forwards to see near objects.

It is often asked if fishes can see colour, and how can one ascertain whether they do or not. The answer is that many fishes certainly can distinguish between different colours, as is shown by training them to respond to coloured discs associated with a food reward. In some fishes, such as skates, colour perception is absent and the fish distinguishes colour according to the brightness of the object; by varying the brightness of coloured objects the fish can be made to confuse different colours. In most bony fishes, as well as in lampreys, colour can be appreciated quite apart from brightness. This can be correlated with the type of visual cells in the retina, which are of two kinds, rods and cones. Both of these contain certain pigments that react chemically to light, thus stimulating a nerve impulse that is transmitted to the brain. The rod cells, which function both during the day and in twilight, are associated with the ability to see fine detail and, as might be expected, predominate in fishes that live in dim waters. The cone cells only function under powerful illumination and are responsible for colour perception. A balance of rods and cones is found in many fishes of clear waters where recognition of a mate, rival, enemy or prey depends on colour, or where background colour matching is necessary, but in deep-sea fishes cones are almost always absent. Cones were once said to be absent also in sharks, so that stories of the danger of wearing highly coloured bathing suits were discounted. It has now been shown, however, that many species of sharks possess cone cells and that they must live in a coloured world.

It might be thought that fishes living in the twilight zone, from about 650 to 3,300 ft (200 to 1,000 m) below the surface, would have abandoned eyes in favour of other sensory systems, but this is not the case. Their eyes are well-developed and are often rather large, with a large lens, wide pupil and a predominance of rods containing a golden pigment highly sensitive to blue light. To increase the amount of light falling on the retina, certain sharks and other fishes have a mirror-like reflecting layer of plates behind the retina. Light passing through the retina is reflected back again, thus triggering a further nervous impulse from the retinal cells. Such eyes glow when light is shone into them. In bright light a layer of dark pigment migrates across the reflecting plates to prevent the fish from being dazzled. Certain sharks have another peculiarity, a movable

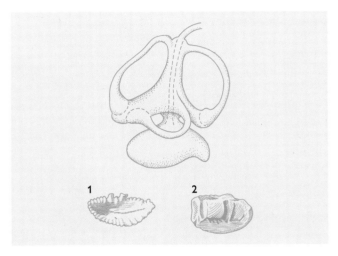

The ear of a fish, showing the three semi-circular canals and the sacs containing the ear stones or otoliths. Below, the largest otolith (sagitta) of a Cod (left) and a Meagre (right).

eyelid or nictating membrane which slides obliquely backwards and upwards across the eye. It is moved by five related muscles, of which the principal one is that which is otherwise associated with the opening of the spiracle; sharks with a well-developed spiracle (Mackerel sharks, Carpet sharks) lack a nictating membrane, while those with a reduced or absent spiracle (Brown shark, hammerheads, Smooth hound) possess one. This membrane seems to afford protection to the eye and is apparently unaffected by strong light; in any case, sharks, unlike many other fishes, are able to contract the pupil in bright conditions. What may be another protection for the eye is the layer of tissue, the so-called adipose eyelid, found for example in shads and Grey mullets, although it may also play a more important role in streamlining.

While eyes are usually large in fishes of the twilight zone (down to about 3,300 ft, say 1,000 m), there is a marked tendency for small, regressed or degenerate eyes in fishes living at greater depths, as for example certain brotulids, liparids and bathypteroids. Degenerate eyes, often so reduced as to be barely recognizable as eyes, occur in certain cave fishes. The parasitic hagfishes also have degenerate eyes, which may be only a millimetre in diameter; although a lens is formed at the embryo stage this subsequently disappears.

Observations and experiments have shown that both the behaviour and the physiology of fishes are frequently dependent on the amount and duration of light. For example, ripening of the ovaries and testes during the breeding season has been shown to depend on day-length, in the Bridled shiner *Notropis bifrenatus*, the European minnow and the Three-spined stickleback; while the migration of White bass *Roccus chrysops* in Lake Mendota in Wisconsin is to a large extent guided by the direction of the sun's rays. Appreciation of light as opposed to actual vision is not, however, solely the property of the eyes. In some fishes the roof of the skull is fairly transparent and reactions to light have been recorded in the pineal body, a small outgrowth from the top of the forebrain (this is the posterior of two such outgrowths, the anterior one being the parietal organ, best known for its development as a 'third eye' in the Tuatara). In certain surface-living fishes, such as the silversides (Atherinidae), herrings (Clupeidae) and anchovies (Engraulidae), a part of the pineal body is greatly extended over the top of the brain and thus presumably enhances the perception of light. Lampreys and hagfishes, on the other hand, have both parietal as well as pineal organs, the former being absent in bony fishes, and each is developed into an eye-like structure. Because of the far greater sensitivity of true eyes, however, it is difficult to establish the exact part played by other light receptors.

In a few fishes the eyes have become highly specialized for particular kinds of vision. The larval stage of the deep-sea *Idiacanthus fasciola* has eyes at the end of long stalks held out from the body by movable cartilaginous rods, which become retracted in the adults. It is thought that this arrangement gives better stereoscopic vision.

As every fisherman knows, fishes in shallow water pay considerable attention to objects out of the water. Trout, for example, certainly see insects before they land on the surface and do not wait for them to do so. The archerfish *Toxotes* sees its out-of-water insect targets clearly enough to be able to hit them with great accuracy even though its aim must compensate for diffraction at the surface of the water. A few fishes are adapted to seeing both in air and in water. The surf-loving Rock blenny *Dialommus* of the Galapagos Islands has an iris with a double opening, the hind part for underwater vision and the fore part for seeing on land. The forward 'window' brings light onto the most sensitive part of the retina and so accurate is its sight that individuals resting in small caves have been seen to catch flies walking above them. A similar 'two-window' eye for aerial vision is also found in the rock-climbing *Mnierpes* of Central America, but the most celebrated species, also from that part of the world, is the 8 in (20 cm) Four-eyed fish *Anableps*. In this case, not only is there a double-window, but there are also two distinct retinas. The fish swims with the upper part of the eye in air and the lower part in water and the lens is so shaped that it focusses in the two elements simultaneously. Other unusual eyes are found in some of the deep-sea fishes and these will be described later.

Hearing and Vibrations. As already emphasized, fishes live in a dense medium. One effect of this is that sound travels almost five times faster than in

A Red sea bream in which the lateral line can clearly be seen running from behind the gill cover to the tail.

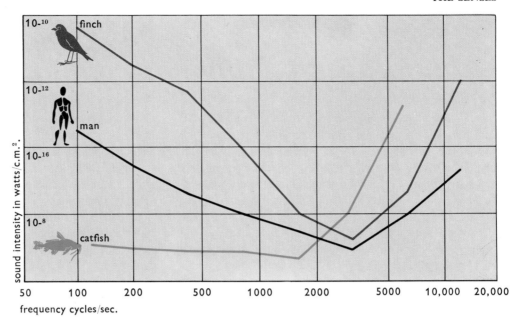

The thresholds of hearing in a bird (finch), a mammal (man) and a fish (catfish).

sound intensity in watts/c.m.²

frequency cycles/sec.

air and vibrations are much more easily perceived. Fishes have taken advantage of these properties and have developed ways of gaining a great deal of information about what is going on around them. Sounds result from high frequency vibrations which, by alternately compressing and expanding the water, produce sound waves. There are also pressure disturbances in the water due to eddies, currents, swimming movements of other fishes, reflection of waves off rocks or the bottom, and so on, and these too are of interest to fishes.

The ears of fishes lie in paired cavities at the hind end of the skull, and are thus near to the most stable point when the fish swims. Only the inner ear is developed, the external and middle ear of land vertebrates being superfluous because of the ease with which sound waves penetrate from water into a solid body. The ear cavity is divided into an upper part, the utriculus, and a lower part, the sacculus, with a small outgrowth, the lagena. It is the lower part that is concerned with hearing. At one time it was doubted that fish could hear and the carp that apparently assembled at the sound of a bell were shown to do so only when they saw the man who rang it. Modern equipment, however, now proves that fishes often have an acute sense of hearing, responding to sound waves up to 7,000 Herz (cycles per second), compared with about 10,000 in man and about 100,000 in bats and mice. The greatest range of hearing is found in the freshwater Cypriniformes – carps, characins, catfishes – in which a unique method of amplifying sounds has been evolved. This is the Weberian apparatus and consists of three or four pairs of small bones modified from the anterior vertebrae. Linked together, they form a system of levers that transmit vibrations picked up by the swimbladder to the ear, thus greatly increasing the ear's sensitivity. This kind of amplification is surprisingly like the system adopted by land vertebrates in which sounds are picked up by the outer ear and transmitted by three little bones, the malleus, incus and stipes. It is not, however, the only method of amplification used. In the herrings, anchovies, tarpons, mormyrids and certain other fishes the swimbladder has small tube-like outgrowths that reach forwards to the skull and in some of these fishes they form vesicles which are closely associated with the ear capsule; the result is something like a stethoscope. In all, over 5,000 species of fishes have some type of connection between the swimbladder and the ears.

Experiments have been conducted on how fishes react to recordings of the noises made by a speared and struggling fish. On one occasion a Tiger shark *Galeocerdo* approached the speaker and gave every indication that it has been attracted by the noise and it appeared that sharks were able to pick up the sounds from about 650 ft (say 200 m) away. Skin-divers claim that shouting will deter an attacking shark, so that the day may come when divers will be equipped with a small gadget to produce a 'repellant' sound.

Fishes pick up pressure waves or sounds from distances well beyond those at which objects can be seen. The information would be of little value, however, if the direction of the sound could not be

89

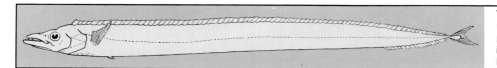

The frostfish *Lepidotus cauda-tus* is highly sensitive to temperature, a sudden drop bringing thousands to the shore in New Zealand.

determined, and here a difficulty arises. A fish's tissues are fairly transparent to sound waves, so that sound entering the right side of the head will be registered only very shortly afterwards by the left ear (in a land animal bone and other tissue effectively insulate one ear from the other). Some fishes, such as Sea robins *Prionotus* and the toadfish *Opsanus*, have a mass of fatty tissue separating the ears and this probably acts as a partial sound barrier, but in the Cypriniformes and the Clupeiformes, both with intricate ear–swimbladder connections, there is no such sound barrier. In this case directional hearing may depend on the special Mauthner nerve cells whose giant fibres produce the sudden muscle contraction needed for a fast getaway. The Mauthner cells are linked with the sensory system (sight and hearing) and their reaction is fast enough to trigger a 'tail flip' in response to sound entering one ear before it is appreciated by the other. Since the Mauthner nerve fibres are crossed over, the effect of the tail flip is to bring the head of the fish towards the noise. Such may be the system by which many fishes orient to sounds.

Compared with our own medium, that of fishes seems so empty of noise that Jacques Cousteau has dubbed it the 'silent world.' In fact, the underwater world is noisy and much of the noise is produced by fishes. Fish sounds are produced in three main ways. The first is by stridulation or the rubbing of rough surfaces together. This is commonly done by grinding the pharyngeal or throat teeth, as in the grunts (Pomadasyidae), but chewing with the jaw teeth can also be audible if the food is hard. A few fishes, and in particular the catfishes, can make high-pitched squeaks by moving the pectoral fin spines, while Sea horses produce sounds by rubbing the hind margin of the skull against the first vertebra. The second method of producing sound is purely hydrodynamic and results from sudden changes in swimming direction or velocity. The third and most successful method is by using the swimbladder as a resonator. Some triggerfishes, *Balistes* for example, beat their pectoral fins against the body in the region of the swimbladder. The most celebrated drummers, however, are the croakers or drumfishes (Sciaenidae) which have a pair of strong muscles (sometimes only present in the male) on either side of the swimbladder. These can be rapidly vibrated to produce short bursts of drum-like sounds. The swimbladder in sciaenid fishes is sometimes a highly complex system of branching tubes reaching forwards to the skull and backwards along the body, but the effect of this upon noise production is not known. In other drumming fishes, such as certain groupers, squirrelfishes and scorpionfishes, the drumming muscles are anchored to the hind end of the skull and connect to the ribs at the front end of the swimbladder or, in the case of some of the catfishes, to a special elastic bone that enhances the vibration.

Fishes produce a wide variety of sounds ranging from squeaks, whines and clicks to grunts, growls, cheeps and plain drumming sounds. In a few cases they can be heard out of water, as for example some of the drumfishes, but for the most part underwater sounds are inaudible to us unless amplified in some way. Native fishermen sometimes locate shoals of fishes by listening in with an oar, trident or pipe, but it was only with the development of underwater recording equipment that the extraordinary range of fish noises became apparent. Since fishes can both hear and make sounds, the question arises of the role of sound production. Some sounds are clearly produced unwittingly when the fish swims, chews hard food or expels air from the swimbladder and these sounds are obviously of interest to a predator. There are, however, other sounds which are purposefully produced and which must be considered as a means of communication.

Quite as important to fishes as sounds are the

Red mullet in search of food 'fingering' the sea-bed with its barbels.

The front rays of the pectoral fins of the gurnard are used to feel for food on the sea bed.

subtle disturbances of the water around them, whether as the result of their own actions in swimming or those of other fishes, or through forces in the environment. Such water movements are registered by the lateral line system, comprising small sensory cells (neuromasts) distributed mainly in lines over the head and body, either freely at the surface or enclosed in canals. Each neuromast contains support cells surrounding fine sensory cells which terminate in hair-like processes. These in turn are surrounded by a gelatinous plate or rod, the cupula, which projects above the surface of the skin. Any movement or vibration of the surrounding water will deflect the cupula and stimulate a signal from the sensory cells to the brain. In both sharks and bony fishes the most obvious part of the lateral line system is the canal that runs along either flank; sometimes there are two or even three canals, as in certain of the flatfishes. In most bony fishes with scales, but not in the herrings and anchovies, each scale covering the canal bears a small pore and the canal itself is filled with mucus. In this way, differences in water pressure are transmitted to the mucus and registered by the neuromasts. On the head, the canal divides into branches behind the eye, a part passing over the eye to the snout, another part running below the eye and a third leading forward to the lower jaw. The multiplication of canals on the head suggests that a considerable amount of information can be monitored in the head region, presumably in connection with swimming movements and appreciation of current velocities or the movements of prey. The lateral line system can react to low frequency sound vibrations but its main function seems to be to detect disturbances close to the fish.

As in land animals, the ear is intimately associated with the organ of balance, a most necessary faculty in fishes since they are often unable to get their bearings by sight alone. As already stated, the upper part of the ear chamber is occupied by the sac-like utriculus. Above it, and joined to it, are three curved membranous tubes, the semi-circular canals, each with a swelling or ampulla at one end and, within the ampulla, a structure somewhat resembling a swing-door. Each canal is at right-angles to the others so that acceleration by the fish in any plane of the canals sets up a surge of fluid which deflects the 'swing-door' and triggers sensory signals to the brain. In addition, the utriculus and the two sacs below, the sacculus and the small lagena, contain limy concretions, the ear stones or otoliths. Sensory hairs lining the sacs register movements of the otoliths; by replacing the otoliths by iron filings and placing a magnet over the fish, the animal can be made to turn upside-down. Experiments have shown that it is usually the otolith of the utriculus (known as the lapillus) that registers gravity, those of the sacculus and lagena (known as the sagitta and the asteriscus) being concerned with hearing. The otoliths are enlarged by additions of lime at a rate similar to that of general body growth. They thus tend to show concentric rings and can be used to calculate the age of a fish.

Before leaving the subject of hearing, mention should be made of the possibility that some sound-producing fishes can use echo-location as a means of navigation. In one instance the sound of a deep-sea fish has been recorded, followed by the echo from the sea bed, which presumably the fish itself was also able to hear. Although there seems no reason why fishes should not employ such a sonar system, it is extremely difficult to find any proof that they do.

Like the catfishes, the Stone loach *Noemachilus barbatulus* has a mouth surrounded by sensory barbels.

Temperature. Observations show that bony fishes seem to be aware of the water temperature around them. They will seek out preferred temperatures, avoid those above and below the optimum and, at least experimentally, show by their behaviour a very fine discrimination of slight rises or drops in temperature. The frostfish *Lepidopus caudatus* is particularly sensitive to sudden drops in temperature and in New Zealand a cold night will bring thousands to the shore. Unlike sight, smell and hearing, temperature appreciation is not localised in paired organs on the head but seems to be a property of nerve endings over most parts of the body. However, there is reason to suppose that nerves that respond to temperature also respond to other types of stimulation, touch for example. Since it is necessary to touch a nerve or nerve ending with an electrode in order to record its activity, it is extremely difficult to isolate responses made purely to temperature. Again, the ampullae of Lorenzini in sharks and rays, described here under electrical senses, also respond to changes in temperature and at one time this was believed to be their sole function. Certainly it is true that temperature is an important feature in the environment of fishes, but for most species it changes rather slowly and within limits which do not require sudden adjustments or evasive action.

Smell and Taste. In land vertebrates, smell and taste can be distinguished from each other by the way in which the chemical stimuli are perceived, whereas in fishes smell and taste both result from substances dissolved in the water around them. Like land vertebrates, however, fishes have paired nostrils in front of the eyes which can be reasonably called organs of smell, while perception of chemicals by cells in the lining of the mouth and gill cavity can be termed taste. The two are distinct in as much as minnows *Phoxinus* trained to respond to a variety of odorous substances will not discriminate between them by taste if the nerves to the nostrils are cut. Fishes also have a third means of sampling substances in water, the common chemical sense. This is a general and less sensitive appreciation of the chemicals which come into contact with exposed parts of their bodies.

In sharks and rays, the nostrils or organs of smell are small pits in front of the corners of the mouth, to which they are sometimes connected by grooves. In bony fishes the nasal pits are on the upper side of the head and the opening of each pit is divided by a flange of skin so that water can flow in at the front and out at the rear. Inside the pit, the skin is thrown into a number of folds, often in the form of a rosette, thus increasing the surface area to as much as 4% of the total body surface in the gudgeon *Gobio*, but only about 2% in the minnow and as little as 0·2% in the pike. The folds of the rosette bear cells that register chemical substances present in the water as it passes over them.

Observations show that some fishes are clearly more dependant on a sense of smell than others. The pike *Esox*, for example, has a very much smaller surface area with which to smell than has the gudgeon, but it has larger eyes, good stereoscopic vision and relies on sight rather than smell to locate its prey. In certain pufferfishes the nasal sacs are dispensed with altogether, whereas in eels the sacs are very elongate, stretching from the tip of the snout to the eye, and these fishes probably have the most acute sense of smell of any species yet tested. To increase the flow of water through the pits some

fishes possess fine cilia which induce a current. In others the pits are pumped by the action of the muscles that work the jaws or those involved with normal breathing movements, usually with the aid of accessory nasal sacs. In a few fishes the nostrils lead through to the mouth just as our own nostrils lead to the throat. This occurs in the hagfishes *Myxine*, the lungfishes (Dipnoi) and in the fossil coelacanths, but not in *Latimeria*; it has also been found in a stargazer *Astroscopus*. Since this arrangement is not for breathing it may be a substitute for a nasal pump.

In bony fishes, but perhaps not in sharks and rays, the taste buds are not limited to the mouth and gill chamber but may also occur on barbels and fins as an additional means of sampling the environment. The 'whiskers' of catfishes and the free pectoral or pelvic finrays of fishes like the Lake gourami *Trichogaster* and some of the cod family (Gadidae) bear taste buds and are used to probe the substrate. In the Sea robin *Prionotus*, however, the finger-like pectoral finrays lack taste buds but have free nerve endings which presumably serve the same function. It is probably such rather unspecialized nerve endings that provide the so-called common chemical sense.

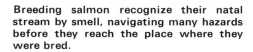

Breeding salmon recognize their natal stream by smell, navigating many hazards before they reach the place where they were bred.

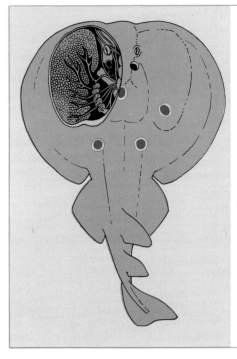

The Electric ray *Torpedo* dissected to show one of the major electric organs with its associated nerve supply. The prismatic areas on the surface of the organ represent the vertical columns of electric plates, of which there may be 500,000 in each organ.

The sensitivity of fishes to smells and tastes is remarkable. It can best be tested by training a fish to respond in some way to a particular chemical, either by linking that chemical with a food reward or by using one that induces fright or sexual reactions. The most sensitive fish yet tested is the European freshwater eel *Anguilla anguilla*. In one experiment, using β-phenylethyl alcohol, the fishes responded to dilutions of one part of 3 trillion, which is equivalent to 1,770 molecules in a cubic centimetre of water or just one molecule in each nasal chamber! Young Sockeye salmon *Oncorhynchus kisutch* were able to detect the chemical at about half that dilution, which is about the sensitivity found in man. Much work is required on this subject, for it is clear that many activities of fishes are motivated by smells and tastes.

Electricity. Electric organs were briefly mentioned in connection with defence, but fishes with organs powerful enough to stun their prey or enemies are rather rare. In the seas there are the Electric rays or torpedoes, which can discharge a current up to 60 volts, and in freshwaters there is the Electric eel *Electrophorus electricus* of South America (more than 500 volts) and the Electric catfish *Malapterurus electricus* of Africa (up to 350 volts). Possibly the stargazers *Astroscopus* of the Western Atlantic should be placed in this category, although they discharge only about 5 volts. The remaining electric fishes, distributed through seven

different families, produce such a weak discharge that their electrical abilities have been recognized only fairly recently. The best known of these are the marine skates or rays *Raja*, the freshwater South American knifefish *Gymnotus carapo* (also members of three related families) and the mormyroid fishes of African freshwaters (*Gymnarchus niloticus* and some of the mormyrid fishes such as *Gnathonemus*). Strong electric fishes tend to discharge only when the occasion arises, whereas weakly electric fishes continually emit pulses or short bursts of pulses.

In most electric fishes the organs are modified from striated muscle fibres and are in the form of blocks of platelets stacked one against the next, either mainly vertically and connected in parallel (torpedoes, stargazers) or mainly longitudinally and connected in series (Electric eel). In some electric

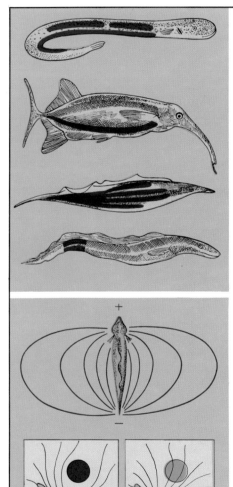

Electric organs in four bony fishes showing their arrangement along the flanks. From top to bottom: Electric eel, Elephant snout fish, African knifefish, South American knifefish. The lines of force produced by the African knifefish *Gymnarchus niloticus* resemble those of a bar magnet (lower part of diagram). Interference in the field of force can be detected by the fish and interpreted to give information on its surroundings.

An underwater photograph of the Black electric ray.

fishes the organs are said to be modified from nerve fibres (Sternarchidae). In the Electric eel there are about 6,000 electroplates, each capable of generating 0·1 volt. The location of the electric organs is highly variable, being on either side of the eyes in the torpedoes, behind the eyes and derived from eye muscles in the stargazers, along the flank in knifefishes and the Electric eel, covering most of the front half of the body surface in the Electric catfish, and confined to the base of the tail in the mormyrids. In the marine species the electric cells are connected in parallel, whereas they are in series in freshwater species, probably because of the higher electrical resistance of the water.

Since weakly electric fishes cannot stun their prey or frighten off enemies, it is clear that these highly specialized organs must have evolved for some other use. Experiments with *Gymnarchus* have shown that the head is positive during discharge and that an electric field is created round the fish. The presence of a non-conducting object will disturb the field and the fish can sense this disturbance. Thus weak electric organs seem to provide information that would otherwise be sensed by the eyes and perhaps

the lateral line. In addition, a number of fishes – sharks and rays, catfishes, knifefishes and mormyroids – have receptors for detection of electrical fields, being modifications of the lateral line organs. In those that produce electricity themselves – knifefishes and mormyroids – it seems likely that the fish operates a system of 'electrolocation' analogous to the echo-location used by bats and dolphins. Those without electric organs may well use their electroreceptors to detect the minute electrical potentials generated by the muscles of gill movements in their prey. The long tubules filled with jelly, the ampullae of Lorenzini, found on the heads of sharks and rays, are now known to be electroreceptors and are probably used in this way.

The sense organs of fishes are extremely intricate, but an understanding of their capabilities is essential in any study of fish behaviour. In turn, fish behaviour can provide a useful experimental tool in determining the scope of the senses. Fortunately, the development of electronics has enabled much more precise measurements to be made and an exciting field has been opened up for further research.

Getting on with Others

The study of ethology or animal behaviour is a comparatively recent branch of zoology, having been pioneered by Conrad Lorenz and further developed by Niko Tinbergen in the years between the two world wars. Ethology is as essential to an understanding of the biology of animals as is morphology (the study of body structure) and physiology (the study of the way the body works). In fact, none of these three fields can be fully explored except in terms of the other two. However, behaviour is by far the most difficult to investigate because of the strong temptation to interpret animal behaviour in terms of our own. Humans clearly have a purpose in their actions, but can one say that animal behaviour is purposive? Does a salmon migrate because it wants to reach the spawning grounds, or is this merely an instinctive drive? Did Henri Fabre's famous processionary caterpillars endlessly marching around the rim of a tub show praiseworthy singleness of purpose, or were they locked in a behaviouristic determinism ruled solely by cold chemical necessity? Much depends on our definitions of 'purpose,' 'instinct,' 'drive' and 'need.' The matter is still much discussed and the best one can do is to try to describe the way that animals behave without reference to aims, wants or desires.

Ethology is a broad subject, covering every relationship entered into by the animal, whether with inanimate objects, with members of the same species, or with other animals. Behaviour in relation to the environment is a rather diffuse category, ranging from methods of swimming or hiding to the ways that behaviour contributes to overcoming adverse or abnormal conditions. It will not be dealt with specifically here since examples occur throughout the book. Associations with members of the same species frequently contain elements of communication and in some cases one can refer to the signals used as a language. Such a language is recognized in bees, for example, where various dance routines indicate direction and distance of food sources. Associations with other animals, apart from those involved in feeding or defence, range from the intimacy of parasitism to an informal sharing of the same dinner table, for which we use the term commensalism. Careful study reveals the way in which these often complex relationships may have evolved, step by step, with modifications in both physiology and morphology. Although lacking a fossil history, ethology often provides clues to the origin of particular body parts or processes. Much of the work done on the behaviour of animals has involved mammals, birds and various insects, but opportunities for underwater observations have now made it possible to supplement aquarium studies of fishes by work in their natural habitat. For example, during the Tektite Project of 1970, 10 missions, each of 10 to 20 days, took place from an underwater laboratory off the Virgin Islands and ichthyologists were able to follow the daily lives of coral reef fishes over a seven month period. The results, such as the recording of a distinct changeover pattern between day and night feeders, were often only made possible by such extended study.

Relations Within Species. The species can be regarded as a very special system of relationships between a number of individuals. Because all individuals share a common pool of genes, that is to say any male can mate with any female so that theoretically the offspring can inherit any hereditary character available within the species, then all individuals within the species will have approximately the same requirements and habits. As will be explained later, the species is the only biological unit which can not only produce but can also preserve novelties. It is thus the unit of evolution. This has a very profound bearing on the kind of relationships that occur between individuals of the same species and it shows why such relationships are quite different in quality from those that exist between individuals of different species.

The relationships within a species fulfil the function of preserving both the existence and the character of the species. From the point of view of behaviour, one method of direct preservation has already been mentioned under breeding, namely the highly specialized methods of brooding the eggs in

The serried ranks of a shoal of marine fishes afford protection, by weight of numbers, for individual members. ▷

cichlid and other fishes. This is a purely individual act, but there are other methods of preservation that require cooperation and thus a relationship between several or many members of the population. An example of this is seen in shoaling behaviour. In this case a mass of individuals of approximately the same size swim together, sometimes in such perfect unison, turning, diving, rising or stopping, that it seems almost unbelievable that each fish is individually motivated. This type of synchronization is probably achieved by two means, by vision and by the lateral line organs. Some species of shoaling fishes have a silver, electric blue or dark stripe down the flank, for example in some of the herrings and anchovies, while others have a conspicuous spot or series of spots, as in certain of the shoaling species of the cichlid genus *Haplochromis* found in Lake Malawi. By using such markers, each fish can visually orientate itself with respect to its immediate companions and any sudden change of direction can be followed. For fishes that swim in a compact shoal, the swimming movements of their neighbours may be registered as vibrations by the lateral line organs and this may be the method by which a constant distance is maintained.

Shoaling behaviour seems always to be linked with plankton feeding, more frequently in juveniles but in a number of species carried over into adulthood. Thus it is striking that among the species of the cichlid genus *Haplochromis* all manner of feeding habits have evolved, but it is only the plankton feeders that shoal. Shoaling has been considered a means of defence, a predator being confused by the sight of so many identical bodies, but it seems that it must also aid feeding in some way. A shoal, after all, is made up of thousands of eyes, ears, noses and lateral lines all on the look-out for danger; perhaps each individual fish can devote more of its attention to feeding than it could if it were swimming on its own. Again, circling shoals of *Tilapia* in some of the African lakes have been found to comprise only females (on one occasion only males), and it has been suggested that by this means the fishes appreciate their population density and regulate their breeding accordingly. In fact, there is no reason why shoaling – or any other kind of behaviour for that matter – should serve only one function.

Some predatory fishes, as for example certain sharks, will congregate to feed, but the relationship between individuals is far looser than in shoaling and may be frankly competitive. The most striking aggregations are those involved in spawning and numerous species that otherwise live an independent life come together in hundreds or thousands during the breeding season. This not only ensures that eggs and sperm are shed at the same time and the same place, but in many cases it forms a kind of mass courtship necessary for stimulating the fishes to discharge their sex products into the water. Mass breeding has, in many groups of fishes, given way to highly specialized individual courtship and spawning, for which there are quite definite requirements.

Male African lyretails *Aphyosemion batesi* have larger fins and brighter colours than the females.

Tilapia tholloni male in breeding dress — the red on throat and belly.

male does zig-zag dance

female enters territory

female approaches male

male leads to nest

female follows

courtship ends

male points at entrance to nest

female enters nest

male quivers at female's tail

female spawns

male fertilises eggs

Diagram showing sequence of movements in stickleback courtship (left); (right), male stickleback constructing his nest, carrying nesting material in the mouth.

Most important of all, the fishes must have some definite place to meet. Having met, they must be able to recognize each other as belonging to the same species and, of course, opposite sexes. They must then be able to stimulate each other to spawn and finally, in certain cases, must show appropriate responses in the brooding and care of the young.

To get this complicated procedure right demands a very exact dove-tailing of behaviour between the parents and it is here that one sees some of the best examples of the interplay between ethology, morphology and physiology. A male visual cue, such as a highly coloured dorsal fin, is emphasized by display – leading to a change in behaviour of the female – an answering response by the male –

The Striped drum *Equetus pulcher* of the Caribbean, one of the croakers or drumfishes, which make sounds, presumably to communicate with their fellows.

triggering the discharge of eggs by the female – which is the cue for release of sperm by the male. To analyse the complete sequence takes much patience and ingenuity. By using models it can be shown what are the essential aspects of colour or shape that find a response in the other fish. The models can, in fact, be surprisingly crude, provided that they contain just the elements involved: a square piece of cardboard may be quite sufficient, as long as it has a red blotch along the 'belly,' to stimulate a female stickleback.

One of the best known aspects of breeding by individual pairs is the establishment of a territory from which rival males are driven away but likely females encouraged to enter. In the nest-building cichlids the territory is the nest, a shallow saucer-shaped excavation with a low rim that may be 1–2 ft (30–60 cm) in diameter. The male will hover over the nest, darting out to investigate any intruder and judging first by approximate size and shape, and then by colour, if it is a member of the same species. Colour distinguishes between a breeding male or a female, but will be reinforced by behaviour patterns, a rival male meeting aggression with aggression, until driven away, but a female showing various postures of 'submission.' Much nonsense has been written equating man's 'aggressive instinct' and 'territoriality' with those of other animals, as if the trench fighting of the Somme had deeper roots than the sheer stupidity of those that planned it; so many layers of psycho-social experience overlie man's instinctive behaviour that a comparison with lower animals can be both misleading and, if manipulated as propaganda, highly dangerous.

Individual territories, and the aggressive behaviour needed to maintain them, are common in fishes either where there is breeding between individual pairs, as in the cichlid fishes mentioned above, or where there is competition for living space. An excellent example of the latter is seen on coral reefs, which are notable for supporting a high density of individuals of many different species. Even a small clump of coral may harbour 50 different species of fish as permanent residents and be visited by a number more. Sheer living space, rather than supplies of food, seems to determine how many individuals live on a coral reef and how they behave towards one another. Many of the residents have their own hole or niche into which they squeeze for safety when not out foraging for food, and in some cases it has been found that the same hiding place is shared between a daytime and a night feeder. With space at an absolute premium, it is obviously necessary to show aggression towards intruders and, in many cases, to advertise ownership by a warning display of colour. The speed with which reef fishes will disappear into their crevices at the approach of danger suggests that colour is of less use in camouflage than in providing visual evidence of the ownership of a territory. The actual size of these territories is generally linked to the size of the fish. Some of the small gobies and blennies may not venture more than a few feet (about a metre) from their hiding place, but many of the residents feed, not on the reef itself, but out on the sand flats surrounding it. In one set of observations made

during the Tektite Project, night feeders such as cardinalfishes (*Apogon*) and soldierfishes (*Holocentrus, Myripristis*) ranged up to 20 ft (7 m) from the reef, whereas daytime feeders (some parrotfishes and damselfishes) often kept closer to the reef, presumably for protection.

One of the crucial aspects of behaviour by individuals within a species is to preserve the identity of the species by preventing cross-breeding with other species, although to some extent this is also done physiologically since relatively few species will breed with another and produce successful offspring. Species are not stable, however, but from time to time give rise to variants which may, under the right environmental conditions, become established as new species. At some stage in this process, members of the new species must no longer regard those of the original species as possible mates but as competitors for breeding sites, so that a new pattern of recognition develops. This may precede the evolution of any physiological barrier to cross-breeding and indeed may remain the principal means of preventing it. Certainly, there are numerous cases where breeding behaviour alone makes cross-breeding highly unlikely or even impossible, the male actively driving a strange female away.

The various patterns of behaviour between individuals of a species have come about through the same processes of natural selection as those that shape the structure and the workings of the body. In other words, specializations in behaviour promote the stability, survival and success of the species, as for example in shoaling or in spawning rituals.

Communication. If one fish can influence the behaviour of another, then this can be judged a form of communication. In man, the eyes are so fre-

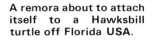

A remora about to attach itself to a Hawksbill turtle off Florida USA.

quently preoccupied in other activities that the voice is the main organ of communication, gestures and facial expressions taking second place. Fishes have available for communication sight, touch, smell, sound and, in a few cases, electricity. For some fishes, sight is obviously of considerable importance, although it can only operate over rather short distances during daylight and in clear water. The heightening of colour (usually in males) during the breeding season and especially during courtship, as well as the intricate sexual displays by movements and fin erections, as in sticklebacks, dragonets *Callionymus* and a host of others, are clearly signals that can be said to constitute a kind of language, albeit a somewhat inflexible one. The vocabulary is rather limited and parts of a spawning sequence may reappear in another context as aggressive gestures, but the correct message is passed across and the appropriate reaction elicited. Touch, on the other hand, seems to be a less common means of communication, whether registered by the skin or, as 'distant touch,' by the lateral line organs. For fishes that copulate, however, touch plays a vital role in calling forth a response by means of nudging, butting and mouthing.

The sense of smell, being highly developed in many fishes, is certainly a channel for communication by means of pheromones or special chemical substances that produce a specific reaction in another individual of the same species. The best known effect of pheromones in fishes is the 'fright reaction' mentioned earlier as a means of defence in the Cypriniformes (carps, loaches, catfishes, characins). Pheromones are produced by special club cells in the skin. Damage to the skin of a minnow *Phoxinus* will release the pheromone into the water and on smelling this the other minnows will quickly scatter. If at the same time the water also smells of a predator, such as a pike, the minnows will soon come to associate this smell with that of the fright reaction pheromone, so that the fright reaction will become

reinforced. In an aquarium, fright reaction can be produced by adding a small quantity of water from a tank containing a damaged minnow or from one containing a pike if the minnows have learned that smell. Communication by smell may also play a part in courtship, or at least recognition of mates, but much work is needed on this aspect.

The properties of sound under water make it an ideal means of communication over much greater distances than is possible by vision and with a greater sense of direction than is possible with smell. A smell, after all, must be followed to its source, but a sound can give immediate information at a distance. Since many fishes produce sounds and have acute or very acute hearing, then it seems reasonable to suppose that sounds are produced for communication. To confirm this is, however, difficult since it requires close observation of the sender and the receiver, but by playing back recorded fish sounds it has been found that courting males can attract females by means of sound. The grinding noises of feeding reef fishes may also be a form of communication. Thus amberjacks *Caranx latus* can be made to feed on hearing their own feeding noises played back to them.

Sound is perhaps most widely used in breeding activities, and fishermen in many parts of the world have long associated the drumming of drumfishes (Sciaenidae) with spawning or spawning migrations. The haddock *Melanogrammus aeglefinus* is another fish that appears to produce sounds during the breeding season. In certain fishes, such as the oviparous (live-bearing) brotulid fishes of the upper continental slope, only the males have large drumming muscles, while in the toadfish *Opsanus tau* both sexes have sonic mechanisms but only the male produces 'boat-whistle' sounds. This strongly suggests that sound plays a part in courting in these fishes. There are, however, instances of sounds produced by schooling fishes, such as Sea robins *Prionotus*, the noisiest fish along the American Atlantic, and Sea catfishes *Galeichthys felis*, choruses of the latter lasting from 5 pm until 11 pm from spring to autumn but with a lull in July and August. Sounds, whether for courtship or for shoaling, must be characteristic for the species, but since virtually the same kind of sound is produced by several species it seems likely that the duration and spacing of bursts of sound, as well as the frequency of the bursts, indicate the species and perhaps also comprise the message ('I am Species A,' 'Danger,' 'Follow me,' 'I am a suitable male' and so on).

Top view of a remora showing the large oval sucker on top of the head. This sucker is derived from a highly modified dorsal fin.

Small cleaner fishes at work picking parasites off larger fishes. The larger fishes present themselves voluntarily for this operation, at times even queueing up to do so.

The final means of communication open to fishes is by electrical discharges and it may be used by those fishes with weak electric organs (skates, gymnotids, mormyrids) both to detect objects around them and to impart information to their neighbours. Indirect evidence for this is the presence of cells capable of recording electric discharges in fishes that are not themselves electric (for example, sharks). If electric signals are important to such fishes, then surely the weakly electric species cannot help but pick up and use electrical information from their fellows.

Relations With Other Species. Relations between members of the same species may involve competition as well as cooperation, but such competition would not survive for long if it were not in the best interests of the species as a whole. Even in direct aggression, as when males dispute over territories or mates, one can see that there is a value in spacing breeding sites or discriminating against less fit members of the species. Relations between members of different species are of another order, each species being adapted to get the best out of the relationship, at the expense of the other, if necessary.

One rather loose association between animals is commensalism, or making use of the same food source but not in a competitive way. Examples among fishes are rare, but the pilotfish *Naucrates ductor* may be a commensal. It lives in close associ-

ation with sharks, swimming alongside its much larger host and apparently feeding on scraps left by the shark. It was once thought that the pilotfish guided the shark towards food and in reward received immunity, but this is unlikely; sharks are perfectly well able to find food by themselves, while the agility of the pilotfish probably saves it from being eaten. It is quite possible, however, that the pilotfish gains a measure of protection, for few medium-sized predators would risk approaching a shark so closely.

An extremely interesting aspect of commensalism has recently been described for some of the cichlid fishes of Lake Malawi. Until now it has been generally held that the closer one species is related to another the less likely it will be that their feeding habits are similar, since the two would thus compete with each other for a limited resource and in the end one would oust the other. This principle, Gause's hypothesis, seems quite contradicted by the 'Utaka' group of *Haplochromis* in Lake Malawi. These are zooplankton feeders in a lake where small drifting animal life is not over-abundant. So the Utaka seem to have abandoned competition between species and to have formed a kind of condominium in which, for feeding purposes, they act as a single species. From the same lake and even more remarkable are the 10 or so species of another cichlid genus, *Diplotaxodon*, which apparently all live together in rather deep water and all exploit exactly the same food resource, the little sardine-like carp *Engraulicypris*. It is generally accepted that the more diverse the habitat, the more diverse are the species that occupy it, but in these examples from Lake Malawi almost identical living conditions are shared by extremely similar species. The situation is rare, however, and closely related species are much more often complementary, exploiting feeding and breeding possibilities that are not used by the other.

Among invertebrate animals there are many cases where one species attaches itself to another and is thus transported around, although itself sedentary. This is known as phoresis. The larvae of the Spanish fly, for example, wait in flowers for bumblebees and then attach themselves to the bee and on arrival at the hive feed on the pollen, honey and bee larvae. The classic case among fishes is found in the remoras or sharksuckers (eight species in the genera *Remora*, *Phterrichthys* and *Echeneis*). These fishes have an unusual sucker on top of the head, which represents one of the most remarkable adaptations among the fishes. The suction disc is in fact a modified dorsal fin, left and right halves of each finray having come to lie horizontally to form a series of ridges much like a louvre with a raised rim. Lowering of the ridges creates a partial vacuum. By this means remoras attach themselves to large fishes, turtles or even ships, the latter habit giving rise to the ancient myth that they could actually hold back a sailing ship, hence the old name 'ship holder.' Fishermen in several parts of the world have put the remoras to good use by attaching a line to the base of the tail, allowing the remora to find a large fish or turtle, and then hauling the two back to the boat. Remoras have been observed entering the mouths or gill cavities of Manta rays, large billfishes and several species of sharks, possibly to feed on parasites.

A closer relationship between animals is that in which both parties benefit from the association. This is known as symbiosis. The habits of cleaner fishes are usually regarded as an example of symbiosis, the cleaners removing external parasites from their hosts, thereby gaining a meal and at the same time ridding the host of unwanted guests. One case involves the two freshwater cichlid fishes *Eutroplus suratensis* and *E. maculatus* of S.E. India and Sri Lanka, in fact the only cichlid fishes found in Asia. For some time *E. suratensis* has been known to perform some curious antics, standing on its tail, flickering its pelvic fins and becoming very dark in colour. Now it has been found that this ritual was an invitation to the related *E. maculatus* to nibble off any foreign matter on the body or fins of its host and especially fungal growth, which shows up white against the darkened body. It has been found that *E. suratensis* is much more prone to fungal infection than *E. maculatus* and also that the 'head up' posture also acts as an appeasement signal at other times. In both species the young make physical contact with their parents by minute nibblings in which mucus is removed and forms a food supplement in early development. Thus one can visualize the possible steps by which this curious arrangement evolved.

Cleaning activities are more frequently found in marine environments and some 15 families of marine fishes have representatives that are cleaners. The best known are wrasses, gobies, species of *Chaetodon* and juvenile *Pomacanthus*. Typical are small wrasses of the genus *Labroides*. These are elongate fishes with rather pointed snouts and a distinctive colour pattern for advertising their services. They set up a territory, a kind of barber's shop, where larger fishes congregate and adopt postures that indicate a readiness to be cleaned. Not only do the larger fishes raise and lower fins for the cleaners to nibble at the interstices but obligingly open their mouths and gill covers for the cleaners to swim right inside and pick parasites, such as copepods, off the gills. For a small fish to swim inside the mouth of a large fish requires a certain degree of confidence and it is clear that visual signals and behavioural mannerisms form a necessary language, spelling out the roles of the host and the cleaner. As mentioned earlier, certain other fishes mimic the cleaners and either avoid being preyed upon or actually nibble at the fins of their unwitting hosts.

There are a number of fishes that form an association of one kind or another with quite unrelated animals, such as sponges, shellfish or anemones, or even with inanimate objects. The rudderfish *Lirus*, for example, is also known as the wreckfish because of its habit of swimming around, under or inside pieces of flotsam or jetsam such as boxes, barrels or logs, presumably both for protection and for the opportunities of feeding on barnacles and other attached organisms. This association with floating

Portuguese man-o'-war eating a fish caught in its long ▷
tentacles, which have contracted and drawn the food up
to the feeding polyps. It is with *Physalia* that the Portu-
guese Man-o'-war fish, *Nomeus*, has a close association,
the fish finding protection and rarely falling prey to its host.

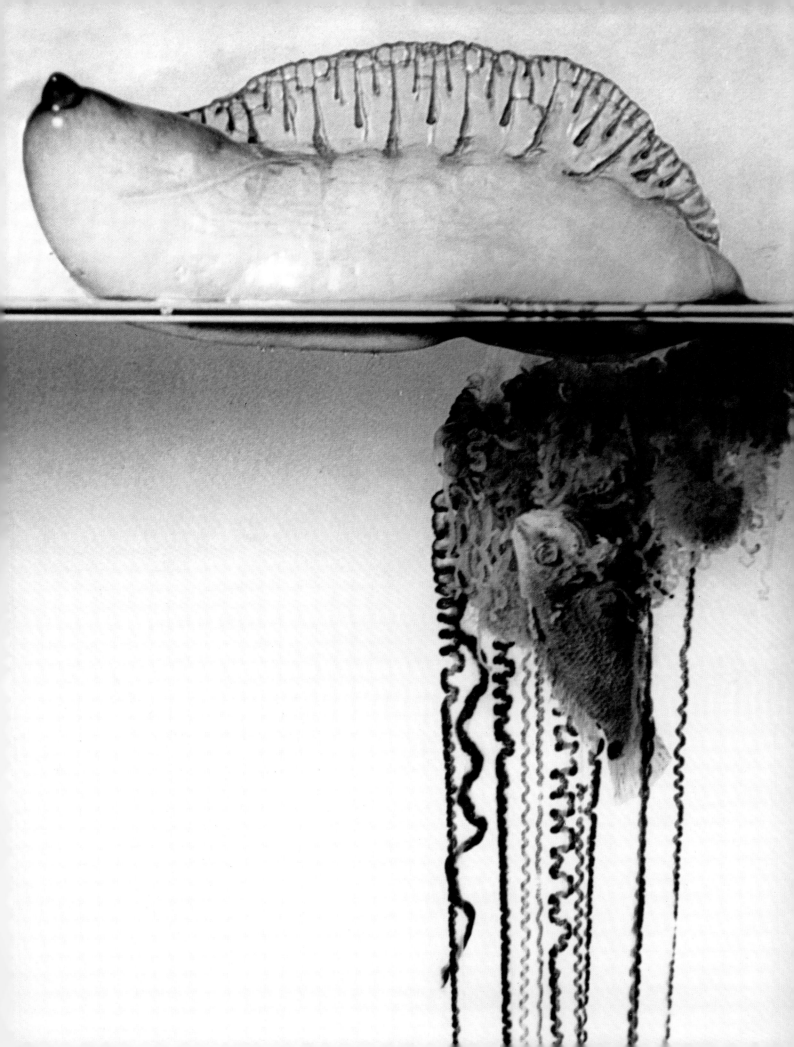

objects is often found in the juveniles of other members of the rudderfish family (Stromateidae), most usually with jellyfishes. A number of world-wide tropical fishes, such as the sergeant-major *Abudefduf saxatilis* and the Scribbled filefish *Aleutera scripta*, probably owe their wide distribution to their habit of accompanying flotsam. One of the very few adult fishes to accompany jellyfish is the Portuguese man-o'-war fish *Nomeus*, which swims

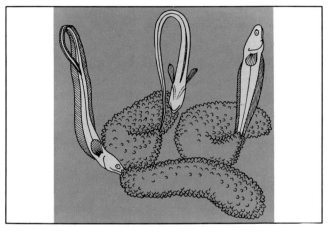

The cucumberfish *Carapus apus* shown entering and leaving a holothurian.

among the highly poisonous tentacles of the Portuguese man-o'-war *Physalia*. One or more fishes may live among the tentacles, rarely moving far from their host and showing signs of panic if forcibly separated. The fishes feed from scraps left by the jellyfish but it is not clear whether the jellyfish benefits in any way. Possibly the fish is less a commensal than a parasite since it also feeds on the tentacles of the jellyfish. There is some question about the immunity of the fish to the jellyfish's stings since on one occasion at least, the partly eaten remains of a *Nomeus* have been found among the tentacles. A number of other fishes associate with jellyfishes, including the Horse mackerel *Trachurus trachurus*, which when young shelters beneath the Sombrero jellyfish *Cotylorhiza borbonica*. Presumably, this is chiefly for protection since the fishes will quickly retreat beneath the tentacles at any sign of danger. The fry of cod, haddock and whiting also have this habit.

Another invertebrate host to fishes is *Acanthaster planci*, the notorious Crown-of-thorns starfish that has wrought such destruction on the Great Barrier Reef and in other parts of the Indo-Pacific. Between the spines on the upper side of the starfish lives a small apogonid fish, *Siphamia fuscolineata*, which

has never been collected elsewhere. Another species of apogonid lives among the spines of the Hat-pin sea urchin *Diadema* and this refuge is also colonized by the shrimpfish *Aeoliscus* and a clingfish *Diademichthys*. Both the latter species are slender fishes with a black on white (or white on black) stripe down the flanks. Their colour and their habit of resting head downwards serves to conceal them, and in any case the spines of *Diadema*, as also *Acanthaster*, are long, pointed and venomous and provide protection from most predators. Such fishes do not have total immunity, however, for triggerfishes (Balistidae) and filefishes (Monacanthidae) feed voraciously on *Diadema*, being apparently undeterred by the sharp spines.

A rather similar relationship exists between the reef-dwelling clownfishes (*Amphiprion*, *Stoichactus*) and certain Sea anemones. About 12 species of clownfishes are known, all highly coloured, usually orange with white or bluish bands. They spend their lives among the waving tentacles and since the latter are used to catch fishes on which the anemone lives, the question arises of how the clownfish manages to survive. Certainly, agility plays no part since clownfishes have been seen actually rubbing the tentacles to encourage the anemone to open. Possibly the biting or rubbing against tentacles immunizes the fish to a particular host since some clownfishes only associate with one species of anemone; however, others will associate with several species. It has been suggested that the fish thereby develops a special mucous coating that affords protection. Although one species of clownfish has been observed to bring pieces of food to the anemone, the latter seems to gain from the relationship in other ways too. Although it can live perfectly well without its guest, whereas the clownfish falls an easy prey when deprived of its shelter, clownfishes have been observed to drive away butterflyfishes *Chaetodon* that feed on the anemone's tentacles.

The reverse of this relationship is found in an Indian scorpionfish *Minous* in which it is the fish's turn to act as host, the guest being a colony of hydroid polyps. This is a true case of symbiosis, the fish gaining an effective camouflage and the polyps being transported to fresh feeding grounds and perhaps gaining a measure of protection.

The habit of many fishes, and especially those of

Clownfish *Amphiprion percula* lives in symbiosis with Sea anemones. The clownfish is protected from predators by the tentacles, while the anemone profits from food dropped by the fish.

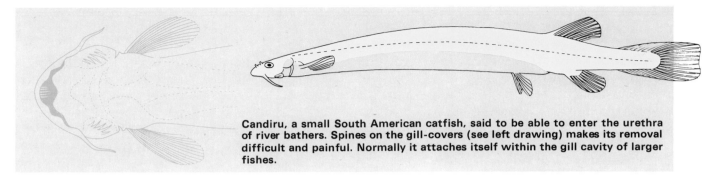

Candiru, a small South American catfish, said to be able to enter the urethra of river bathers. Spines on the gill-covers (see left drawing) makes its removal difficult and painful. Normally it attaches itself within the gill cavity of larger fishes.

coral reefs, of seeking shelter in holes and crevices has led to many unusual associations with other animals. Some 40 marine fishes have a permanent or temporary relationship with sponges, retreating inside the sponge for protection. The water currents set up by the flagellated cells of the sponge ensure an adequate supply of oxygen and for some residents the invertebrate inhabitants of sponges (alpheid or snapping shrimps, and polychaete and annelid worms) supply a ready-made meal. Some permanent sponge-dwelling fishes (*Evermannichthys, Risor*) are specially adapted, having elongate bodies and reduced scales; in *Risor* the canine teeth are curved upwards and downwards as if used to dilate pores in the sponge in order to extract small invertebrates. These fishes are found in the massive sponges (*Spongia, Ircinia*), but the large tubular or candle

sponges (*Verongia, Callyspongia*) also harbour permanent fish residents and in particular species of the goby genus *Gobiosoma* and at least one species of cardinalfish *Phaeoptyx*, none of which show any particular specialization in form to this way of life. The remaining sponge-dwelling fishes probably use the sponges as a convenient retreat when the occasion demands.

Similar to the sponge-dwellers are those that seek shelter in Sea cucumbers (Holothurians). Species of pearlfishes *Carapus, Jordanicus* have been recorded in Sea cucumbers, where they live on the internal organs of their host, including the gonads, and at the same time gain shelter and concealment. Other species of *Carapus* have been found inside the Cushion starfish *Culcita* and members of the related genus *Onuxodon* have been taken from the mantle

A batfish *Platax* showing the wing-like dorsal and anal fins. These fishes similate both leaves and wriggling invertebrates.

cavity of the Rock oyster *Pycnodonta*. Pearlfishes are elongate fishes and in *Carapus acus*, at least, enter the Sea cucumber backwards by inserting the pointed tail into the host's anus and wriggling in. Their way of life is partial, or in some cases perhaps total, parasitism, some leaving the host to forage for food but others gnawing away at the Sea cucumber itself.

Full parasitism is rather rare in fishes, although this cannot only be due to their relatively large size when compared with invertebrate parasites. Lampreys, and more particularly hagfishes, are external parasites, the latter often burrowing deep into its host, and the same habit is found in certain South American catfishes (Pygidiidae), which attach themselves to other animals and suck their blood. Members of another South American family (Trichomycteridae), the candirus or carneros, live within the gill cavities of larger catfishes and by

biting start a flow of blood on which they feed. The most dreaded of these is the small and slender candiru *Vandellia cirrhosa* of Brazil which has the unpleasant reputation of entering the urinogenital apertures of both men and women, probably when they urinate in the water, the fish perhaps mistaking this for the flow of water from the gill openings of another fish. The erectile spines on the gill cover make the fish impossible to remove without surgery. The candiru thus has the distinction of being the only vertebrate to parasitize man.

The relationships between fishes, and between fishes and other organisms, is a fascinating field of study, as much for its own sake as for the light that it throws on the interaction between structure and function. Relationships are the result of individual facets of behaviour and there is as much exciting work to be done on this topic as there was on the morphology of fishes a century ago.

Shrimp fishes *Aeoliscus* hover head downward amongst the long spines of the Hat-pin sea urchin, thus gaining protection from most predators; the black stripe down the body helps to camouflage the fish.

Getting into Deep Water

Until about the middle of the last century men had little notion of how deep the oceans were nor what their waters might contain in the way of animal life. For thousands of years seamen hugged the coasts, but even when ships ventured out across the oceans there was no way of telling how much water lay beneath the ship once the end of the sounding line had been reached. Posidonius (c. 135–50 BC), the Stoic philosopher, is said to have stated in his lost book on the oceans that the Sardinian Sea had been sounded to a depth of about 1,000 fathoms. Whether the ancients really knotted such a rope or could have carried over a mile of it in their ships is difficult to say, but clearly they appreciated that considerable depths existed. Small wonder that these dark and forbidding zones should be populated by monsters that would rise to the surface, grapple with a ship, seize a seaman perhaps, and then sink back into their murky world.

For many more centuries the oceans remained, literally as well as figuratively, an unknown quantity, as much in breadth as in depth and content. What went on below the surface could only be inferred from the observations of sailors and fishermen and, as Aristotle ruefully acknowledged, 'no theory has been handed down to us that the most ordinary man could not have thought of.' It was not until the Renaissance that better measuring devices were evolved and it is worth remembering that a reliable method of calculating longitude at sea (by means of an accurate chronometer) had to wait until the mid-18th century and the voyages of Captain Cook; up to that time the distance travelled east or west had to be crudely calculated by tossing a piece of wood – the log – overboard and timing its passage, thus giving the speed of the ship. Complicated astronomical methods were equally unreliable.

The Age of Discovery brought the first realization that the greater part of the earth's surface (in fact 70·8%) was covered by liquid. The 19th century, and particularly Victorian ingenuity, added the third dimension, depth, thus laying the foundations of a new science, oceanography. Twentieth century know-how has shown just how immense the oceans are. The *average* overall depth is 12,460 ft (3,800 m)

The distribution of ocean fishes and factors affecting their distribution. The amount of plankton living in the water drops off sharply below a depth of 1,000 metres (A). Light is only able to penetrate to a depth of up to 1,000 metres (B) and at this depth one enters the sunless zone. As may be expected, the temperature of water in the surface layers is considerably higher than that deeper down (C). Finally, the amounts of food available on the sea bed (D) are greatest in shallow waters. The fish shown here are: (1) rat-tail, (2) *Anoplogaster*, (3) lancet-fish, (4) Giant swallower, (5) lantern-fish, (6) Hatchet fish, (7) star-eater, (8) notacanth, (9) brotulid, (10) Deep-sea angler fish *Melanocetus*, (11) whale-fish, (12) gulper-eel *Eurypharynx*, (13) gulper-eel *Saccopharynx*, (14) halosaur, (15) tripod-fish, (16) Deep-sea angler fish *Linophryne*, (17) rat-tail, and (18) sea-snail.

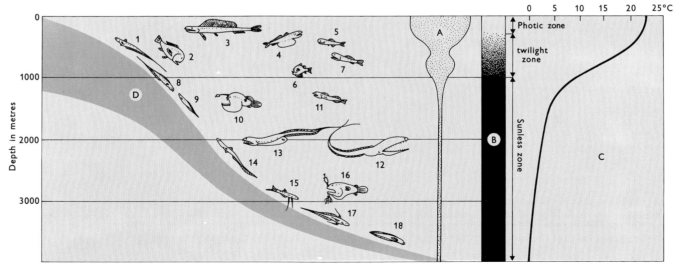

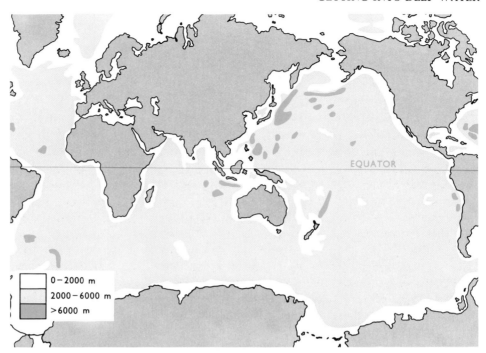

Map showing the location of exceptionally deep oceanic water.

0—2000 m
2000—6000 m
>6000 m

or twice the depth that Posidonius no doubt thought a maximum, while the greatest depth was established in 1962 by HMS *Cook* in the Mindanao Trench off the Philippines, the sea floor lying 37,780 ft (11,515 m) below the surface, nearly a mile and a half deeper than the height of Mount Everest. About 86% of the world's oceanic water is over 3,000 ft (1,000 m) deep.

Towards the middle of the last century men began to consider more seriously the question of whether life existed in the deep oceans and what kind of life that might be. The notion of sea monsters is with us still, but marine biologists were concerned to know whether the less spectacular forms of life, the sponges, seaweeds, sea urchins or even fishes, could exist at depths. One of the pioneers in this study, and the man whose mistaken ideas dominated the field for nearly 20 years, was Edward Forbes, the Manx naturalist. In 1842, Forbes sailed in HMS *Beacon* and surveyed the eastern end of the Mediterranean. He found, quite corrèctly, that animal life in the Aegean fell into distinct zones according to depth, but it apparently petered out at about 230 fathoms (1,380 ft or about 396 m). He concluded, therefore, that below this there was a lifeless or Azoic Zone. The idea appeared reasonable since pressure, temperature and lack of oxygen would seem to be limiting factors to the ordinary shallow-water forms. Unfortunately, Forbes's Azoic Zone developed into a kind of dogma, with records of animal life at greater depths being discounted.

By the 1860's, however, Forbes's theory was seen to be untenable. George Wallich found starfishes clinging to a sounding line that had plumbed 7,560 ft (2,304 m) and the argument that the creatures had attached themselves much later when the line was nearer the surface was disposed of when animals were found firmly anchored to the submarine telegraph cables between Sardinia and Africa at 7,087 ft (2,160 m). Meanwhile, Darwin had published his *Origin of Species* and a new question arose. If life exists in the depths, does it represent the earliest forms from which later species developed? Thomas Huxley, Darwin's great protagonist, had solemnly given the name *Bathybius* to a sample of deep-sea ooze and pronounced it to be the primaeval life form. After all, life had apparently begun in the oceans and here was exactly the simple, almost structureless 'life-stuff' one would expect. *Bathybius* had a short life, however. During the cruise of HMS *Challenger* (1872–76), the voyage that heralded the birth of oceanography, the chemist John Buchanan showed conclusively that *Bathybius* was nothing more than the result of the precipitation of calcium sulphate by alcohol, which occurred when a bottom sample was bottled and preserved.

Bathybius was discredited, but there still remained the possibility that within groups like fishes some 'missing link' would be brought up from the depths. Some support for this idea comes from *Neopilina*, a primitive mollusc dredged up from 11,670 ft (3,551 m) by the Danish deep-sea research ship *Galathea*.

111

Neopilina has such molluscan features as the tongue-like radula, but at the same time it shows signs of the segmentation of the body characteristic of the annelids or ringed worms. Since its discovery in 1952, further specimens have been brought up from twice that depth, but this really proves no more than that some primitive forms have found the depths attractive. Certainly, as far as fishes are concerned, almost the reverse holds true: the midwater twilight waters are inhabited by fairly primitive soft-rayed fishes, whereas the depths produce fishes belonging to highly specialized families that evolved much later in time. It is a popular misconception to think that the coelacanth, sole survivor of an ancient line of primitive fishes, is a deep-water fish in the true sense of the word, for the majority of specimens have been taken at a mere 300 to 1,000 ft (91 to 305 m). If the deeps were not to solve evolutionary problems, however, they were to pose some baffling physiological questions, for how was it possible that such complex animals as fishes could survive the tremendous pressures encountered on the sea floor?

During the last century, the presence of fishes in deep water was difficult to prove, but modern midwater trawls and bottom dredges have now shown that some 2,000 different species live below 820 ft (250 m). This represents about a tenth of the known species of fishes, so that clearly fishes have not neglected the depths in their gradual spread to all possible types of habitat. In conjunction with nets, the presence of fishes can also be deduced from the so-called Deep Scattering Layer (DSL) that appears on echo-sounder traces between 820 and 2,297 ft (250–700 m), but which moves upwards at night. The sound signals are reflected mainly by shoals of small lantern-fishes that migrate towards the surface after dark, their large swimbladders providing an excellent means of bouncing supersonic waves back to the transmitter. Nowadays, there is also the possibility of direct observation. In 1934 William Beebe and Otis Barton, using a spherical steel container, the *Bathysphere*, sank to a depth of 3,000 ft (913 m) off Bermuda and for nearly 20 years this record went unchallenged, being broken in 1948 by Barton's dive to 4,500 ft (1,369 m) in his *Benthoscope*. Remarkable as this was, it was still less than a mile below the surface and the Belgian Auguste Picard saw no reason why much greater depths could not be achieved. Having already earned fame from his record balloon ascent, Picard and his son Jacques designed the *Bathyscaphe*, the first deep-diving vehicle with its own self-contained supply of

electricity and air. In it, Picard passed the one mile mark, and then the two mile mark, reaching a depth of 13,284 ft (4,042 m). Finally, in 1960, Jacques Picard and Don Walsh showed that no part of the oceans is inaccessible to man. In a new craft, the *Trieste*, they descended the Marianas Trench to 35,800 ft (10,894 m). The last 10 years have seen a whole new family of underwater vehicles designed for observations in deep waters and together with the development of automatic underwater cameras it has been possible to glimpse something of the lives of fishes otherwise known only from dejected corpses which are often badly deformed through decompression in their journey to the surface.

Regions of the Oceans. From a geological point of view, the oceans can be divided into two major realms, the shallower seas fringing the continents and the remaining deeper areas. The shallower parts, the continental shelf areas, are like submerged shoulders of the land masses and although as narrow as only 10 miles in some places they always provide a step before the sea bed plunges to the depths. It is on the continental shelves that the vast majority of marine fishes live and virtually all the world's sea fish production comes from this narrow fringe around the continents. At depths of between 300 and 600 ft (about 100–200 m) rather suddenly the shelf gives way to the continental slopes. These descend to the abyssal floor of the ocean and are themselves cut by deep and winding V-shaped canyons which, were they not concealed from view, would provide scenery to rival the Grand Canyon. Adding to the topographical diversity of the oceans are the deep trenches that in some cases plunge nearly seven miles below the surface, and also the Mid-Oceanic Ridge, the greatest mountain range on earth, that stretches in an unbroken chain from the Arctic through the Atlantic to the Antarctic, Indian and Pacific Oceans, a distance of some 40,000 miles.

Dramatic though this scenery may be, however, it is not the primary factor in the distribution, abundance and life of fishes or other marine organisms. The controlling factor is quite simply light, for the marine plants that provide the first step in the chain or web of food relationships depend on sunlight for their energy. At about 600 ft (say 180 m), the light becomes insufficient for photosynthesis and plant life virtually comes to an end. This thin

A stareater *Astronesthes* common in the twilight or ▷ mesopelagic zone.

surface layer, the epipelagic or photic zone, is obviously a discrete and important ecological unit and, as one would expect, where it coincides with the continental shelf the production of animal and plant life is greatest. Below this, from 600 to 3,000 ft (say 180–950 m) lies the mesopelagic or twilight zone, inhabited solely by animals. Here the rich bloom of planktonic organisms found at the surface rapidly dwindles and the animals must prey on each other, catch what drops from above, or migrate upwards for a meal. Below the twilight zone of mid-water fishes is the vast area, and volume, of sunless water, the bathypelagic zone, reaching down to the abyssal floor at 13,120 ft (approximately 4,000 m) and beyond. Here the plankton becomes minimal and not so long ago it would have seemed impossible that any fishes could thrive in this cold, black, inhospitable world. Finally, there are the deep trenches, extending from 19,000 to 36,000 ft (say 6,000 to 11,000 m), referred to as the hadal zone.

In shallow waters, seasonal heating and cooling result in an overturn in the water and a return of nutrients to the surface. In the open oceans the vast bulk of the water is below this seasonal influence, so that what drops from above in the way of animal and plant remains, and the nutrients that they contain, is lost to surface-dwellers unless physically returned, either by animals migrating up to feed or spawn, or by upwelling currents. In fact, such upwelling occurs both in the tropical oceans, where counter-flowing currents produce rising masses of nutrient-rich waters from below, and also along certain continental coasts, as well as in Antarctic waters. These are the most productive oceanic areas, contrasting strongly with the relatively deserted central water masses.

Deep-sea fishes that live in water below a depth of 650 ft (200 m) where no light penetrates: (top left) viperfishes; (bottom left) a Deep-sea angler; (top right) juvenile anglerfish and (bottom right) _Anoplogaster_.

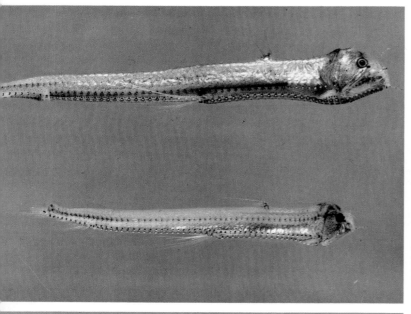

The transition from the twilight to the sunless regions of the sea is a gradual one, but the sea bottom forms a distinct ecological unit and brings with it a characteristic way of life. Here is the eventual resting place for all detritus produced above and not consumed during its drop of several miles to the sea floor. Here a fauna that breaks down detritus can sustain a chain of predators that ultimately reaches upwards to the twilight zone where, in turn, there are food links with the bright surface layers. Thus the flow of energy, although drawn downwards by gravity, is not entirely in one direction. The colonization of the depths could only become possible after the surface layers were well inhabited, which argues that primitive forms of life must later have sought the deeper parts of the oceans.

Fishes of the Twilight Zone. The fishes of the twilight zone, from 600 to 1,000 ft (say 180 to 305 m), form a mesopelagic fauna with certain characteristics. Plankton in this layer of the oceans has rapidly thinned out and is about a tenth as abundant as in the well-lit photic zone. The fishes themselves are generally small, less than 6 in (15 cm) in length, and have been aptly referred to as Lilliputians. For the most part these are rather primitive soft-rayed fishes formerly placed in the order Iniomi but now grouped with the Salmon-like fishes and a number of others in the superorder Protacanthopterygii. Two main groups are represented, the stomiatoids and the myctophoids.

Of stomiatoids, some of the best known are the viperfishes *Chauliodus* with long canine teeth in the jaws and a filamentous first dorsal finray; the hatchetfishes *Sternoptyx, Argyropdecus* with highly compressed, deep bodies that earn them their name, Scaly dragons *Stomias*, bristlemouths *Cyclothone*, stareaters *Astronesthes*, Black dragonfishes *Melanostomias* and *Idiacanthus* whose stalk-eyed young stage has already been mentioned. The myctophoids include the lanternfishes (Myctophidae), rather undistinguished looking fishes except for their rows of pearly light organs, the barracudinas (Paralepididae) and the lancetfishes *Alepisaurus*, the latter veritable giants that reach 3 ft (about 1 m) or more. Other elements in this mesopelagic fauna are the alepocephaloids *Searsia, Alepocephalus* and some argentinioids *Opisthoproctus*, and its allies. Some of the mesopelagic fishes of the twilight zone are pale or translucent, but others are dark brown or black, sometimes with silvery flanks as in the hatchetfishes, representing three different types of camouflage: disappearing from view, reflecting no highlights and exactly reflecting what dim light filters down from above.

The majority of mesopelagic fishes are found below tropical and subtropical waters where plankton is most abundant. As might be expected, a number of species have wide distributions since the barriers to their dispersal are chiefly vertical, at least within the tropical and subtropical belts. The Black bristlemouth *Cyclothone microdon*, however, also ranges into temperate and antarctic waters, but this is an exception.

Fishes of the Sunless Zone. Below 3,200 ft (say 1,000 m) there is a rather different fish fauna, the bathypelagic species that live in a zone devoid of even a glimmer of the sun's light. Not only are these regions dark, but they are also cold, temperatures ranging from 5°C to zero. Plankton is even less abundant than in the twilight zone and the biomass or total weight of living creatures is about 1/50th of that at the surface. Nevertheless, there is a diverse fish fauna, the commonest elements being the deep-sea anglerfishes, comprising about 100 species from no less than 10 distinct families – an indication that even here evolution has not stood still; deep-sea eels; Gulper eels *Saccopharynx*; Great swallowers *Chiasmodon*; Whalefishes, but hardly rivalling their namesakes in size; melamphaeids, and a few stomiatoids, especially the bristlemouths, *Cyclothone*.

Like the fishes of the twilight zone, these bathypelagic species are generally less than 6 in (15 cm) long. Exceptions, such as the Gulper eels, are usually attenuated, ribbon-like or rat-tailed, although in one fairly robust deep-sea anglerfish *Ceratias holboelli* the females may reach 4 ft (1·2 m). Bathypelagic species are mostly a deep velvety brown or black, presumably to reduce shine when caught in the light of luminescent flashes. The brotulids, however, are pallid, while the whalefishes have a reddish tinge to the body or may even be bright orange-red (for example, *Barbourisia rufa*), a colour more commonly found in deep-sea shrimps, worms, copepods and squids. Red reflects very little blue or green light and since most of the luminescence is blue-green, these animals appear black.

Bottom-living Fishes. The bottom-living or benthic fishes of deep water form a rather distinct community. Where the midwater fishes tend to belong to rather primitive groups, the benthic fishes are generally representatives of more highly specialized families. The commonest species are rat-tails or grenadiers (Macrouridae, with about 300 species) and brotulids (Brotulidae), but there are also sea-snails (Liparidae), eel-pouts (Zoarcidae), deep-sea cods (Moridae), tripodfishes (Bathypteroidae) and a number of others. In contrast to the midwater fishes, these bottom-living forms are often larger than 6 in (15 cm) in length, but like their colleagues in the water layers above them, they tend to be concentrated in areas below the plankton-rich tropical seas since their source of nourishment ultimately depends on what rains down from above.

The shallow bottom-living fishes of the continental shelf region, down to about 650 ft (say 200 m), form a very distinct fauna. Beyond the edge of the shelf is a rather abrupt change as one progresses down the continental shelf. Upper and lower slope faunas can be distinguished, the transition being at about 3,000 ft (914 m). Below 9,000 ft (2,743 m) an abyssal zone is recognized and some authors refer to a hadal fauna in the trenches (below 19,685 ft or 6,000 m). The majority of the deep-water fish species are found at depths of 800 to 5,000 ft (say 250–1,500 m), that is to say, on the upper parts of the continental slopes, but one brotulid *Bassogigas* and three sea-snails *Careproctus* have been caught at 19,685 to 22,966 ft (6,000 to 7,000 m) and the record is a sighting made by Jacques Picard in the bathyscaphe *Trieste* in the Marianas Trench where he saw a sole-like fish at no less than 33,793 ft (10,300 m). However, some say this was not a fish but a holothurian.

Fishes of the deep-sea floor either remain on the bottom (bathybenthic species) or cruise around just above the bottom (benthopelagic). A number of the latter, for example the rat-tails, have long, attenuated bodies, sturdy heads and prominent snouts. Undulation of the hind part of the body probably tends to thrust the head down so that the snout can 'root' through the bottom deposits and the mouth is in the right place for taking food (invertebrates, detritus). As with the amount of plankton in the midwaters, so food available on the bottom de-creases rapidly with depth. Falling several miles from the upper layers, the remains of animals are largely broken down by a chain of organisms, from bacteria to fishes, before they settle on the sea floor. Enough penetrates, however, to support a bacterial and invertebrate fauna sufficient for the needs of fishes and, in turn, the fishes that prey on other fishes.

After the initial surprise that fishes can exist at all in the deep oceans, the question arises as to how they have managed to adapt to these apparently inhospitable watery deserts. Food and oxygen are scarce, temperatures are low, pressures are enormous (over 1,000 atmospheres or six tons to the square inch in the deepest parts), sunlight absent and communication difficult. Yet some 2,000 fish species survive and multiply under such conditions.

Depth and Buoyancy. Problems of buoyancy were outlined earlier and it was noted that many fishes make use of a gas-filled swimbladder to compensate for the weight of their body tissues. Among the fishes of the twilight zone, nearly half have a well developed swimbladder. These are species of lanternfishes, hatchetfishes and so on, that generally feed on plankton. In the predatory species, such as viperfishes, Scaly dragons and Black dragons, the swimbladder is either reduced or absent altogether. Progressing down into the sunless zone (below 3,280 ft, 1,000 m) one finds that there are no fishes with swimbladders (or at best, only rudimentary ones) and it is tempting to think that the immense pressures encountered have made swimbladders unworkable. Certainly, many fishes of the sea floor also lack a swimbladder. But another group of bottom-living fishes, those that cruise above the sea floor, possess swimbladders and are able to maintain gas pressures equal to the water pressure outside.

The explanation seems to be that the midwater fishes of the sunless zone have lost their swim-

Rows of light organs on the deep-sea fish *Bonapartia*.

A deep-sea or ceratioid angler fish, showing its 'fishing rod' with luminous 'bait' at tip.

bladders as one of a number of economy measures forced onto them by an extremely poor food supply. Compared with their relatives in the twilight zone, they have greatly reduced skeletons and musculature, and many other features, such as their brains, eyes, gills and kidneys, are also less well developed. As a result, they are lighter than their relatives and so require little muscular effort in order to maintain a constant depth. The bathybenthic fishes, on the other hand, spend their time on the sea bottom and so have no need to be buoyant, whereas a swimbladder is essential for those that hover over the sea bed. Finally, the predators of the twilight zone may have lost their swimbladders as an economy measure since their food – other fishes – is far less abundant than the food – plankton – on which their prey feeds.

Eyes, Light and Luminous Organs. As already explained, the zone of full light penetration, the photic zone, is a relatively thin upper layer comprising the top 600 ft (say 20 m) of the oceans.

Below this, in the twilight zone, the amount of sunlight is too weak to allow plant growth and by about 3,300 ft (say 1,000 m) even a faint glow that would indicate the surface has disappeared. Not surprisingly, the eyes of deep-sea fishes have become adapted to these different regimes.

The majority of fishes in the twilight zone have well developed or quite large eyes. Small eyes occur in species of *Cyclothone* but there are no fishes with regressed or rudimentary eyes. Typically, the eyes have a large pupil and lens so that the maximum amount of light can enter. With the exception of the lanternfish *Omosudis*, the retina of the eyes contains no cones – colour sensitive cells – but only rods – responsible for visual acuity – so that the fishes live in a grey world. In fact, if colour can be said to exist in this dim region, it is in the blue/green range of the spectrum and accordingly many species have golden pigments in the retina that are especially sensitive to blue light. Significantly, it is blue/green light that most deep-sea fishes emit from light organs. Yet

117

another method of increasing the sensitivity of the eyes is by multiplying the layers of rod cells in the retina. Another curious specialization is the development of tubular eyes, as for example in the hatchetfish *Argyropelecus*, and in members of no less than 10 other families, mostly from the lower layers of the twilight zone. Tubular eyes concentrate the image onto a small area of retina and may, therefore, give better binocular vision in dim light, a useful attribute for a predator.

In the sunless zone below 3,300 ft (say 1,000 m) the bathypelagic fishes tend to have small eyes which in some cases are regressed. Evidently there is not much to see. An exception is found in the free-living males of the anglerfish family Linophrynidae, in which tubular eyes are developed, presumably to enable the male to find its light-bearing mate. Bottom-living fishes of the sunless zone invariably have regressed eyes, although their relatives further up the slope, often members of the same genus, may have well-developed or even large eyes. Obviously, much depends on the luminous displays by fishes and other organisms at these depths.

From time immemorial sailors in warm seas have admired 'phosphorescent' displays at the surface and for centuries speculated on their cause. This 'living light' emanates from enormous numbers of the minute dinoflagellate *Noctiluca* which discharge light, by oxidation of luciferin, when disturbed. Many other organisms emit light and in most deep-sea fishes the same process is used as in *Noctiluca*. An exception is found in the rat-tails (Macrouridae) and a few deep-sea cods (Moridae), in which the light is produced by luminous bacteria, a method otherwise found in certain shallow water fishes *Anomalops*, *Monocentris* and in the lures of deep-sea anglerfishes. It has been suggested that these luminous bacteria are relics of a time when the planet was without oxygen. When atmospheric oxygen first accumulated and dissolved into the seas it would have been lethal to existing life and the quickest and easiest way to get rid of it was perhaps

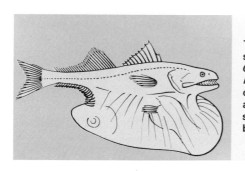

The Black swallower *Chiasmodon niger*, capable of swallowing a fish its own size or even bigger.

its conversion to water, with the liberation of energy sufficient to stimulate light emission.

Most of the fishes with light organs are found in the twilight zone, but if all midwater fishes are considered then some six or seven hundred species are capable of producing light. All the lanternfishes (Myctophidae) and most of the stomiatoids, which together dominate the twilight zone, have light organs and in the sunless zone light organs are present in almost all females of the hundred or more deep-sea angerfishes. In the bottom-living deep-sea fishes, however, light organs are rather rare, being confined to the rat-tails and some deep-sea cods. The frequency of light flashes was measured in deep water off New York, giving a frequency of 160 per minute at 300 ft (say 90 m), 90 at 2,952 ft (900 m) and only 1 at 12,630 ft (3,750 m), the deepest at which flashes have been recorded. Thus, luminous activity decreases with depth and the regression of eyes in the deeper living species is understandable.

In many luminous fishes the light organ is a simple pit and the light merely shines through a membrane or through the scales. Some, however, have a silvery screen or reflecting layer behind the light organ, as for example in the hatchetfishes, which enhances the power of the light. More complex still are those fishes, such as the lanternfishes, in which the scale overlying the light organ is thickened to form a lens. The disposition of the light organs varies greatly, depending on the use to which they are put. In the lanternfishes the organs form lines of pearly buttons along the body, each species having a different and characteristic pattern which presumably enables an individual to recognize one of its own species. The same is probably true of other families but it has also been suggested that the position of the luminous organs may play a part in camouflage. By illuminating the underside of the body – and many luminous fishes have light organs along the belly – the shadow along the underside is eliminated and at the same time the flanks, when seen from below, take on much the same hue as the brighter water above. It would also seem that the predominant placing of light organs along the lower flanks stems from the fact that predators are more abundant in the upper layers and thus live above the luminous fishes.

In addition to aiding in identification, and so discriminating between a prospective meal or mate, light organs undoubtedly play a part in courtship and in other aspects of communication where a fish signals its internal state (ready to feed, breed, fight

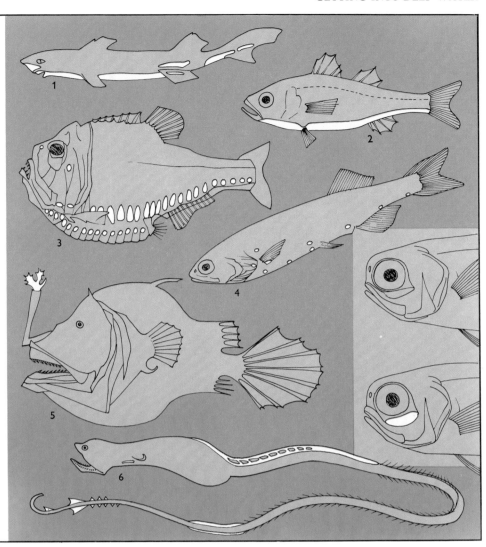

Luminous fishes: (1) Squalid shark, (2) *Acropoma*, (3) *Sternoptyx*, (4) *Searsia*, (5) Deep-sea anglerfish, (6) *Saccopharynx*. (Right) The light organ below the eye in *Anomalops katopteron* which can be exposed or retracted.

or escape). In three stomiatoid fishes (*Stomias, Idiacanthus* and *Chauliodus*) minute light organs are found along the upper and lower profiles of the body and on the fins. The effect of these, far from camouflaging the fish, is to emphasize its outline. This kind of silhouetting may be important in mating, in spacing out individuals as they hunt for their food, and perhaps as an indication to predators of their relatively formidable size.

Yet another use for light organs is as a lure in feeding, best developed in the deep-sea anglerfishes. The shallow water anglers (Lophiidae) have an esca or a modified tip to the first dorsal ray which can be dangled in front of the mouth exactly as a human angler might do. In their deep-sea relatives the tip of the finray bears an organ containing luminous bacteria and the same fishing principle is followed. As pointed out earlier, the ultimate in this kind of fishing is found in the bottom-living *Galathea-*

thauma, which has the lure actually inside the mouth. The viperfishes *Chauliodus* also have a filamentous second dorsal finray with a luminous tip which must be used in the same way. In stareaters (Astronesthidae), Black dragonfishes (Melanostomiatidae) and Scaly dragonfishes (Stomiatidae) there is a luminous chin barbel and possibly this too is used as a lure. Most of the stomiatoids also have a curious arrangement of light organs that shine into the eye, which would seem to be a rather illogical system until it is remembered that the eye must be at all times prepared to receive flashing signals which, under normal circumstances, would temporarily dazzle it. Finally, the Searsidae have a curious shoulder organ which can emit a sudden stream of blue-green sparks that temporarily illuminate the fish.

Feeding. Since the amount of available food decreases sharply with depth, the feeding regimes

119

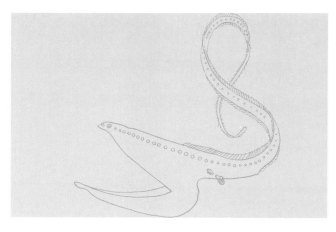

A Gulper eel *Eurypharynx pelecanoides*, one of the deep-sea eels characterized by their enormous mouths.

of the twilight, sunless and bottom-living fishes are rather different. In the twilight zone many of the plankton-feeding lanternfishes and stomiatoids show a strong diurnal rhythm, moving upwards to the rich waters of the photic zone after sunset and descending again before sunrise. It is these fishes that contribute to the Deep Scattering Layer, the echo-trace that registers their daily rise to the surface and return to depths of 820 to 2,620 ft (250–800 m). Predators of the twilight zone, such as viperfishes and stareaters, may well follow the plankton-eaters upwards and feed on them during their migration.

The fishes of the sunless zone do not make this upward migration and must either take what drops down or feed on their neighbours. Locating prey is clearly a problem since a fish that is being persued would surely extinguish its light organs. Bathypelagic fishes generally have well developed lateral line sensory systems in which the sensory cells (neuromasts) are in free contact with the outside or are even on the ends of long stalks, unlike the system of closed canals generally found in shallow water fishes. Response to water disturbances is probably more sensitive and such disturbances will usually be the near presence of another but most likely invisible fish. Fishes such as the deep-sea anglers do not hunt but quietly await some activity at the end of their lighted fishing lure. Other fishes may well use their light organs suddenly to illuminate the possible prey around them, making an immediate dash before it flees. Because of the sparseness of the fish population, fishes such as the Gulper eels *Saccopharynx* and in the twilight zone the Giant swallower *Chiasmodon* have developed large mouths and distensible stomachs and are thus capable of swallowing prey as large as themselves or larger.

The bottom-living fishes subsist mainly on invertebrates which, by successive links in the food chain, depend on the bacteria that break down falling debris and the remains of other bottom-living animals. The amount of available food matter on the sea floor, however, is greater than the amount available in the sunless midwaters and it is for this reason that the bottom-living fishes are better built and more robust than their bathypelagic counterparts.

Breeding. As with feeding, the problem with breeding in the deep oceans is the sparseness of the population and thus the difficulty of finding a mate. Light organs must surely play an essential role in species recognition. Smell may also play an important part, for it is noticeable that in anglerfishes and in bristlemouths *Cyclothone* the olfactory organs, as well as the nerves and that part of the brain that serves them, are well developed in males but regressed in females, suggesting that the male smells its way to the female. Yet another means of making sexual communication is probably by sound, although only the benthopelagic fishes (rat-tails, deep-sea cods) seem to be sound producers.

The anglerfishes have one of the most extraordinary reproductive patterns of any fish. At a certain stage the males cease to grow and, having found a female, attach themselves to some part of her body, sometimes more than one male to a female. So closely is the male joined to the female by its mouth that it derives nourishment from the blood of the female and becomes virtually an attached testis. In a full-grown anglerfish female her dwarf 'husband' may be less than a tenth her size.

The fishes of the twilight zone either spawn in the upper waters or produce eggs that float up to this rich feeding ground. Similarly, the bathypelagic fishes also produce floating eggs that have been spawned in the depths and develop near the surface. Of the bottom-living species, the rat-tails, deep-sea eels and some of the brotulids are known to have floating eggs, although others of the latter group are live-bearers. Possibly some of the deepest living fishes, such as sea-snails *Careproctus*, lay eggs on the bottom; not only is food more abundant, but the five or six mile journey to the surface and back would seem to be too great a risk. Yet one more adaptation to deep-sea conditions is found, for example, in the tripodfishes (Bathypteroidae), the lancetfish *Alepisaurus ferox* and the ipnopids (Ipno-

Two species of deep-sea fish that have lures with which prey is attracted. (A) *Chauliodus sloani* in which the front ray of the dorsal fin is elongate and bears a luminous bait which can be dangled in front of the fish's mouth. (B) *Stomias affinis*, in which a luminous barbel attached to the lower jaw performs a similar function.

pidae), mature individuals being hermaphrodites. This may mean that an encounter with any mature fish of the same species can lead to spawning, and perhaps, in extreme circumstances, a fish can be self-fertilizing.

As in other environments, the fishes of the deep seas have shown themselves to be equally resourceful in surviving and maintaining their populations. It must be borne in mind, however, that although conditions of light, temperature, pressure and available food are often extreme, actual variations in the habitat are rather small so that the fishes can, in a sense, concentrate all their energies into coping with adverse but closely circumscribed conditions.

Extreme Conditions

The incentive, if one can speak of it that way, towards the evolution of new species is provided by the possibility of exploiting different living conditions. This may merely involve differences in the relationships between the animal and its surroundings, as for example in the use of a new food source, in the development of a better means of camouflage, or in an adjustment in the interactions with other organisms. It may, however, mean reaching out beyond the normal range of tolerance to temperature, salinity, pressure or any of the other purely physical factors that limit the distribution of the species.

As already noted, fishes have shown a quite amazing ability to colonize the more inhospitable regions of the earth. Each new step has been a gradual extension of the range of a few members of a particular species, but once established the species has often adapted further, flourished, and from time to time given rise to other species even better equipped for the new conditions. In some cases the half-way stages still exist and one can deduce the manner in which the more highly specialized forms came to solve their problems.

Judging by the sheer abundance of species, the shallow tropical shores seem to have offered the optimum conditions for fishes, tropical lakes and rivers coming next on the list. The temperate continental shelves, which support fewer species but more individuals of each, must also be considered well suited to fish life. It is from such regions that fishes have explored into the less favourable habitats. One possibility, exploited by both pelagic and bottom-living (benthic) species of the seas, has been a gradual extension into the ocean depths. Another has been the conquering of what would normally be lethal temperatures, either cold or hot. On the whole, freshwaters provide more extreme conditions than do the seas, yet fishes have managed to colonize waters that periodically dry out, that lack sufficient oxygen for normal respiration by gills, or that are excessively alkaline. Fishes have also found their way into subterranean caves, where light is absent and food scarce, and have worked their way upwards into torrential hill streams.

Although extreme habitats cannot support large numbers of fishes, either in terms of species or of individuals, it is remarkable that they have been colonized at all. It is a measure of the suitability of fish design, as much in physiology and behaviour as in structure, that it can allow for such diversity.

Extremes of Temperature. From the point of view of temperature, the temperate seas and inland waters are the least stable, with seasonal fluctuations of 10°C or more. The tropical and polar waters show much less variation in temperature, and while this has contributed to a rich diversity in the tropics, the arctic and antarctic seas have a rather poor fish fauna. Nevertheless, well over a hundred different species live in the polar seas where temperatures may be close to $-2°$C. Although some of these fishes spend their time lurking on the bottom, they are by no means inactive and it has been claimed that the tempo of their lives, as measured by oxygen consumption and with due allowance for temperature, is biologically higher than that in fishes from warmer waters. In other words, these fishes cannot be compared with the sluggish carp hibernating at the bottom of a pond.

Of the polar regions, the Antarctic is the richer in species, of which about three-quarters belong to the antarctic cods, the suborder Notothenioidei (families Bovichthyidae, Nototheniidae, Bathydraconidae and Channichthyidae). These are slim-bodied fishes with large heads and mouths, pelvic fins set forward near the throat, and flexible spines in the fins (unlike most of the perch-like fishes). Antarctic waters also harbour skates, eel-pouts (Zoarcidae) and sea snails (Liparidae).

The central problem of how these fishes are able to survive in water below 0°C has not been fully solved. If the blood freezes or ice crystals form in the cells of the tissues, then normal biological processes

The Alaskan Blackfish *Dallia* can withstand extremely low temperatures, but its ability to survive when frozen into ice is an exageration.

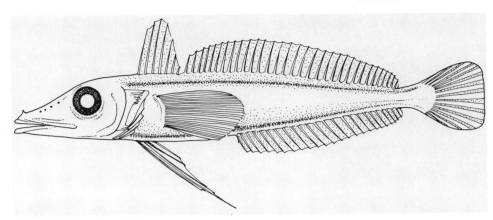

Chaenodraco wilsoni, one of the Antarctic ice fishes, a group that lack red blood corpuscles and can survive in water close to freezing point.

come to an end and the fish dies. Just as salts in sea water lower the freezing point from 0°C (i.e. that of freshwater) to about −1·9°C, so also do the salts dissolved in the fish's blood and body fluids. As explained earlier, skates and other cartilaginous fishes allow urea to accumulate in the blood so that the concentration of salts is about that of the surrounding sea water. Skates of polar seas can thus survive in all but freezing water. For bony fishes it is not so simple since the salt concentration in their blood is less than that of sea water and the blood will therefore freeze at a higher temperature (from −0·4°C to −1·9°C). One common nototheniid from McMurdo Sound, *Trematomus bernachii*, for example, has been observed to live throughout the year at or near temperatures of −1·9°C, and this would seem to leave far too fine a margin for safety. In the case of certain arctic fishes living off northern Labrador it was found that their blood froze at

about −0·8°C in summer but at −1·5°C during the winter months, yet such fishes are able to survive water temperatures of −1·75°C. To account for this it has been suggested that they are able to secrete some kind of organic 'anti-freeze' into the blood.

Yet another peculiarity of the blood of these fishes, in this case known only from those of antarctic waters, is the absence of a respiratory pigment. Reports of 'bloodless' fishes were brought back by men from whaling expeditions and were at first disbelieved, but in the 1930s antarctic fishes were examined on the spot and although clearly possessing blood, this was almost transparent. The bloodless fishes, usually called icefishes because of their colourless or even translucent bodies, belong to the family Channichthyidae (*Chaenocephalus*, *Chaenodraco*, *Champsocephalus* and a number of other genera). In these fishes red blood corpuscles

Cynolebias nigripinnis, one of the South American annual fishes whose eggs hatch after a period of complete desiccation.

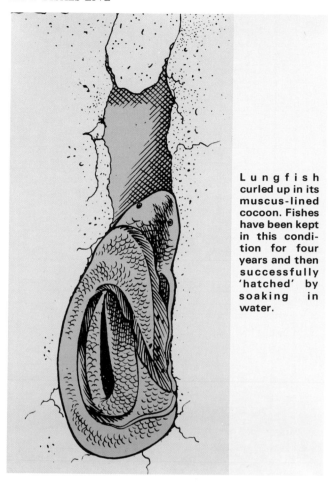

Lungfish curled up in its muscus-lined cocoon. Fishes have been kept in this condition for four years and then successfully 'hatched' by soaking in water.

are either absent or extremely few, while the respiratory pigment haemoglobin, which gives the blood its red colour, is also absent or only present in minute quantities. This poses some difficult problems in oxygen transport since haemoglobin is the chemical agent that combines with oxygen, allowing it to be carried around the body and released where needed. In the icefishes it has been found that the only oxygen present in the blood is the small quantity dissolved in the blood plasma, the watery fluid that normally carries the blood corpuscles. Since polar waters are well supplied with oxygen and the fishes themselves are fairly inactive, it seems that this rather inefficient method of oxygen transport is enough for their needs.

In some antarctic fishes, contact with ice is a critical factor. A zoarcid *Rhizophila* and a sea snail *Liparis*, for example, appear to tolerate temperatures of 0·4°C and 1°C below the theoretical freezing point of their blood. However, if such fishes are caught and raised to the surface through the upper water layers which are laden with small ice crystals, they will freeze and die, while other antarctic fishes

will actually perch on platelets of ice in the water.

At least two species of the family Nototheniidae, the most diverse family of antarctic fishes, have a reduced number of red blood corpuscles and less haemoglobin than is normal in bony fishes, although such small quantities are not unusual in the jawless fishes (Agnatha) and the cartilaginous fishes (sharks and rays). Are such fishes on the way to losing their respiratory pigment? At present there is no satisfactory explanation.

Antarctica is devoid of freshwater fishes, but there are fishes like the pike *Esox lucius* and the Arctic char *Salvelinus alpinus* in arctic rivers and although temperatures are not so extreme as in the antarctic these fishes have to face near-freezing conditions. The celebrated blackfish *Dallia* of Alaska and Siberia, and the North American mudminnows *Umbra*, both related to the pike, have been said to survive in solid ice and while this may be an exaggeration it seems possible that, like some of the arctic marine fishes, they can withstand contact with ice crystals. As explained earlier, the blood of freshwater fishes is saltier than the water in which they swim and its freezing point is thus lower, so that in theory at least their blood and body fluids should not freeze when the water turns to ice around them.

The area of water offering minimum temperatures to fish life (i.e. the polar waters) is large compared to the isolated bodies of hot water where the upper limit of temperature tolerance is encountered. In the tropics, shallow sun-heated pools on the exposed coral reef or beside flooding rivers are colonized by juvenile fishes or the adults of small species and these can well tolerate temperatures of 30°C. It is in hot springs, however, that the real test comes since there is often a gradient from warm to hot to very hot and the penetration of fishes towards the source of the spring can be readily observed. An example is found in the hot springs that fringe Lake Magadi in Kenya. These bubble up and run in shallow pools and channels down to the lake. In the pools live shoals of a dwarf species of the widespread African genus *Tilapia* (*T. grahami*) and they feed on the abundant algae attached to the rocks. A clear 'browse-line' shows how far up they will penetrate and this corresponds to a temperature of about 40°C. It has been claimed that females will quietly brood eggs at 44°C, but active movements are perhaps impossible at this temperature.

Salt Concentration and Alkalinity. The Magadi *Tilapia* are remarkable not only for their tolerance of high water temperatures, but also for their ability to live under strongly alkaline conditions. The water from the springs contains high concentrations of sodium carbonate and bicarbonate, as well as some other salts (sodium chloride, sodium sulphide and sodium fluoride) and the water is correspondingly alkaline (pH of 10·5 – cf. 7·0 for neutral water). Like marine fishes, these *Tilapia* face a problem of salt regulation and must presumably drink copiously, excreting the excess salts. Other members of the genus *Tilapia* can withstand brackish or even fully salt water and it would seem that, as Lake Magadi slowly dried out and increased in alkalinity, it was only a species of *Tilapia* that had the physiological plasticity to survive; the catfishes and carp-like fishes that must have inhabited the lake were evidently unable to tolerate the new conditions.

In the open oceans the concentration of salts (chiefly sodium chloride) varies rather little, ranging from 33 to 37 parts per thousand (‰), with an average of about 35‰. There are, however, small areas where this average is doubled or even tripled, yet even this has not proved a total barrier to fishes. In Southern California, for example, shallow bays and lagoons may rarely be flushed out by the tide during the summer, with the result that salinities are raised by evaporation to 70, 90 or exceptionally to over 120‰. Such pools are inhabited by the California killifish *Fundulus parvipinnis*. These fishes are able to maintain the concentration of salts in the blood at a constant level until the salinity of the water rises to about 65‰. There is then a rise in the concentration of their own salts, followed by a further period of control. In other words, this remarkable fish, having reached the limit of its power

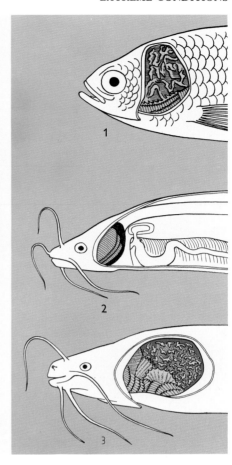

Accessory air breathing organs in: (1) Climbing perch *Anabas testudineus*, (2) Indian catfish *Heteropneustes fossilis* and (3) African catfish *Clarias lazera*.

The Australian lungfish *Neoceratodus* has a single lung, but the bichir *Polypterus* and also the African and South American lungfishes have two, thus showing a strong resemblance to the lungs of the land vertebrates or tetrapods.

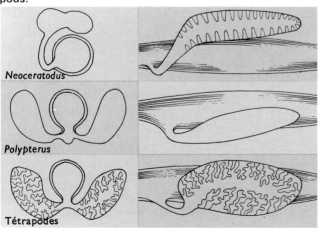

to regulate its own salts against the concentration outside it, allows and tolerates an increase in blood salinity and then starts afresh to regulate at this new higher level. Of equal interest is the fact that the California killifish can survive just as well in freshwater.

This is obviously exceptional, but so too are the environmental conditions. Fishes are so adaptable that the rarity of species able to stand high temperatures or salinities may reflect, not some inherent physiological inability, but the lack of opportunities seriously to tackle the problem and to evolve suitable forms.

Desiccation. Large areas of tropical inland waters suffer from seasonal extremes of flooding and drought, or from successive years of poor rainfall and a dwindling of lakes and rivers. Certain crustaceans have mastered this kind of environment, notably the Fairy shrimps (Cheirocephalidae) which lay tough-coated, drought resistant eggs that hatch out once the pools in which they live are re-flooded. Such pools may also contain fishes, the so-called annual fishes, and these too have found the way to cheat an inhospitable environment. Before the start of the dry season, these fishes deposit their eggs in the mud. As the pools dry out the adults die but the eggs remain until, months later, the pools are refilled. The eggs then hatch and begin the next cycle.

Annual fishes are toothcarps (Cyprinodontidae) and in Africa include members of the genera *Notobranchius* and *Aphyosemion*. In India another toothcarp *Oryzias melastigma* also shows delayed hatching of the eggs, although in this case the eggs are not dried out but await a freshening of the water. A number of South American toothcarps (about 24 species) of the genera *Austrofundulus*, *Pterolebias*, *Rachovia* and *Cynolebias* are annual fishes, including the beautiful Argentine pearlfishes. In Florida the brackish water killifish *Fundulus confluentus* is an annual fish but a rather unusual one, in that the eggs are not buried in the mud but are left exposed to the atmosphere, lying stranded on the marshy ground among the plant litter as the swamp dries out. In one experiment, the eggs hatched out after three months and five days, but in Africa the incubation period must not only be longer than this but on some occasions must be doubled or more when the seasonal rains fail in certain years.

The hatching of such eggs is an extraordinarily rapid process. The eggs of *Fundulus confluentus*, for example, hatch within 15 to 30 minutes of flooding. Deferred hatching until the conditions are ripe seems to be a characteristic of the toothcarps, but it is also found in the grunion *Leuresthes tenius* whose eggs remain stranded on the beach until the next high tides.

Air breathing Dwarf gourami *Colisa lalia*.

Aestivation, or survival in seasonally hot or dry conditions, is obviously easier in the egg stage before the development of complex organ systems that require large amounts of oxygen and food. Some of the lungfishes, however, have solved such physiological problems and can survive several years without water. In West Africa *Protopterus annectens*, an inhabitant of small streams and swamps, burrows down into the mud as the water level drops, forming a tube with a slightly enlarged chamber into which the fish doubles up. As the surface of the swamp dries out, the fish secretes quantities of mucus which hardens to form a cocoon around it, perforated at the top and thus allowing air to filter in from the barely closed entrance to the mud tube. As in hibernation, the metabolic processes of the aestivating lungfish are drastically slowed down and energy for essential processes like blood circulation is derived from body tissues and especially from the muscles. When the waters return once more the cocoon dissolves, the fish frees itself and soon recovers from its months of incarceration. Aestivation seems to be a regular habit in the West African lungfishes *Protopterus annectens* and *P. dolloi* but is rarer in the East African species *P. aethiopicus* and *P. amphibius*. The South American species *Lepidosiren paradoxa* makes a less elaborate chamber, with no cocoon, but the Australian species *Neoceratodus forsteri* is unable to aestivate, which is curious because the ability to do so has surely been of great value in the survival of this ancient line of fishes. Fossil lungfishes have been found in cocoons dating back to the Triassic period (180–225 million years ago) showing that the colonization of extreme habitats has not been a recent experiment. Since lungfishes have been 'hatched' successfully from cocoons kept dry for some four years, it would seem that this method of drought resistance should confer considerable advantages on the species that employ it.

Hibernation. Among warm-blooded animals of high latitudes a torpid period during winter is not uncommon, but rather few fishes actually hibernate. An exception is the carp *Cyprinus*, which is said to move into deeper water and to cluster in immobile groups at the bottom, respiration and other activities being at a minimum. Tench *Tinca* also hibernate, burying themselves in the mud, and the same is true of eels *Anguilla*, but the majority of fishes, although perhaps more sluggish in winter, maintain their normal activities.

Another possible exception is the huge Basking

The labyrinthfish *Ctenopoma ansorgei* from the freshwater of West Africa.

shark *Cetorhinus maximus*, a fish that grows to about 30 ft (9 m) in length and may approach 4 tons in weight. As explained earlier, this shark loses its gillrakers in winter and, being unable to feed, it perhaps hibernates at the bottom until spring and the growth of new sets of gillrakers.

Air-breathing Fishes. In the majority of fishes respiration, the absorption of oxygen and elimination of carbon dioxide, is accomplished by the gills and it is by refinements in these organs that they compensate for low oxygen concentrations in certain habitats. In shallow waters, however, and particularly under stagnant conditions, fishes have the possibility of gulping air directly at the surface. At first this may have been no more than a matter of drawing the well-oxygenated surface layer of water over their gills, but the development of absorbent surfaces associated with the gill chamber or the pharynx, in the form of accessory breathing organs, must have accompanied a tendency to retain air bubbles beneath the gill covers.

Several unrelated groups of fishes have adopted this method of breathing air. In certain African and Asian freshwater catfishes (e.g. some species of *Clarias*) the gills are stiffened to prevent their collapse in air and in a special part of the gill chamber are spongy arborescent (tree-like) organs growing from the upper ends of the gill arches. These, and the skin surrounding them, are well supplied with blood vessels and operate efficiently in water lack-

ing in oxygen or when the fish is out of water. In the Asiatic snakeheads *Ophiocephalus*, the air-breathing organs are rather simpler, being pouches in the pharynx lined with folds of skin, but the principle is the same, namely the gulping of air and extraction of oxygen. Another Asiatic freshwater fish, the catfish *Heteropneustes*, has organs rather similar to those of *Clarias* but the air chambers are tubular and extend back along the body as far as the tail, thus resembling lungs. Yet another freshwater group that has developed air-breathing organs is the synbranchid eels (Synbranchidae) of India and Burma, which have a pair of sacs budded off from the pharynx. Finally, and unrelated to any of the previous fishes, there is the celebrated Climbing perch *Anabas testudineus* and its relatives, known as labyrinthfishes because of the labyrinthine breathing organ in the upper part of the gill chamber.

This is not the only method used by fishes to absorb oxygen from the atmosphere. In some of the loaches (Cobitidae), and also in the mailed catfishes of South America (Loricariidae), air is swallowed and oxygen subsequently absorbed by means of special blood vessels in the intestine, the remaining gases being passed down the gut and expelled at the anus. Another curious method is that found in the goby-like estuarine fish *Dormitator latifrons* of western Panama. In this species the top of the head is flat and the skin richly supplied with blood vessels. When oxygen levels decline, the fish raises its head

Mudskippers *Periophthalmus* from the Indo-Pacific clamber out of water on mud banks and stay for several minutes before returning for another gulp of oxygenated water.

above the surface and absorbs oxygen directly from the air. This use of a special external organ for breathing seems to be unique among adult fishes, although in embryos and larvae the blood vessels are near enough to the surface for the exchange of gases; in some cases the flap of skin covering the gill cavity takes on the duties of the gills before the latter are developed.

From the standpoint of an amphibian, a reptile, a bird or a mammal, the various air-breathing organs described above might be regarded as rather make-shift arrangements when compared with the system of lungs universally adopted by the 'professional' air breathers. In fact, lungs were first developed in primitive fishes as paired pouches budded off from the gullet. During the course of evolution the pouches fused together, lost their respiratory function, and served a hydrostatic role, as a swimbladder such as those found in most modern fishes. However, in the African and Australian lungfishes *Protopterus* and *Lepidosiren* and in the African bichir *Polypterus* there are paired lungs which, as in reptiles, birds and mammals, join by a tube to the *floor* of the pharynx, as also does the single lung in the Australian lungfish *Neoceratodus*. On the other hand, when swimbladders retain a connection with the pharynx, it is by a pneumatic duct leading from the *roof* (occasionally one side) of the pharynx,

suggesting that the development of a buoyancy organ was a quite separate line of evolution.

In the lungfishes the lungs are well supplied with blood vessels and in their spongy lining resemble the lungs of land vertebrates. The same is found in the two surviving families of the holosteans, the bowfin (Amiidae) and the garpikes (Lepisosteidae), although in this case the 'lung' is a swimbladder (joined to the top of the pharynx). The use of the swimbladder as a lung is not confined to the primitive holosteans, however, but is found also in the tarpon *Tarpon*, the bonytongues *Clupisudis* and the African freshwater butterflyfish *Pantodon*, the featherbacks *Notopterus*, the Electric catfish *Gymnarchus*, a characin *Erythrinus unitaeniatus* and the mudminnows *Umbra*.

Whatever the method used, whether lungs, intestine, swimbladder or specialized organ, none of the modern air-breathing fishes has sought to compete with the land vertebrates. They have merely extended their aquatic range into habitats so poor in oxygen that normal respiratory methods would not work. Many of these fishes live in tropical swamps where a mat of aerial vegetation (such as papyrus roots) prevents light penetration and thus the production of oxygen by photosynthesis. Such fishes must gulp air where the surface is exposed and some species, such as the synbranchid cuchia *Amphip-*

nous cuchia are so dependant on air that they can be drowned if prevented from reaching the surface. The nearest that the air-breathing fishes have come to existing on dry land is in aestivation, as in the lungfishes, the Asiatic gouramis *Osphronemus* and the North American bowfin *Amia*. A few even make active overland journeys, the best-known being the so-called Climbing perch *Anabas testudinosus* and the snakeheads (Channidae), the former gaining purchase from its spiny gill covers while pushing forward with its pectoral fins and tail, the latter making 'rowing' movements with its pectoral fins. In this way, new water bodies can be sought.

It might be thought that air-breathing is essential to an aerial life, but the mudskippers *Periophthalmus* are an exception. Living chiefly in mangrove swamps, they skitter across the surface of the water and with their highly mobile pectoral fins climb the stilt roots of the trees. Although they can remain out of water for several minutes, this is achieved by trapping a quantity of water under the gill covers and absorbing the oxygen from it.

Hillstream Fishes. Fishes of torrential mountain streams have already been mentioned in connection with locomotion and it was shown that the flattening of the underside of the body, often combined with frictional ridges or some form of sucker, help to prevent the fish from being washed away by the current. Melting snows in the Himalayas or the Andes produce spates of such force that boulders of 4 ft (over a metre) in diameter are tossed downstream like pebbles. Under such conditions it is remarkable that fishes can hold their own, yet this inhospitable environment has been colonized independently by several groups of the order Cypriniformes, including the Naked catfishes of the Andes and various carps, loaches, suckers and catfishes of Asia, India and the Malayan Archipelago. It has even led to the evolution of a distinct family, the sucker-like Homolopteridae.

In addition to the purely mechanical problem of 'staying put,' those species that use the mouth as a sucker have a further difficulty since they cannot at the same time use the mouth to take in water for breathing. A Southeast Asian carp-like fish *Gyrinocheilus* has solved this problem by not using the mouth for breathing. Instead, the gill opening is divided into two parts, water entering the upper part by a kind of syphon, passing over the gills and being expelled from the lower part. Other hillstream fishes, the Homolopteridae, have the ability to suspend normal breathing for a while, presumably using up the oxygen in the well-aerated water held in the mouth and gill chamber. Hillstream fishes mostly subsist either on algae scraped from the rocks or on insect larvae. The virtual absence of predators has made defence a minor consideration and has enabled the fishes to specialize in the solution of the purely physical problems of their environment.

Cave Fishes. Not content with colonizing even the most unlikely surface waters of the world, fishes have also managed to gain a foothold in certain subterranean caves and artesian wells, not merely as

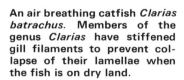

An air breathing catfish *Clarias batrachus*. Members of the genus *Clarias* have stiffened gill filaments to prevent collapse of their lamellae when the fish is on dry land.

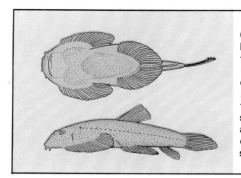

One of the hillstream-fishes is the Bornean sucker *Gastromyzon*. Its paired fins form suckers, which are used to cling to the stream bed.

temporary retreats but for permanent residence. Altogether some 32 species of cave-dwelling (troglobiotic) fishes have been recorded, belonging to 12 different families. Over half of these (18) belong to the order Cypriniformes, of which 11 are catfishes of one kind or another, five are carps and two are characins. This reflects both the predominance of cypriniform fishes in freshwaters (about four-fifths of all freshwater species) and also perhaps a certain proclivity to cave life. The remaining cave fishes belong to the families Synbranchidae (1), Amblyopsidae (6), Brotulidae (3) and Gobiidae at (4). In most of these families, the cave-living forms represent only a small proportion of the known species, but in the Amblyopsidae only three other species are known. It is worth noting that the cave fishes are mostly found among the less highly evolved and not among the more advanced orders of fishes, although this is less pronounced in the marine forms.

Perhaps the most striking feature of the cave fishes is the degeneration of the eyes, since the majority of these fishes live in total darkness and, unlike the fishes of the sunless oceanic midwaters, none has developed luminous organs. *Caecobarbus geertsi*, the Blind cave barb from Thysville in the Congo, resembles its surface-living relatives (*Barbus* species) but lacks eyes and is a general flesh colour. A few were brought to Europe in 1956 for aquarists, but their export is now rigidly controlled. The most common aquarium species is the Blind cave characin *Astyanax jordani* from caves in Mexico, a species that closely resembles its surface-living relative, *A. fasciatus*. In fact, the two have been cross-bred experimentally and there is a possibility that the blind fishes are merely a cave form of *A. fasciatus*, for cave populations include fishes with varying degrees of development of the eyes, with a high proportion of eyed individuals in those caves connected with a surface river. In many cave fishes the eye tissues regress, in addition to being covered over by skin, but where a connection with the optic nerve still exists, there is a possibility that light can be appreciated. The pineal body is also sensitive to light and may be of use to those fishes living in caves connected to the surface.

Although stemming from very different stocks, cave fishes share several other features. They are usually very small fishes, the largest being the Cuban brotulid *Stygicola dentatus*, which reaches 6 in (15 cm) and the slightly larger Kentucky blindfish *Amblyopsis spelaeus*, which grows to 8 in (20 cm). This probably reflects the paucity of food in a cave environment since the lowest levels of the food chain must be derived from outside, plant life being impossible in the absence of light. However, there is no dramatic reduction in tissues such as that characteristic of certain deep-sea fishes. Cave fishes often show a tendency towards constant swimming, which again may be a response to an environment in which food must be carefully sought. Since camouflage is unnecessary, the skin lacks dark pigments and is usually white, pink or flesh-coloured. The sensory system of the lateral line in many cave fishes is often better developed than in their surface-living relatives and this presumably compensates for the lack of vision. The senses of taste, smell and hearing, on the other hand, are not especially developed, except perhaps for the more sensitive barbels in the catfishes and carps, but these are senses that are already very acute in normal fishes.

Rather little is known of the breeding habits of cave fishes. The Cuban brotulids are live-bearers, as also are some of their normal relatives, while the Kentucky blindfish female incubates the eggs within the gill chamber. The Blind cave characin is the only species to have been bred in aquaria and in this case the adhesive eggs drop to the bottom.

Blind cave characin of Mexico, *Astyanax fasciatus*.

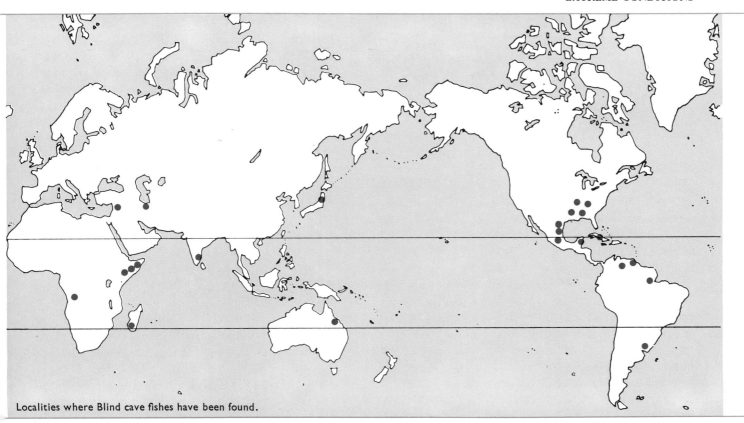

Localities where Blind cave fishes have been found.

Cave fishes are found throughout the world, mainly in the warmer zones. Some inhabit vast caves while others are confined to small subterranean wells or springs. In the New World there are 21 species, in Africa five, and the remainder come from the Middle East, India, Japan and Australia. Curiously enough, there are no true cave species in Europe, although partial cave forms are known (*Paraphoxinus*). Surface-living species may have cave populations but, apart from being a little pale, they are indistinguishable from those in the open waters.

Even in this short survey it is clear that fishes have shown an extraordinary capacity for exploiting what might be considered marginal habitats. It should be remembered, however, that in a sense all habitats become marginal once there is competition for their resources. To the purely physical problems of 'making a living' are added those of making that living at the expense of others. To this extent one can say that the cave-dwelling fishes, as also those of hillstreams, stagnant pools, polar seas and hot springs, have opted for a simpler if harsher way of life.

131

Distribution Patterns

From earliest times men have been aware that the distribution of animals and plants is not uniform but falls into distinct patterns. Thus, to explore a new area was to discover a new flora and fauna. Ancient myths are full of the exotic animals to be found outside the range of a particular society's normal territory and although such beasts were often wholly or partly imaginary, they were nonetheless expressions of the principle that a new locality harboured new forms of life.

Plants, and the animals ultimately dependant on them, are susceptible to quite small changes in soil or in regimes of temperature, humidity or rainfall and so, in this sense, a different spectrum of animal and plant life can be encountered on a journey of only a few miles. But it is noticeable, and early man understood this quite well, that similar environments tend to produce a similar array of living forms. It was this repetition that enabled the hunter or plant gatherer to seek new areas of exploitation and nowadays it gives the ecologist confidence that his efforts to probe the relationship between plants, animals and their environment will result in the discovery of 'natural laws' governing the association of organic and inorganic matter.

Even before the Age of Discovery – essentially, the crossing of broad oceans to new continents – it was realized that animal and plant life does not vary solely with habitat. When the armies of Alexander the Great returned from conquests in the east they brought back to Europe the first parrots (probably ringed parakeets) and stories of such animals as the Indian rhinoceros. These confirmed that beyond Greece could be found all manner of zoological curiosities and this provided a rich source for the later writers of bestiaries. With the great voyages of Columbus and the explorers of the 16th century it was found that the remote regions held such a different assemblage of animals and plants that some other principle must be at work beyond the one that seemed to place similar organisms in similar environments. Before Darwin discovered the key it was difficult to explain these often strikingly different forms, but evolutionary theory showed the importance of isolation in producing diversity.

Zoogeography, or the study of animal diversity in geographical terms, is thus more than ecology on a global scale: its basis is historical, being essentially the results of alternate dispersal and isolation. Since this is intimately associated with the history of landforms, there is a fruitful exchange of ideas between zoogeography and geology. The changing patterns of landforms throw light on the distribution of animals and in turn the latter serves to confirm or refute the earth's history as interpreted from the rocks. It should not be forgotten, however, that the habits of the animals and their relations with their environment form the essential background to the processes of dispersal and isolation, while the capacity to evolve decides whether isolation will lead to extinction or to the flowering of a whole new branch of animal life.

Isolation. The most obvious factor in the distribution of animals, whether aquatic or land-living, is the disposition of land masses, for the demarcation between land and sea is a fundamental barrier for the vast majority of animals. The classic example is Australia, whose profusion of marsupials reflects isolation at a time when the placental mammals were making their successful bid for supremacy on other continents. Australia's isolation is reflected also in its freshwater fish fauna, for there are only two true freshwater fishes, the Australian lungfish

The lungfishes are members of a primitive group that once had a wide distribution but is now represented by only three genera in three families, which are widely separated. Members of the Dipteridae are known only as fossils.

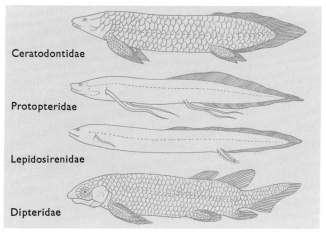

Ceratodontidae

Protopteridae

Lepidosirenidae

Dipteridae

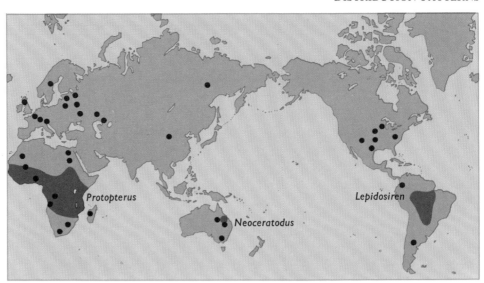

Distribution of living (brown) and fossil lungfishes (the purple dots) showing that the group was once widespread.

Neoceratodus and a bonytongue *Scleropages*, both of which are from archaic lineages and are thus as much relics of bygone days as are the marsupials. All other Australian fishes found in freshwaters are members of families that are otherwise marine, such as the herrings, mullets, sandsmelts, sea perches and gobies. Madagascar presents a rather similar picture of long isolation, for it lacks almost entirely the rich diversity of freshwater fishes found on the African mainland; only the perch-like cichlid fishes are shared and these have evidently entered from the sea.

In the case of the Australian marsupials, isolation has resulted in the evolution of about 170 species, yet the Australian lungfish and bonytongue failed to proliferate in this way. Certainly, there was no question of competition since the dominant freshwater group, the cypriniform fishes (carps, catfishes), is absent, except for certain marine catfishes that have come into the freshwaters. However, neither the lungfishes nor the bonytongues have produced more than a handful of present-day species elsewhere in the world and their conservatism has thus been maintained in spite of the opportunities afforded by isolation. In certain other cases quite the reverse has occurred and from one or two ancestral species a remarkable proliferation has occurred. Some of the best examples are seen in the great lakes of Africa, where the perch-like cichlid fishes have multiplied in a most extraordin-

The distribution of the Bonytongues or Osteoglossidae: (1) *Osteoglossum bicirrhosum*, (2) *Arapaima gigas*, (3) *Clupisudis niloticus* and, (4) *Scleropages leichhardtii*.

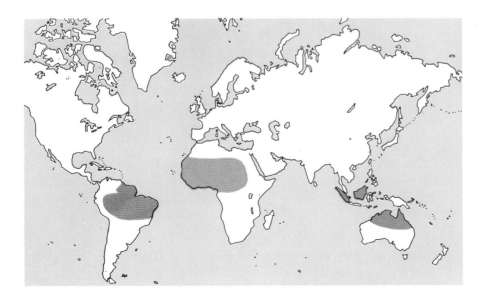

The distribution of the perch-like fishes of the family Percidae.

ary way and often with great rapidity. In fact, Lakes Malawi, Victoria and Tanganyika contain more fish species than any other lakes in the world, the bulk of these being cichlids. Lake Malawi has the most (over 200 cichlids), followed by Victoria (over 170) and Tanganyika (about 126). The degree of isolation is shown by the fact that almost all these species are confined to their particular lake basin.

This kind of explosive evolution is one result of isolation. It shows how, given a new territory in which to expand, a wholly new fauna can arise and one which, in its myriad interrelationships with the plant life of the region, often bears the stamp of surprising novelty. Such was the impression that the first European explorers had of the Americas, Africa, India, Australia and many other lesser regions once they paused from conquest to examine their surroundings. The other result, the inability of the isolated stock to seize its chance, as in Australia, is rarer; usually there is at least some degree of proliferation, even where the habitat is uninviting, as in Antarctic waters.

For strictly freshwater fishes, the distribution of land and sea produces gross barriers to dispersion. Less permanent barriers are provided by the divides between river systems. For example, the Nile contains a number of fish genera (*Lates* or Nile perch, *Polypterus* or bichirs, *Hydrocynus* or tigerfish, *Malapterurus* or Electric catfish), which are absent from the rivers in the east or south of Africa. These 'Nilotic' fishes are found, however, in the Niger and other rivers of West Africa, showing that isolation between these river systems was not so complete in former times. Waterfalls provide minor barriers to dispersal. The Murchison Falls have prevented the entrance of Nilotic fishes into Lake Victoria, so that *Lates, Polypterus* and *Hydrocynus* are unknown in this huge, shallow basin, but the processes of erosion will eventually remove the barrier. Finally, there are purely ecological factors preventing the exchange of fishes, for example, temperature may confine a particular fauna to the upper reaches of a river.

The tailing off of the continents in the Southern

After a period of growth in the sea, salmon return to their natal river to spawn, scraping the sand and gravel to make a trough or redd in which the eggs are laid. The sand is pushed back over the eggs by bodily movements. After hatching the alevins remain in the river, growing to the stage known as parr. Losing the black parr marks, the juveniles, now known as smolts, pass down to the sea.

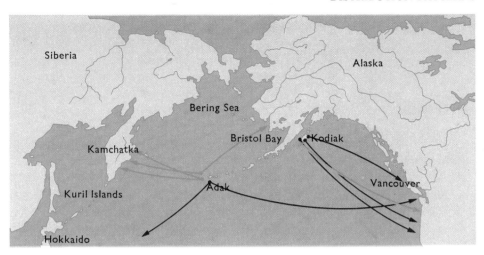

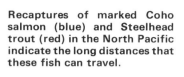

Recaptures of marked Coho salmon (blue) and Steelhead trout (red) in the North Pacific indicate the long distances that these fish can travel.

Hemisphere makes gross isolation of marine fishes less complete but a glance at the map suggests that three major ocean basins exist. The most complete is the Atlantic, with its offshoot the Mediterranean. Then come the Indian Ocean and the Pacific. In fact, the Indo-Australian Archipelago, the string of islands that stretch between Malaysia and Australia, is no barrier to shore fishes but rather the reverse, the centre of their dispersal, so that the Indo-Pacific can be regarded as one huge zoogeographical unit. The real longitudinal barriers are the Americas and Africa and between these two colossal fences the oceans are wide enough to allow for a rather different fish fauna on either side. These four major vertical zones are cut off to the north and south by a latitudinal temperature barrier, the line (isotherm) bounding areas of sea that are 20°C in the coldest month. This generally marks the division between the tropical fauna and that of temperate and colder seas. Since in the Southern Hemisphere this isotherm cuts the tips of South Africa and South America, it serves to contain most tropical forms within the two major ocean basins, the Atlantic and the Indo-Pacific. Yet another important latitudinal barrier is the 12°C isotherm.

As in freshwaters, there are numerous smaller isolating barriers of a less permanent nature. The Isthmus of Panama is a comparatively recent feature, being about 3 million years old, and even if man does not breach it with a sea-level canal it will eventually fail to serve as a fence, as a result of the normal processes of erosion. At the entrance to the Red Sea is another important barrier, a low sill that has no effect on surface living forms but which separates fishes of the colder depths of the Indian Ocean, where temperatures drop to 2–3°C, from those of the warm Red Sea (about 21°C at all depths

below 1,000 ft or 300 m). Salinities and other physical features of the oceans can also prove to be barriers.

Isolation is a powerful force in the creation of distinct faunal units, but one which also presupposes an initial dispersal period.

Dispersal. A number of adaptations have already been described whereby fishes can extend their ranges. Aestivation, air-breathing, and tolerance to extremes of heat, cold, pressure, salinity and the lack of light, are all ways in which fishes have managed to spread and to hold their own in new regions. In this way, the lesser barriers to dispersal, the ecological hurdles, have been overcome. Gross barriers, such as an entire continent or thousands of miles of open ocean, are almost insuperable; if this were not so, then there would not be such distinct faunal regions. The arrival of Asiatic catfishes (families Ariidae, Plotosidae) in Australian freshwaters, however, shows that members of an otherwise freshwater group can turn first to the seas and then later revert to freshwaters again, having in the meantime crossed one of the most famous of all zoogeographical boundaries, Wallace's Line, between Borneo and Celebes and between Bali and Lombok, thus separating the Oriental from the Australasian regions. Similarly, a number of shore fishes have managed to span opposite sides of both the Pacific and the Atlantic Oceans. It is these exceptions that not so much prove the rule as ensure the development of new patterns of distribution.

One of the strongest barriers to dispersal in fishes is the boundary between salt and freshwater. Groups which are euryhaline or tolerant of a wide range of salinities, such as the Grey mullets (Mugilidae), often have a considerable geographic range; the Common grey mullet *Mugilcephalus* of Atlantic shores, for example, is met with again in Australia

135

Female Sea trout migrating up a river to breed, leaping the rapids.

as well as off the intervening coasts. The primary freshwater fishes, being those that have evolved in freshwaters and cannot tolerate saltwater, are largely dependent on changes in topography for their dispersal. The spreading of a genus or even a species over a whole continent is a surprising feat and in the past it was often postulated that this must be achieved by the transport of fish eggs on the feet of birds. Those who mark birds by ringing find, however, that birds' legs are remarkably clean. A quite adequate explanation of fish dispersal can be found in terms of river capture, of uplift and tilting of the earth, and of an exchange of fauna towards the end of the river erosion cycle when the head-waters of two systems drain adjacent marshy areas.

The adults of some fishes have minute ranges, as for example some of the smaller reef fishes that hardly stray from their place of concealment in a burrow or mollusc shell. By contrast, certain large oceanic fishes, and in particular the tuna-like fishes,

have vast ranges and may encircle the globe in tropical or subtropical waters. In recent years the sailfish *Istiophorus platypterus* has been shown to comprise a single wide-ranging species present in all warm oceans, rather than a number of species confined to particular basins as was formerly thought. The sailfish, and also the swordfish *Xiphias gladius*, are able to range into temperate waters to feed and can thus round the capes of the two major land barriers, South Africa and South America.

Dispersal in fishes, as in other animals, is a rather slow process. Individuals at the edge of the range inch slowly outwards, advancing but sometimes retreating according to the balance of ecological forces. For a while, the geographical boundary is smaller than the ecological one, but when the two coincide the fish must either adapt or await some environmental change in its favour. A large number of fishes, however, have adopted another solution.

136

Although strictly limited by environmental conditions to a particular spawning area, they make migrations at other times of the year and thus enormously extend their feeding range.

Migration. Perhaps the best known of the migratory fishes are the salmons – the Atlantic salmon *Salmo salar* of the North Atlantic and the six Pacific salmons belonging to the genus *Onchorhynchus* of the Pacific coasts of Canada and the northern part of the USA, with one species from the Pacific coasts of northern Asia. The construction of the salmon's gravel nest or *redd* in the upper reaches of rivers and subsequent egg-laying have already been mentioned. On hatching, the larvae or *alevins* of the Atlantic salmon remain among the pebbles of the stream-bed, but having used up their supply of yolk they then lead a secluded life in shallow waters, feeding principally on small insect larvae. Young of about 5 in (13 cm) are known as *parr* and develop 8–10 dark oval blotches or 'parr marks' on their flanks, each separated by a red spot. Usually in their second year, but sometimes in their first or third, a silvery pigment develops over the parr marks and the fish, which is now ready to migrate to the sea, is referred to as a *smolt*. Some of the Pacific salmons follow a different pattern, the young making their migration to the sea shortly after emerging from the gravel and while still only about an inch (2·5 cm) long. This is the case with the Pink and Chum salmons *O. gorbuscha* and *O. keta* and sometimes occurs in the Chinook *O. tschawytscha*; juveniles of the Coho and Sockeye salmons *O. Kisutch* and *O. nerka* spend one or one to three years in rivers before making their migration.

The advantages of feeding in the open ocean can be seen by comparing normal Sockeye adults with those that for one reason or another have become land-locked. Those that spend between four and six years in the sea grow to about six times the size of the ones left behind. Once in the sea, salmon make considerable journeys. An Atlantic salmon, marked in the southwest of Sweden, was apparently recaptured off the west coast of Greenland, some 2,500 miles away, while a Pink salmon, marked in the Gulf of Alaska, was recaptured not far from Korea, a journey of over 3,000 miles. Although these are probably exceptional, there is no doubt that the fishes are widely dispersed and this makes their migration back to their natal stream even more remarkable, for it has now been shown that many if not all salmon return to breed in the very stream in which they themselves were spawned.

As yet little is known as to how salmon navigate in the open sea but it has been suggested that they orient by means of the sun, the so-called solar compass method or celestial navigation used by migratory birds. The recognition of the 'home' river and finally of the exact stream is now known to depend on a very acute sense of smell. Because of particular local conditions of vegetation, soil, type of bottom and general geology, each stream has its own peculiar odour. By training fishes in tanks, it was found that salmon will appreciate quite minute concentrations of chemicals in water, while the experimental plugging of their nostrils showed that the accuracy of their homing behaviour could be severely upset if they were denied olfactory clues. Finally, the tagging of smolts on their downward journey and their recapture during the spawning run confirms the precision with which they locate their original river.

The journey up-river is itself no mean feat, for Sockeye may travel as much as 700 miles at a rate of 30 miles a day and this may involve the leaping of waterfalls of 10 ft (3 m) or more. The Atlantic salmon drift slowly downstream after spawning and

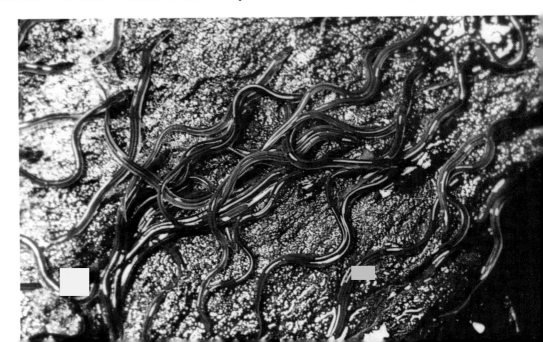

Elvers 'roping' up rocks. Even adult eels show remarkable dexterity in climbing.

are known at this stage as *kelts*. They return for a second or even a third spawning, but the Pacific species spawn only once and then die.

The term anadromous is applied not only to the salmons but also to those fishes that breed in rivers but extend their feeding range into lakes. The reverse, the catadromous fishes, are those that evidently have a marine origin but migrate up rivers to feed, of which the best examples are the freshwater eels. Most eels live and feed in the sea, but members of the genus *Anguilla* spend the first weeks, months or even years of their lives as frail leaf-shaped leptocephali. These drift slowly towards coasts where they transform into cylindrical elvers and continue their migration, entering rivers and remaining for up to seven years before migrating back into the sea.

Fishermen have long been used to seeing ripe eggs in the ovaries of breeding female fishes and the milky exudation from ripe testes, but the European freshwater eel presented a problem since it never appeared to produce eggs or milt. Aristotle and Pliny can hardly be blamed for assuming some form of spontaneous generation. Not until 1777 was an ovary described and since the eggs were immature even this was doubted. More than a century later a sexually mature female was caught in the Straits of Messina and in 1903 a male with ripe gonads was caught off Norway. Evidently the eels bred in the sea, but their early life remained a mystery. In fact, the leptocephalus or larval stage of the eel was described by Gronovius as long ago as 1763, but this leaf-like creature was so different from the adult that he and later authors placed it in a new genus, *Leptocephalus*, which they felt might be allied to the eels. In 1896 two leptocephali were caught in the straits of Messina and by very good fortune they were on the point of metamorphosing into elvers, much to the surprise of their discoverers. The life history of the eel was almost complete and only one problem remained: where did they breed?

The discovery of the European eel's breeding grounds resulted from the collection of leptocephali across the Atlantic and the careful plotting by Johann Schmidt of the length of each specimen against the place where it was caught. Smaller and smaller leptocephali were found as one progressed westwards across the Atlantic until in an area centred on the Sargasso Sea, between 20° and 30° north and 48° and 65° west, were found leptocephali of only 10 mm, the smallest yet discovered. Here then were the breeding grounds.

This was not the end of the story, however. Very few adult eels have been caught in the sea and all of these have had the alimentary tract so constricted that they could not possibly feed. Commenting on this, Dr Denys Tucker concluded that the eels die before ever reaching the spawning grounds; but in that case, how can the species maintain itself? Dr Tucker's ingenious answer was that the parents of the European eel are actually American freshwater eels *A. rostrata*, a closely related species that has a slightly lower number of vertebrae. Since there is good evidence in other fishes that the number of body parts, and especially vertebrae, are higher, the lower the temperature at which the embryos and larvae develop, it seemed that the American eel was not a different species but a population developed under slightly warmer conditions. The American mainland is considerably closer to the spawning grounds, so that there is no problem in the adults returning to breed. The discovery of an undoubted European eel at the spawning grounds would topple Dr Tucker's theory, but until then it deserves consideration.

Very many fishes make some sort of migration, however small, between feeding and breeding grounds and this has undoubtedly aided in their dispersal. In the Atlantic herring *Clupea harengus* it has been accompanied by the development of various races which in the North Sea and the Baltic

The common European eel *Anguilla anguilla*. It is yet not known for certain if these are the same species as the American eel.

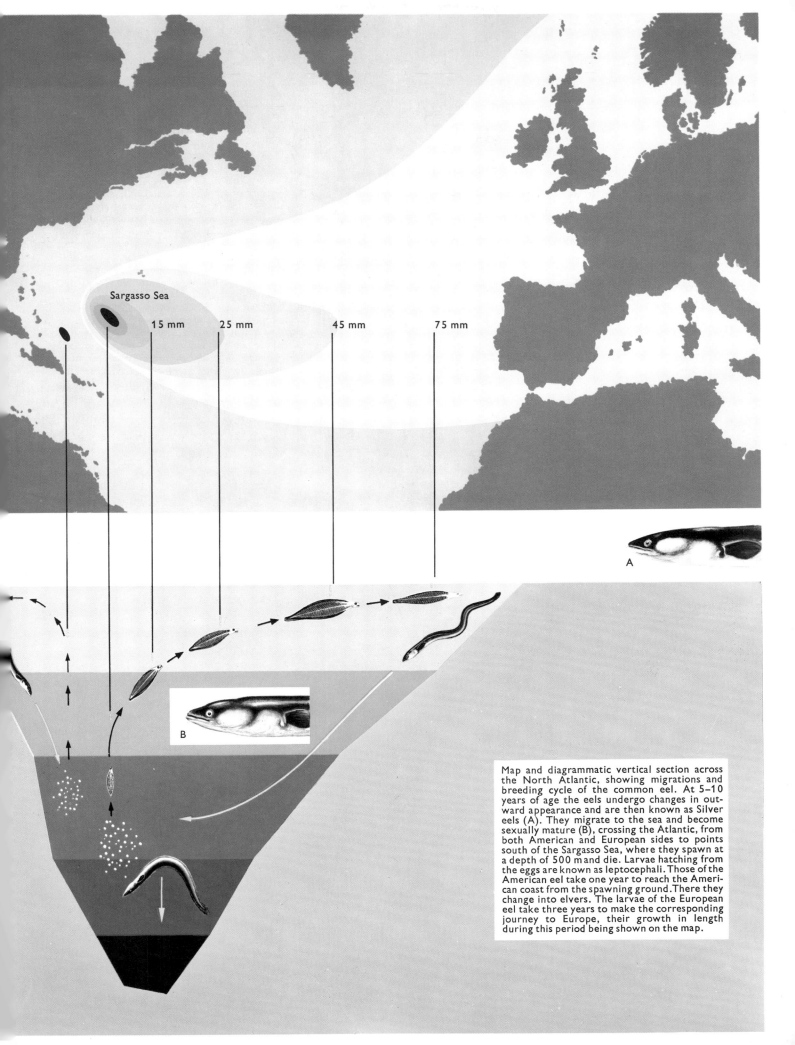

Sargasso Sea

15 mm   25 mm   45 mm   75 mm

A

B

Map and diagrammatic vertical section across the North Atlantic, showing migrations and breeding cycle of the common eel. At 5–10 years of age the eels undergo changes in outward appearance and are then known as Silver eels (A). They migrate to the sea and become sexually mature (B), crossing the Atlantic, from both American and European sides to points south of the Sargasso Sea, where they spawn at a depth of 500 m and die. Larvae hatching from the eggs are known as leptocephali. Those of the American eel take one year to reach the American coast from the spawning ground. There they change into elvers. The larvae of the European eel take three years to make the corresponding journey to Europe, their growth in length during this period being shown on the map.

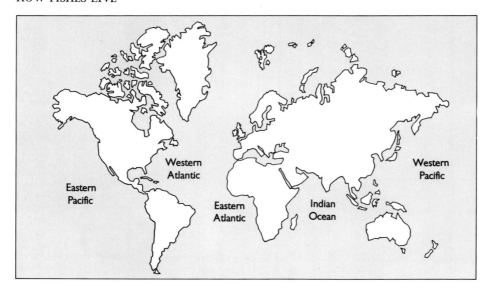

The major zoogeographical regions of the world.

spawn at different times and at different places throughout the year. Complete separation of breeding stocks could be the first step in the evolution of distinct species, which in their turn might specialize under new conditions, leading to a further fragmentation and a further extension of the range.

Distribution Patterns. The continents provide the basis for dividing the world into convenient faunal units. Modified in accordance with the distribution of land animals, one arrives at five major zoogeographical zones – the Holarctic, Ethiopian, Oriental, Australasian and Neotropical, of which the Holarctic can be further divided into Palaearctic (Old World) and Nearctic (New World). In general, the distribution of freshwater fish faunas coincides with these major zones, to which can be added Madagascar because of its long isolation

from the African mainland. Each region has its characteristic species, genera, families and sometimes even orders, and its equally characteristic absence of certain species, genera or families that occur elsewhere. By mapping both the shared and unshared elements, some interesting patterns emerge.

The largest and most important of all the orders of freshwater fishes, the Cypriniformes, are found in five of the major zoogeographic zones, being absent from Australasia and Madagascar. Evidently, these fishes became dispersed at a fairly early period, but after Australia and Madagascar had become isolated. The Cyprinidae or carp-like fishes, one of the largest families within the Cypriniformes, follows approximately the same distribution pattern except in one major respect: it is entirely absent from the

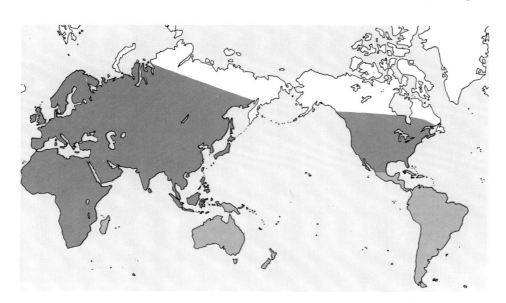

Distribution of the Cyprinidae or carp-like fishes (purple), absent in the yellow regions.

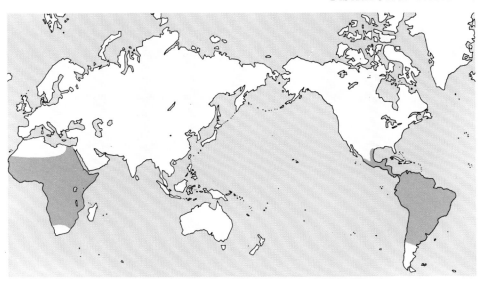

The distribution of the Characinidae or characin-like fishes. Note the absence of characins from North America, Europe, Asia, Australasia and Madagascar.

Neotropical region (South America). To explain this, one can assume that the carps evolved in Asia, migrated southwest into Africa and also eastwards via the Bering Straits into North America but were then stopped by the lack of a land-bridge down into South America. This seems reasonable since the fish faunas of North and South America are very different and indeed there is no overlap between them, even though a substantial land-bridge has existed for the last 1 to 3 million years. There is, however, a complication. The Characinidae or characins, a second large family of the Cypriniformes, are today found in Africa, are absent entirely from Asia and North America, but reappear in South America. Is it possible that they could have crossed Asia and North America and left no trace? The perch-like Cichlidae also occur in South America and Africa, but are represented in Asia by about three species of a genus endemic to southern India and Sri Lanka.

The explanation for these curious zoogeographic patterns hinges on the relationship between Africa and South America. As well as sharing characins and cichlids, the two also have in common lung-fishes and bonytongues (Osteoglossidae), as well as catfishes, although the latter are also shared with Asia. The African region shares with the Asiatic not only the carps and catfishes, but also the Spiny eels (Mastacembelidae), the labyrinthfishes (Anabantidae), the featherbacks (Notopteridae) and to a minor extent the Cichlidae. Taken as a whole, however, the fish fauna of South America and Africa show closer relationships than do those of Africa and Asia. The most reasonable explanation is that Africa and South America were in the past able to exchange elements of their faunas. A land-bridge

had been postulated, while others favour Wegener's theory that the two continents were once joined and later drifted apart. The modern plate theory, which visualizes vast crustal plates sliding imperceptibly to new positions, lends strong support to Wegener's 'continental drift' theory, and very simply explains the similarities between the fish faunas of Africa and South America. This would suppose that the carps reached Africa after it has lost its connection with South America, and indeed the relatively recent nature of this carp invasion is shown by the fact that Africa and Asia share several genera, whereas no characin genera are shared between Africa and South America. In the meantime, Africa has generated the evolution of certain families found nowhere else, such as the elephant snoutfishes (Mormyridae), the characin-like moonfishes (Citharinidae) and the bichirs (Polypteridae), but similarly South America has seen the development of highly specialized catfishes and characin-like fishes.

Zoogeographic division of the marine fish fauna, both in the Atlantic and in the Indo-Pacific, has also been affected by drifting plates or continents. This is seen very clearly in the New World land barrier, of which the Isthmus of Panama forms the narrowest strip. It has been in existence for a maximum of 3 million years and in this time the original fish fauna has gradually diverged on either side. In a number of cases it is possible to find pairs of similar species that evidently had a common ancestor before the two areas were split.

More important in the oceans, however, have been the enormous distances between opposite shores and the ocean currents between them. In the Atlantic, for example, only 118 shore fishes are

Before continental drift occurred, the continents were joined together. If outlines of continental shelves, rather than coastlines, are used, the close fit of eastern North and South America with western Europe and Africa can be seen. The past and present distributions of fishes have been used in support of the theory of continental drift.

common to both sides. Of these, 24 seem to have come from the Indo-Pacific via the Cape of Good Hope; the remainder all evolved in the Western Atlantic and managed to colonize eastwards, comprising, off West Africa, no less than 30% of the shore fauna. Similarly, the very much greater distances in the Pacific have proved a major barrier to most shore fishes, only 53 species being found on both sides, excluding a further nine species also found in the Atlantic. Once again, the migration has taken place in one direction, from west to east, and in both cases this must be explained in terms of ocean currents.

It would appear that the two outer boundaries of the Indo-West Pacific, that is to say the Cape of Good Hope in the west and the East Pacific barrier in the east, act as one-way filters that allow species to escape but do not favour invaders. The Indo-West Pacific area, and the Indo-Australian Archipelago in particular, is very rich in species. These appear to have pushed outwards into areas where the fauna is poorer and the competition therefore less, so that in this sense the Indo-West Pacific can be considered as *the* evolutionary and distributional centre for shore fishes, the Western Atlantic region being a secondary centre.

It must be remembered, however, that pure transport is only one side of the picture. For an invasion to be successful, the newcomers must succeed in competing with existing residents. Thus, in freshwaters as in the oceans, the patterns of distribution reflect a subtle combination of geology, hydrology, ecology and evolutionary potential. To which, in the modern era, one must add yet another factor – man.

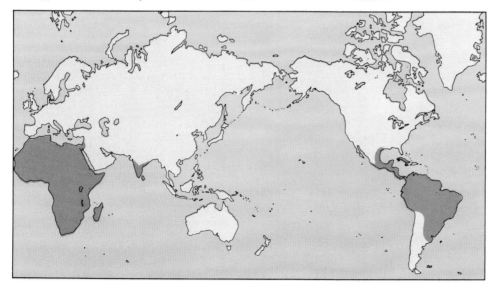

Distribution of the cichlid fishes.

Characins are found in South America and Africa but not in Europe, Asia or North America. The species shown here is a member of the genus *Myleus*, a relative of the piranha.

Introductions. With man's increasing mobility came the unwitting transport of plants and animals around the globe, quite apart from any intentional introductions of crops or domestic animals. Compared with plants or insects, however, fishes are less likely to be accidentally transferred from one area to another, but the Suez Canal offers at least one example in which man has assisted in the uncontrolled movement of fishes. Since the opening of the canal in 1869 at least 24 species of Red Sea fishes have penetrated into the eastern Mediterranean; it is of interest to note that no Mediterranean species has been able to establish itself in the Red Sea, once again demonstrating the filter principle between the faunistically rich Indo-Pacific region and the relatively poorer areas surrounding it. This makes it likely that, were the Isthmus of Panama cut by a sea-level canal instead of the mainly freshwater passage that exists at the moment, the much richer western fauna would quickly dominate that of the east, with the extinction by competition of hundreds or even thousands of eastern fishes and invertebrates.

Of deliberate introductions of fishes, chiefly freshwater, there are numerous examples. One of the best documented is *Tilapia mossambica*, a cichlid from East Africa that appeared in Java just before World War II and rapidly established itself in streams and irrigation channels. Because of its value as a pond fish it spread throughout Indonesia and the Philippines, passing from Malaysia to Thailand and reaching Taiwan where it dominated the local fish fauna. It was introduced into India and Pakistan, has been tried in Trinidad, Haiti and St Lucia, and was then taken to Texas. This is one of the most rapid and spectacular of all fish introductions, but it is matched in scope by the more gradual spread of the goldfish *Carassius auratus*, valued as an ornamental fish but with inevitable

143

A typical goldfish, household pet for the last 2,000 years. It has been taken all over the world by man and, by accident or design, is now found in many natural waters.

escapes into natural waters. Carp *Cyprinus carpio* and the mosquito-eating gambusia *Gambusia affinis* are also species with wide artificial distributions. It was said earlier that Lake Victoria was formed in isolation from the Nile system and thus lacked a number of fish species typical of the Nile. This is no longer true since the predatory Nile perch has now been introduced in an attempt to 'convert' the myriad small *Haplochromis* species into large units of edible protein. In addition, many extra species of *Tilapia* have been put into the lake, while their use in pond culture and their escapes into natural waters have meant that the original zoogeographic patterns are becoming increasingly difficult to recognize.

Marine fishes have been less frequently intro-duced to new areas but the anadromous salmons have been transferred and the King salmon is now well established in New Zealand, while the Pink salmon has been brought to British waters. Rainbow trout *Salmo gairdneri* from North America are in English streams, while European trout *Salmo trutta* are in American waters. The temptation to transfer fishes seems irresistible, although the biological consequences are often not properly investigated beforehand.

Although the results of artificial introductions cause but a fraction of the environmental upsets that have through the ages brought about the present patterns of distribution, they should not be undertaken lightly.

How it all Happened

In the previous chapters something of the diversity of fishes has been described, although it has been impossible to mention more than a handful of the 20,000 known species. Each species is subtly different from the next, if only in minor details of structure, physiology and behaviour. Again, each has slightly different requirements and each is adapted to a slightly different ecological situation or niche. If the way this diversity arose were known in detail, then we would be many steps nearer towards being able to engineer the kind of changes most in the interests of mankind. Unfortunately, this is not the case. The broad outlines are understood, but individual aspects are all too frequently blurred, both from lack of fossil material and also because there simply has not been time to investigate all the problems posed. To establish the relationship of one species or group of species to another, and to relate both of these to their probable common ancestor, is a lengthy business, demanding painstaking comparative studies of the skeleton, muscles, nerves, brain, blood vessels and so on, together with aspects of their biology and early development. This requires sufficient and well-preserved material, though even the best of museums has great gaps in its collections of modern forms, let alone fossils. Thus the evolution of our present-day fishes must be pieced together from a very incomplete jig-saw.

To understand the evolutionary history of fishes, one must first get to grips with their diversity. Faced with diversity, whether in fishes or the pieces of a jig-saw, the individual objects appear quite meaningless until similarities are found and the various elements classified into groups. For thousands of years men have done just that with the objects around them. At first things were either edible or inedible, dangerous or harmless, useful or useless. The major animal groups were fairly obvious, but gradually subsidiary zoological groupings were noticed and by the 4th century BC Aristotle was able to produce a classification of which many elements are still valid. He noticed, for example, that horns are found in mammals with cloven feet but not in hoofed mammals. Based on observation, this hypothesis, which incidentally ruled out the possibility of there being such creatures as unicorns, could be tested by further observation. It did not explain *why* the relationship should occur, but for the first time men were able to consider such a question.

For about 18 centuries thereafter, little or no progress was made in Western Europe beyond Aristotle's work, and indeed much of his common sense was obscured by fanciful beliefs that had no basis in observation. With the rebirth of interest in the natural world in the 16th century, however, men began to examine and describe once more the animals around them and to explore more complex groupings. Objects brought back from the expanding empires of the Spanish, Portuguese, Dutch and English became much-prized curiosities that increasingly found a place in museums and collections. They were classified on their general appearance as well as on some simple notions of their structure. By the 18th century such numbers of animals and plants were known that it was only through the work of the Swede Carl Linnaeus and his associates that order was brought to the assemblage, both by more workable classifications and by the development of our modern system of nomenclature.

The earliest classifications of animals and plants were based on the close resemblance between parent and progeny, and since this was repeated from generation to generation, there were evidently sorts of animals and plants with a greater resemblance to one another than to any other sort. From this concept grew the idea of a unit of classification – the

A fossil fish with some fine detail preserved, enabling scientists to reconstruct much of its appearance in life.

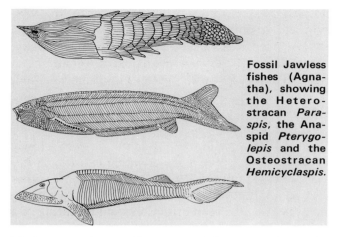

Fossil Jawless fishes (Agnatha), showing the Heterostracan *Paraspis*, the Anaspid *Pterygolepis* and the Osteostracan *Hemicyclaspis.*

kind or species – well expressed for example in the story of Noah and his ark.

A second and equally important observation was that no two individuals resembled each other exactly, even when of the same parents. This, coupled with confusion between variation within the species and variation outside it, led to the notion that there might be a continuous variation from the lowest to the highest in the animal and plant kingdoms, the extremes separated only by gradual degrees of difference.

These two principles, of discreteness and hierarchical groupings, as against a gradual *scala naturae* without distinct breaks, seemed irreconcilable until the notion of evolution and its mechanism, natural selection, were discovered. Before the causes of diversity were known only the phenomena themselves could be recorded. Interpretations were for centuries made solely in the light of non-scientific, religious and philosophical ideas.

It was almost an accident of history that Europe adopted an ancient Hebrew myth to explain the origin of life on our planet. For nearly 2,000 years this myth was firmly upheld and with great determination, for some explanation was needed to account for what could not be understood except by a technology and body of observation unattainable until the 19th century. If each animal species was created at the beginning, then their classification was merely a useful way of summarizing knowledge; relationships between species were no more than chance similarities or expressions of the creator's will. The gradual realization in the 18th century that fossils were not just tricks of nature but actual remains of extinct animals, was an embarrassment, but it was neatly explained, first by Noah's flood and later – when distinct layers of fossils were discovered – by a series of floods and catastrophes.

Finally, in 1859, came Darwin's *Origin of Species*, in which diversity was rationalized and given a history. From now on diversity was not arbitrary but the result of a process, namely evolution. The classification of diversity became the attempt to sketch the evolutionary threads that produced it, and questions about similarity made possible by Aristotle and later classifiers could now be answered in terms of historical relationships. Darwin's hypothesis was accepted because he provided a plausible mechanism for change – natural selection. If variation within domesticated species of animals and plants could be manipulated by human selection, then natural variation must be the result of natural pressures. The overriding pressure, which Darwin derived from Malthus' essay on human populations, was the so-called 'struggle for survival' and 'survival of the fittest.' The final link in the argument, published in 1865 but overlooked until 1900, was Gregor Mendel's pioneer studies in genetics, for these pointed to the actual mechanism of inheritance and opened up the way for modern work on the biochemical basis of variation.

Fossil Fishes. One of Darwin's arguments for evolution was that it provided the most reasonable explanation for the succession of fossils found in progressively younger rocks. The older rocks yield the remains of invertebrates, the next oldest the first fishes, and so on through the amphibians, reptiles, mammals and birds. Unfortunately, the fossil record is highly imperfect (a fact often siezed upon by the few who would still believe in some form of Special Creation) but very many evolutionary trends are now well illustrated by successions of fossils that supply the essential links in the chain of progressive development of new characters, and thus of new ways of life.

The earliest fossil remains of a vertebrate animal occur in the Middle Ordovician, nearly 400 million years ago. These are isolated bony plates from the external skeleton of a group of jawless fishes (Agnatha) known as the Heterostraci. Heterostracans, of which *Pteraspis* and *Poraspis* are good examples, were generally small fishes, usually not more than 12 in (30 cm) in length, with an armour of bony plates enclosing the head and front of the body, the rest of the body being covered by plate-like scales. The earliest Heterostracans were evidently bottom-living forms, but later species probably fed in mid-water or even at the surface judging by the position of the mouth (opening dorsally in *Doryaspis*); yet others returned to the bottom again, but now equipped with highly specialized heads and snouts for grubbing in the bottom muds.

Two other groups of jawless fishes appeared in the later part of the next geological period (Silurian, about 430 million years ago). These are the Osteostraci and the Anaspida. In general appearance an Osteostracan like *Cephalaspis* or *Hemiclaspis* is not unlike the Heterostracans in having a bony head shield, but the body appears to have been much more flexible and some species have pectoral fins. Since the head is internally well ossified, the various organs within it being lined with bone, it has been possible to cut a series of very thin sections through the fossils and thus reconstruct the brain, nerves, blood vessels and other features that otherwise could only be guessed at. The mouth was on the underside of the head and the fishes probably sucked in mud and extracted their food from it.

The second group, the Anaspids, much more resembled modern fishes, being fusiform (cigar-shaped), lacking a bony head shield, and bearing scales which in some species were thin and flexible. In fact, the earliest of the Anaspids, *Jamoytius* from Upper Silurian rocks in Scotland, was remarkably like the living jawless lampreys. The Anaspids had a small mouth and no jaws or teeth, so that they too must have sucked in their food (probably from the bottom since some fossils have a fine sediment in their guts). A curious feature of the Anaspids was that the vertebral column turned downwards at its tip, thus supporting the lower lobe of the caudal fin and not the upper.

By the Upper Devonian (about 375 million years ago) these three early groups of jawless fishes, the Heterostracans, Osteostracans and Anaspids, had all died out. The characters that they shared – absence of jaws, presence of two semicircular canals in the inner ear (three in all other fishes), possession of gill pouches – are those now found in the modern jawless fishes, the lampreys and hagfishes. One would have expected, therefore, that the next chapter in the record would have been fossil lampreys and hagfishes, but until quite recently there was

nothing to span the 375 million year gap. In 1968, however, a single fossil lamprey, *Mayomyzon*, was found in rocks of Carboniferous age, that is to say, shortly after the demise of the early Agnathans in the Devonian. For the other group of modern jawless fishes, the hagfishes, there is no such link and one can only guess at the point at which they diverged from their early Agnathan ancestors.

While the primitive Agnathans were slowly evolving, flourishing and becoming extinct, an important development had taken place in another early group, the evolution of true jaws, thus making possible the seizing, biting, chewing and eating of a far wider range of foods, including other fishes. The earliest fishes with jaws were the Acanthodians, first found in the Upper Silurian, that is to say, at about the same time that the Anaspids and Osteostracans appeared. The Acanthodians were small, fusiform fishes with a covering of shagreen-like scales, and their outward resemblance to more modern fishes was heightened by the presence of paired fins (pectorals and pelvics) as well as dorsal and anal fins supported in front by a spine. There were three semicircular canals in the inner ear, an indication of a greater need to maintain equilibrium, being the result of more complex swimming movements. Also, the bony arches supporting the gills were of a surprisingly modern design, and the jaws often had teeth capable of handling a variety of foods. The Acanthodians had large eyes but small nasal capsules and probably fed in the well-lit upper waters and not on the bottom; advanced forms, which often lacked teeth in the jaws, had long and slender gillrakers and probably fed by filtering off small invertebrates in the water. By the Lower Permian, however, about 200 million years ago, the Acanthodians had in their turn become extinct, having been ousted by even more advanced forms.

At some time before the end of the Upper Silurian there lived a common ancestor of the two major modern groups of fishes, the bony fishes (Osteichthyes) and the cartilaginous fishes (Chondrichthyes). However, the cartilaginous Chondrichthyes,

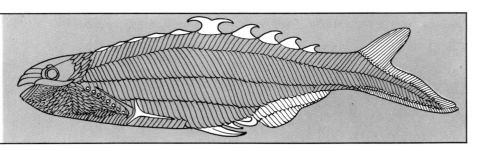

Reconstruction of an Anaspid. Note the eight gill pores behind the head and the down-turned tail lobe.

represented nowadays by the sharks, rays and chimaeras, were preceded by the Placoderms, a group in which the head was covered by bony plates that hinged to another shield covering the front of the trunk; the rest of the body tapered and was usually naked. The Placoderms are almost wholly restricted to the Devonian. The main stock belonged to a group known as the Arthrodires, for example, *Coccosteus, Titanichthys,* fairly heavily armoured fishes that lacked teeth but sometimes developed serrations in the jaws. A second and rather bizarre group was the Antiarchs, for example, *Bothriolepis,* with jointed pectoral fins that give them a crab-like appearance. But neither the Arthrodires nor the Antiarchs could compete with the cartilaginous fishes and all remnants of these and other Placoderms disappear from the record by the early part of the Carboniferous period.

Because of the absence of bone, the skeletons of the Chondrichthyes or cartilaginous fishes are rare and these fishes are often known only from their teeth and spines, making the interpretation of their evolution much more difficult than in other groups. They first appear in the Lower Devonian, flourish during the Carboniferous, and continue down to the present day. Right from the start their separation into shark-like fishes (Elasmobranchs) and chimaera-like fishes (Holocephalans) is already established, so that some common ancestor must have lived still earlier. In addition to their wholly cartilaginous skeleton, they had a covering of tooth-like scales, which were sometimes enlarged into spines on the head or preceding the fins, and the fins were supported by horny rays. Of great interest is the presence of claspers in the males in some species, showing that internal fertilization was already established, although it is not known whether the young were born live or in egg cases.

The shark-like Elasmobranchs were often much like their modern representatives, having an underslung mouth, biting or crushing teeth in the jaws, and a prominent snout and small eyes. This suggests that, like their present-day descendants, they were scavengers that sought their prey by smell. One of the best-known but less typical members was *Cladoselache* of the Upper Devonian, which had large eyes and a short snout and was probably a pelagic predator that hunted by sight. Later forms specialized in a bottom-living way of life, developing the pavement-like crushing teeth and flattened body form that led on to the modern skates and rays.

The Holocephalans, known as chimaeras or rabbitfishes, were the dominant marine fishes of the Carboniferous. Some had shark-like teeth, but the main stem of Holocephalans had crushing plates. For a time they replaced the Placoderms as the principal bottom-living fishes, but in their turn they were superseded by the bottom-living sharks. Less than two dozen species survive today.

The evolution of the fishes, as of any other major group, is one of continual replacement by more efficient forms. On the bottom, the Placoderms were superceded by the Holocephalans and these in turn were ousted by sharks and then by bony fishes. In midwaters the same thing happened, the acanthodians being dominant for a while but later yielding to the bony fishes. Each succeeding group of fishes brought new possibilities of structure, physiology and behaviour, and the success of each group is a measure of the extent to which old ecological niches could be better exploited and new ones explored. The bony fishes brought to this competitive struggle a bodily organization of such potential that few watery habitats have not been colonized by them.

The Osteichthyes or bony fishes possibly evolved as early as the Upper Silurian, before the appearance of the cartilaginous fishes, but definite remains occur from the beginning of the next period, the Devonian. Typically, the skeleton is of bone, the biting edge of the upper jaw is formed by external plates of bone (maxilla and premaxilla) and not an internal bone or cartilage (palatoquadrate), teeth are now fused to the jaw bones, and a gas bladder is present, either as a lung or as a hydrostatic swimbladder. These might not appear to be very fundamental but in combination they provided a structural formula that made possible the vast diversity of present day forms. The bony skeleton, for example, provided light, but rigid, support for body parts and enabled moving elements like jaws, fins and gill apparatus to articulate in a manner suited to competitive needs. The new bones serving as jaws were capable of liberation from the rigid part of the skull, eventually forming a mouth that could bite, suck, protrude, nibble, chew or pluck an amazing variety of different foods. The development of a gas bladder was no less revolutionary. As a breathing organ, its future lay with the land vertebrates, but as a hydrostatic swimbladder the possibilities that it opened up in the field of controlled swimming were profound. Each of these innovations aided the others in their gradual evolution until the bony fishes had far outstripped all other groups. Of the jawless fishes, only 31 species of lamprey and 15 species of hagfish survive; of sharks, some 220 species; of skates and rays about 300 species; and of chimaeras, 20 species. On the other hand, the bony fishes, with some 20,000 modern species, are not only the most diverse modern group but have produced many more species than any other group in the past.

The fossil record shows that three distinct lines of bony fishes evolved towards the end of the Silurian and beginning of the Devonian. These were the lungfishes (Dipnoi), the tasselfinned fishes (Crossopterygii) and the rayfinned fishes (Actinopterygii). The lungfishes or Dipnoans, which reached their zenith in late Devonian and early Carboniferous times, are represented today by the three genera *Protopterus* (Africa), *Lepidosiren* (South America) and the most primitive, *Neoceratodus* (Australia). The evolution of the lungfishes has been one of reduction, bone being gradually replaced by cartilage, the external armour of scales and bones being reduced and the tail being replaced by mere extensions of the dorsal and anal fins. Teeth were not present along the edges of the jaws but comprised an upper and lower plate for crushing and cutting. The single or paired lungs enabled these fishes to survive in swampy conditions, an adaptation of great value during certain geological periods but one which limits the fish to rather shallow waters since it must constantly rise to gulp air.

The second line of bony fishes, the tasselfinned fishes or Crossopterygians, is now represented by a single species, the famous coelacanth *Latimeria chalumnae*, of which the first specimen was caught in 1938 off South Africa, and the next off the Comoro Islands, near Madagascar, in 1952; about 70 have since been caught, all in the Comoros area. To have come across a living dinosaur would have been scarcely more surprising since the coelacanths were thought to have become extinct about 70 million years ago. The living form was so similar in appearance to those known only from fossils that it was of the greatest value to explore, at last, the internal anatomy of these primitive fishes. A characteristic feature of all the Crossopterygians is the curious joint in the middle of the skull, enabling the front half to hinge upwards and presumably widen the gape of the mouth. Another feature is the muscular lobe-like base to the paired pectoral and pelvic fins, foreshadowing the articulated limbs of

The resemblance between *Undina* of the Jurassic and the modern *Latimeria* is striking and the latter well merits the term 'living fossil.'

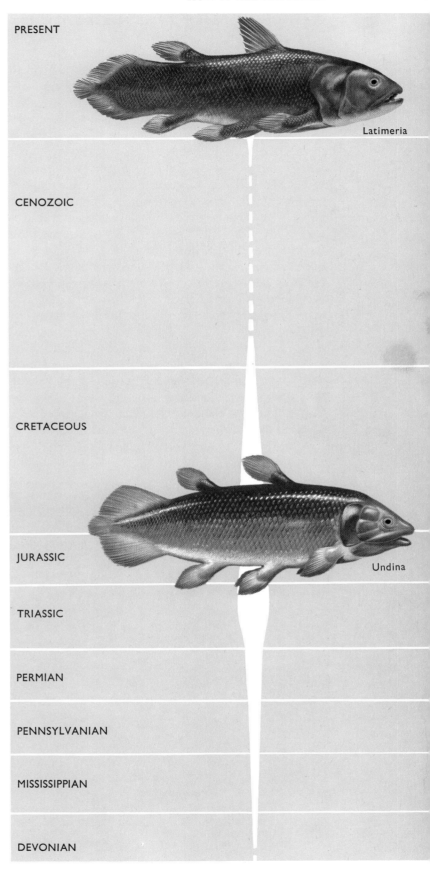

PRESENT

Latimeria

CENOZOIC

CRETACEOUS

JURASSIC

Undina

TRIASSIC

PERMIAN

PENNSYLVANIAN

MISSISSIPPIAN

DEVONIAN

149

the land vertebrates. It was in fact from the Crossopterygians that the early amphibians evolved, not unfortunately from the coelacanth stem, the Actinistia, but from a related group, the Rhipidistians, of which *Eusthenopteron* is the best known.

The third line of the bony fishes, the rayfinned fishes or Actinopterygians, has proved in the end to have been the most successful in terms of diversity, numbers of species, range of adaptations and sheer persistence, for the group as a whole extends from the Upper Silurian to the present day. The earliest members, the Palaeoniscoids, were carnivorous fishes with strong conical teeth in the jaws and an elongate or fusiform body. They reached their acme in the Carboniferous and Permian, and died out in the Cretaceous. Surviving relatives of the Palaeoniscoids are the bichirs and reedfish of Africa, the sturgeons of the Northern Hemisphere and the paddlefishes of the Yangtse and the Mississippi. The Palaeoniscoids were superseded by the Holosteans, of which only two families still survive, the bowfins, a single species, and the garpikes, seven species, both now confined to North America. Appearing in the Permian, most Holosteans had died out by the Cretaceous and the stage was set, so to speak, for the triumphant radiation of the final group of Actinopterygians, the Teleosts. It is these fishes that dominate today, for all but about 600 of the 20,000 modern species are Teleosts.

Some Major Trends. It was once thought that cartilage provided the skeleton for the most primitive fishes and that bone was an innovation that ushered in the more advanced forms. This seemed to be borne out in Haeckel's dictum of recapitulation, that the development of the individual repeats the evolution of the group. Thus the external or dermal bones of vertebrates are formed directly, but the internal skeleton is always laid down as cartilage first and only later does it transform to bone. Therefore, the evolutionary series of fishes would run from the cartilaginous and jawless Agnathans, through the cartilaginous but jawed sharks, to the modern fishes that have a bony skeleton and jaws.

In fact, it is a cartilaginous and not a bony skeleton that seems to be a relatively recent 'discovery' among the vertebrates. The early jawless fishes had a bony skeleton and in one well documented group of Osteostracans, the Cephalaspids, it was the later forms that had the more feeble skeleton. A similar trend of reduction seems to have taken place in the Placoderms, it has already been mentioned above in the lungfishes, and it is repeated in the coelacanths, the earlier forms having a highly ossified skeleton and the modern survivor, *Latimeria*, having a high proportion of cartilage.

Cartilage, it seems, is a structural necessity in embryonic development. External bones present no growth problems because they are not intimately associated with organs, but internal bones, such as those surrounding the brain, are more than just simple plates to which a new outer layer can be added. Bone is too inflexible for such precise three dimensional growth, hence a cartilage template is laid down first, and this ossifies only later on. The very early appearance of bone in the evolution of the vertebrates is puzzling. A possible explanation is the need for defence against the still dominant invertebrates, of which the most dangerous would have been the scorpion-like eurypterids. Since the early fishes were rarely more than a few inches long, whereas the eurypterids were relatively enormous (growing in exceptional cases to about 10 ft or 3 m), bone was of obvious advantage to the first vertebrates before they had mastered their environment.

A second major trend in the history of fishes has been the evolution of the jaws. Aspects of this have already been mentioned above and in the chapter on feeding, and the overall picture can be stated quite

Trout hybrid, result of crossing Brown trout *Salmo trutta* and Brook trout *Salvellinus fontinalis*.

Garpike, freshwater fish of the United States, in which the scales fit together as in a mosaic – a feature of almost all primitive fish.

simply. The jawless Agnathans could suck in their food, but were incapable of chewing it or biting it or scraping it. These fishes had a series of half-hoops of cartilage, the branchial arches, that supported the gills and it was the first of these half-hoops that went to form the jaws, the lower arm being termed Meckel's cartilage and the upper the palatoquadrate. Primitively, all the gill-arches bear small teeth, but only those on this first arch became enlarged. The second half-hoop or gill arch, known as the hyoid arch, also lost its function as a support for the gills and became in part a support for the tongue and in part a means of suspending the jaws from the skull.

Jaws of this nature could deliver a straightforward bite, but more than this was needed if all the rich feeding possibilities of the seas, rivers and lakes were to be exploited. The answer was found in the development of those bony plates that surrounded the mouth into tooth-bearing struts along the upper edge of the mouth. Two paired units evolved, the premaxillae at the front of the mouth and the maxilla behind them. Subsequently the jaws evolved through a gradual squeezing of the maxillae away from the edge of the jaw, to act as levers both to open the mouth and to force the premaxillae out to make the mouth protrusile. From this relatively simple set of levers and struts has developed a mechanical system of surprising efficiency and precision.

The third major trend has been in the evolution of a complex swimbladder from a primitive lung.

Lungs were – and still are – present in the lungfishes and primitive Actinopterygians (bichirs, holosteans, some teleosts) and they were present too in the Rhipidistians and perhaps in some coelacanths, although the modern *Latimeria* has a degenerate 'lung' that no longer functions as such. The effect of transforming lungs into hydrostatic organs has already been described. In essence, it meant the release of fins and muscles, and thus of energy, from the constant drudgery of maintaining the fish's position in the water column, thus enabling all swimming movements to be directed towards going places and freely performing movements that were no longer dominated by gravity. The ceaseless, hungry cruising of sharks, or the rays' enforced life on the sea bottom, could through such adaptation be transformed into the intricate manoeuvres of the modern bony fishes. When it is considered how important these manoeuvres are in escape, courtship, feeding and the many other activities of fishes, one might conclude that the swimbladder is the most fundamental of all the evolutionary trends.

Many other trends can be seen, whether one is looking at a whole class of fish-like vertebrates, or at a subclass, an order, a family or merely a genus. What such trends represent are responses to environmental factors. The bony plates fringing the upper edge of the mouth were potentially capable of forming a jaw, the lungs of forming a swimbladder, and the muscles of acting as electric organs. Intense specialization precludes the evolution of more general adaptations, or to put it the other way

151

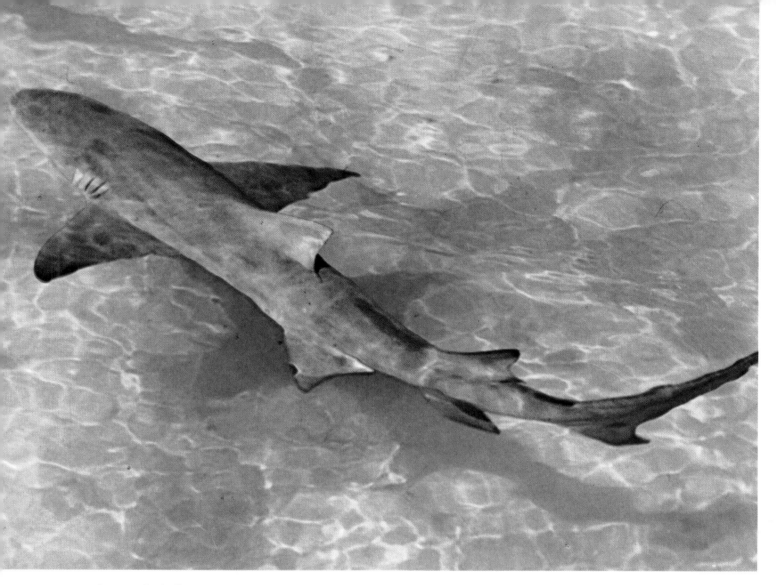

Lemon shark *Negaprion brevirostris*, 8 ft (2·5 m) long, one of the commonest sharks in inshore waters of the American Atlantic coast.

around, specialized forms have radiated from some more generalized ancestor. Thus the evolution of fishes has involved successive radiations of new forms from an ancestor that was both an advance on its own ancestral stock yet not so specialized that it represented an end point. To trigger an advance, each new feature – whether a bony skeleton, a spine supported fin, a protrusile jaw or a series of plate-like scales – had to have the potential for numerous permutations. Whether another fundamental innovation is yet to be made and a new major radiation triggered off is difficult to say; to a man living in Carboniferous times it would have been difficult to envisage the eclipse of the sharks and chimaeras by the rather obscure bony fishes.

Species and Speciation. Darwin called his book the *Origin of Species* and it is with species that evolution is concerned. Darwin's starting point was the noticeable variation among individuals. At what

point did such variation within a species become so marked that one could recognize the birth of a new species? Much depended on what a species was considered to be and it is here that the apparent contradiction mentioned earlier – between continuous variation and discrete clumps of forms – could at last be resolved. A species is nowadays defined as the largest natural assemblage of individuals capable of sharing the same pool of genetic possibilities and thus transmitting the characters of the species to the offspring. Within a species there can be no insuperable barriers to the exchange of genetic material.

The sharing of the gene pool occurs, of course, during breeding when genetic material from males and females both determines the nature of the offspring and equips them to participate in the same process of transmission in the next generation. Thus the origin of a new species is the origin of a group of individuals no longer able to share the ancestral collection of genetic possibilities.

A problem arises in the case of hybrids, for here genetic material from different species is mixed. The first record of a fish hybrid, between a carp and a goldfish, was made by Conrad Gesner in 1558, but in the present century interest in hybrids has increased and they have been recorded in 56 families of bony fishes, most particularly in sturgeons, sunfishes, carps, toothcarps, darters and salmons. However, crosses between two different species frequently result in malformed offspring or else offspring that are either sterile or all of one sex. Rather rarely can the hybrids breed among themselves or back-cross with one or other of the parent stock. When they do breed back with a parent species, a situation more common in plants than in animals, such 'introgressive' hybridization serves to transfer genetic possibilities from one species to another, but clearly this is highly unusual and quite contrary to the normal process of evolution.

Essentially, evolution is the origin of new genetic possibilities and their expression as new kinds of structure, physiology or behaviour when appropriate conditions occur. Vast numbers of genetic mutations are either eliminated because the individuals are unsuited, or are masked by dominant genes. New variations arise within breeding populations, that is to say among only a part of the aggregate of individuals that comprises the species. However, the species is the true unit of evolution because it acts as a ratchet that prevents the wheel of progress slipping back again. It is the species that both consolidates past experiments and at the same time ensures that certain new experiments will evolve into new species and not be absorbed back into the parent stock.

In fishes, as in any other organisms, the barriers to breeding between species are largely extensions of the causes that separated the species in the first place. These may be purely physiological, in that fertilization is impossible, or the hybrids are sterile or malformed; or behavioural, in that the courtship patterns are incompatible, or the care of the young is neglected; or structural, in that the male copulatory organ, such as the gonopodium of toothcarps, is mechanically unsuited; or geographical, ecological or seasonal, the variant population being isolated totally, or at the critical point, the breeding season. In one way or another a population is denied access to the ancestral gene pool and if the isolating mechanism is severe enough to continue perfecting itself, then a new species will have arisen.

This is essentially how an experiment in supporting the length of the body internally, made 400 million years ago, could lead on to the radiation of the vertebrate animals, of which the fishes are still the most diverse group. Competition supplies the incentive, genetics the potential permutations, and environment the actual opportunities for the progressive changes we call evolution. This evolutionary thread is the key to understanding contemporary forms which, in a protein hungry world, are of deep interest to mankind.

It is said that 90% of all scientists that have ever lived are alive today. This may be so, but in the study of fishes the questions that are asked, many of them vital to the well-being of fisheries, far outnumber the resources and especially the manpower needed to answer them. This brief excursion into the way fishes live carries with it the hope that more young research workers will turn to this fascinating group of vertebrates, for much remains to be discovered.

Classification of Fishes

1. Class AGNATHA – Jawless fishes
   Jaws and true teeth absent, as also paired fins, skeleton of cartilage, gills contained in pouches.

   A. Cephalaspidomorphi – Cephalaspids
      1. Osteostraci*
         Order Tremataspidiformes*
         Order Cephalaspidiformes*   *Cephalaspis*
         Order Ateleaspidiformes*   *Hemicyclaspis*
         Order Kiaeraspidiformes*
         Order Galeaspidiformes*
      2. Anaspida*
         Order Jamoytiiformes*   *Jamoytius*
         Order Endeiolepidiformes*
         Order Lasaniiformes*
         Order Birkeniiformes*   *Pterygolepis*
      3. Petromyzonida – Lampreys
         Order Petromyzoniformes   *Mayomyzon*, modern Lampreys (31 species freshwater or anadromous;
                          parasitic or non-parasitic; antitropical)
      4. Myxinoidea – Hagfishes
         Order Myxiniformes   Hagfishes (15 species; marine; antitropical)
   B. Pteraspidomorphi – Pteraspids
      1. Heterostraci*
         Order Astraspidiformes*
         Order Eriptychiiformes*
         Order Cyathaspidiformes*   *Poraspis*
         Order Pteraspidiformes*   *Pteraspis, Doryaspis*
         Order Psammosteiformes*   *Drepanaspis*
         Order Cardipeltiformes*
         Order Amphiaspidiformes*
      2. Thelodonti*
         Order Thelodontiformes*   *Thelodus*
         Order Phlebolepidiformes*

2. Class PLACODERMI* – Placoderms
   Teeth, jaws and paired fins present, bony skeleton; known only as fossils from the Devonian.

     Order Arthrodiriformes*   *Coccosteus, Arctolepis, Titanichthys*
     Order Ptyctodontiformes*
     Order Phyllolepidiformes*
     Order Petalichthyiformes*
     Order Rhananiformes*
     Order Antiarchiformes*   *Bothriolepis*

3. Class CHONDRICHTHYES – Cartilaginous fishes
   Teeth, jaws and paired fins present, skeleton entirely of cartilage, body covered with denticles; no swimbladder, intestine with spiral valve; fertilization internal (male with claspers).

   1. Elasmobranchi – Sharks and Rays
      Gillslits 5–7, spiracle present (used to inhale water in Rays and some sharks); breeding oviparous, ovoviviparous or viviparous; worldwide, mostly marine but some freshwater.

      Order Cladoselachiformes*
      Order Xenacanthiformes*
      Order Cladodontiformes*
      Order Polyacrodontiformes*
      Order Hexanchiformes   Comb-toothed and Frilled sharks
      Order Heterodontiformes   Port Jackson or Horn sharks (about 10 species)
      Order Lamniformes   Other modern sharks (about 200 species)
      Order Rajiformes   Skates and Rays (about 300 species)

154

2. Bradyondonti – Chimaeras and Rabbitfishes

Gills (4) opening to exterior by single slit, spiracle absent; breeding oviparous; marine, in fairly deep water.

Order Chimaeriformes   Chimaeras and Rabbitfishes (about 20 species)
Order Chondrenchelyiformes*
Order Edestiformes*
Order Psammodiformes*
Order Copodontiformes*
Order Petalodontiformes*

4. Class OSTEICHTHYES – Bony fishes
Adult skeleton of bone, jaws capable of many remarkable modifications, swimbladder typically present, as also paired fins; body typically covered by scales.

1. Acanthodii* – Acanthodians
Fossil fishes from Upper Silurian to Lower Permian; strong spines in the front of dorsal, anal and paired fins; the earliest fishes to have true jaws.

Order Climatiiformes*   *Climatius*
Order Ischnacanthiformes*
Order Acanthodiformes*   *Acanthodes*

2. Sarcopterygii – Fleshy-finned fishes
   a. Rhipidistia* – Rhipidistians (ancestors of the amphibians)
      Order Porolepiformes*   *Porolepis*
      Order Osteolepiformes*   *Osteolepis*
      Order Rhizodontiformes*
   b. Actinistia – Coelacanths
      Order Coelacanthiformes   Coelacanths, the modern *Latimeria*
      Order Laugiiformes*
   c. Dipnoi – Lungfishes
      Order Dipteriformes*   *Dipterus*
      Order Holodipteriformes*
      Order Rhynchodipteriformes*
      Order Phaneropleuriformes*
      Order Uronemiformes*
      Order Ctenodontiformes*
      Order Ceratodontiformes   *Ceratodus* and the living *Neoceratodus*
      Order Lepidosireniformes   African and South American genera

3. Actinopterygii – Ray-finned fishes
From Lower Devonian times three groups have successively come to dominance, of which the first two are now represented by only about forty relict species.
   a. Chondrostei – Chondrosteans
      Order Palaeonisciformes*   Palaeoniscids
      Order Polypteriformes   Bichirs (10 species) and Reedfish
      Order Acipenseriformes   Sturgeons (23 species) and Paddlefishes (2 species)
      Order Haplolepiformes*
      Order Tarrasiiformes*
      Order Phanerorhynchiformes*
      Order Dorypteriformes*
      (And a number of Mesozoic orders)
   b. Holostei – Holosteans
      Order Pachycormiformes*
      Order Semionotiformes*
      Order Pycnodontiformes*
      Order Amiiformes   Garpikes (7 species) and Bowfin
      Order Aspidorhynchiformes*
      Order Pholidophoriformes*
      Order Leptolepiformes*

c. Teleostei – Teleosts
The dominant group of modern fishes, comprising all but about fifty of the twenty thousand living bony fishes.

Division I

   i. Elopomorpha
      Order Elopiformes   Tenpounders, Tarpons
      Order Anguilliformes   Eels
      Order Notacanthiformes   Spiny eèls
  ii. Clupeomorpha
      Order Clupeiformes

Division II

   i. Osteoglossomorpha – Bony tongues
      Order Osteoglossiformes   Bony tongues, African butterflyfish
      Order Mormyriformes   Mormyrid fishes

Division III

   i. Protacanthopterygii
      Order Salmoniformes   Salmons, Trouts, Chars
      Order Ctenothrissiformes
      Order Gonorhynchiformes   Beaked salmon, Milkfish
      Order Cypriniformes   Carps, Characins, Loaches
      Order Siluriformes   Catfishes
      Order Myctophiformes   Lanternfishes
  ii. Paracanthopterygii
      Order Polymixiiformes
      Order Percopsiformes   Trout perches
      Order Batrachoidiformes   Toadfishes
      Order Indostomiformes
      Order Gobiesociformes   Clingfishes
      Order Lophiiformes   Anglerfishes, Frogfishes
      Order Gadiformes   Cods
 iii. Acanthopterygii
      Order Atheriniformes   Flying fishes, Garpikes, Toothcarps
      Order Lampridiformes   Opah, Dealfishes, Oarfish
      Order Beryciformes   Squirrelfishes
      Order Zeiformes   John Dories, Boarfishes
      Order Gasterosteiformes   Sticklebacks, Sea horses, Pipefishes
      Order Channiformes   Snakeheads
      Order Synbranchiformes
      Order Scorpaeniformes   Scorpionfishes
      Order Dactylopteriformes   Flying gurnards
      Order Pegasiformes   Sea moths
      Order Perciformes   Perches and perch-like fishes
      Order Pleuronectiformes   Flatfishes
      Order Tetraodontiformes   Triggerfishes, Boxfishes, Puffer fishes

* Entirely fossil groups

Index

Italics are used for generic and specific names and also to indicate pages on which illustrations appear.